Governments at Work
Canadian Parliamentary Federalism and Its Public Policy Effects

In this innovative analysis of how government works, Mark Sproule-Jones examines the underlying arrangements, or 'rules,' that operate between levels of government and the execution of public policy.

He begins by identifying three levels of rules. Rules at the lowest or operational level determine how policies are delivered. Next, at the institutional level, are the rules that determine which institutions operate at the lowest level. Finally, rules at the constitutional level define which institutions can make the determinations. These layers are reproduced in multiple hierarchies throughout the national and international structures in which Canadian public policy operates.

The author then explores three public policies as they converge in one location: commercial shipping, pleasure boating, and water-quality management in the harbour at Hamilton, Ontario. In the context of rule configurations, Sproule-Jones evaluates these public policies with reference to legal doctrine, technical matters, the operation of political institutions, and constitutional constraints.

MARK SPROULE-JONES is a member of the Department of Political Science, McMaster University.

MARK SPROULE-JONES

Governments at Work

Canadian Parliamentary

Federalism and Its

Public Policy Effects

UNIVERSITY OF TORONTO PRESS
Toronto Buffalo London

© University of Toronto Press Incorporated 1993
Toronto Buffalo London
Printed in Canada

ISBN 0-8020-2855-1 (cloth)
ISBN 0-8020-7355-7 (paper)

Printed on acid-free paper

Canadian Cataloguing in Publication Data

Sproule-Jones, M.H.
    Governments at work

    Includes index.
    ISBN 0-8020-2855-1 (bound) ISBN 0-8020-7355-7 (pbk.)

    1. Federal government – Canada. 2. Canada –
    Politics and government — 1984–   .* I. Title.

    JL65 1992.S67 1993   320.471   C92-095271-2

76659

This book has been published with the help of a grant from the Social
Science Federation of Canada, using funds provided by the Social
Sciences and Humanities Research Council of Canada.

Contents

Introduction / 3

PART I Public Policies and Rule Configurations / 19

1 A Framework for Institutional and Policy Analysis / 21
2 Foundations of Understanding / 34
3 The Design and Meaning of Rules-in-Use / 58
4 Constitutional Rules / 79
5 Institutional and Operational Rules / 104

PART II Policy Cases / 125

6 The Setting and the Site / 127
7 Commercial Shipping / 153
8 Pleasure Boating / 188
9 Water-Quality Management / 209
10 Rules and Cases / 249

PART III Conclusion / 261

11 Evaluation / 263

References / 275
Index / 285

GOVERNMENTS AT WORK

Introduction

Scholarship, like a Victorian marriage, requires an early declaration of intentions. This book attempts to explain the basic logic of government in Canada. It focuses on those elements – basic logic – of government that most succinctly explain its operations. And it is concerned with the machinery of political arrangements as they are manifested in one part of the world. Further elaboration, like an extended courtship, can better reveal these honest intentions.

Explanations come in many forms. Some useful ones in everyday life consist of metaphors and analogies. Provided people have some common understanding of the context in which metaphors and analogies are used, these forms of ordinary discourse can provide immediate insight into the topic that is being discussed or written about. Most Canadians can readily understand, for example, what is implied by the comment that 'the government is attempting to "stick handle" the bill through Parliament.' Scots can appreciate how 'the prime minister "splits open" the opposition defence.' Americans can sense how 'Congress has again "fumbled" important legislation.' These metaphors can provide an adequate bridge of understanding between the speaker or writer and the audience or readership. In an older tradition, such bridges were formed by parables that encapsulated shared understandings of general knowledge.

On occasion in this book I use metaphors, analogies, and parables as the bridge of understanding between the author and the reader to explore the meaning of politics. For example, parts of this book are concerned with public policies as they are experienced or manifested in the world in which Canadians live. Other parts are con-

4 Governments at Work

cerned with the institutional rules by which individual Canadians or their political representatives collectively order their politics. Still other parts examine constitutional rules that allow institutions to develop, change, and wither over time. Each of these three elements – operational rules or public policies, institutional rules, and constitutional rules – is linked with the others, with important consequences for the average person. Let me explain the linkage with an analogy.

When people drive cars, their major concern is for convenient and safe transportation between two points. They can achieve this goal with relatively little knowledge of how the car operates. Their knowledge can be limited to how to start the car, use the steering wheel and pedals, read the dials, and pay attention to the other vehicles on the road. The car has operational value to them. Many drivers wish to know more, however, especially those who have had experience with false starts, bumpy roads, and so on. Those drivers will explore the machinery that drives the engine or the organizations that provide and maintain the roads. Some might acquire knowledge of the constitution of cars and roads – of, say, the laws of thermodynamics or the principles of scale economies in the mass production of vehicles. All of these levels of knowledge are linked, but people can disaggregate them, concentrating on those levels appropriate to their interests and concerns.

Similarly, citizens operating within the body politic possess different levels of knowledge of government, depending on their interests and concerns. For most Canadians – indeed, for most people in the Western industrialized countries – knowledge of the operational level of government is enough. Four decades of survey research indicate that relatively few people possess detailed knowledge of institutional and constitutional rules. (The readership of this book is surely an exception!) Indeed, in Canada, a country continually beset by constitutional crises, it is difficult to understand why more people do not possess more information about institutional and constitutional rules.

The book relies on more than metaphors, analogies, and parables to explain the basic logic of government in Canada. Parts of this book use what logicians call deductive-nomological explanations, in which conclusions are validly deduced from a set of premises and determining conditions. This form of explanation will facilitate the understanding of the content of this book for some of its readers, particularly those who gain insight from more formally presented analysis. Other parts of the book use empirical evidence to facilitate readers' understanding. The evidence is both quantitative and non-quantitative in nature. It is organized and presented in a theoretical fashion, however, in the sense that it provides a measure of the proof of generalizations made about the operational, institutional, or constitutional conduct of government. Put concisely, these kinds of data are not presented without analysis or ordering principles. Thus, the presentation of evidence will appeal to those readers who rely on knowledge of the empirical world to reach agreed-upon understandings about politics. In all cases, this book undertakes what can be called 'contextual explanation'; that is, explanation is made not only of a topic but also *to* those to whom the book is addressed. Some deeper implications of this technique are discussed later.

Reference has already been made to the operational rules, the institutional rules, and the constitutional rules of Canadian politics. These provide the core of knowledge from which the basic logic of Canadian government can be found. The phrase 'basic logic' may be perplexing to the reader. It simply refers to probable consequences of the major factors that best account for the conduct of government. Walter Bagehot once referred to the difference between the 'dignified' and the 'efficient' parts of the English constitution (Bagehot 1964). The 'efficient' parts, in his terms, of the Canadian polity comprise those elements that produce 'the basic logic.' By the combination and interaction of those elements, a general range of consequences can be predicted. Understanding of 'the basic logic' leads to an understanding of the major features of Canadian government.

It may be argued that all understanding of the social world is based on an understanding of basic logics (Sproule-Jones 1972). Understanding – in more formal language, theory – about the social world is an inevitable simplification in which many features of the experiential world are excluded from analysis. Some factors, like the prime minister's breakfast or the sex of the Albertan senators, make little difference to the workings of the Canadian polity and may safely be excluded from analysis. Other factors, like a bargaining session between the Albertan and the federal ministers of the environment over a proposed river dam, may be a critical instance of intergovernmental negotiations over water resources, and such intergovernmental negotiations may comprise part of the basic logic. The factors affecting intergovernmental negotiations in Canada – such as shared jurisdiction between provinces and the federal government over international rivers – lead to a range of predictable consequences. These kinds of dynamics constitute the basic logic.

It is, of course, perfectly possible for a scholar, or active politician, or reflective member of the general public to misspecify the basic logic in question. Academics are often characterized as esoteric disputants in specifying a basic logic. Thus it will come as no surprise to the neo-Marxist scholar or to the political psychologist that this book somehow misspecifies the basic logic in question. Many Canadian scholars have a deep distaste for some of the factors given primacy in this book's basic logic – such as the factor that Canadian politicians and public servants often act from a position of self-interest (Borins 1988). But the basic logic as set out in this book offers a form of understanding that can be taken into account, modified, or rejected by readers as they reach their own conclusions about 'the state' in which they live. The conjectures in this book, and their refutations by readers, are a way in which knowledge of the real world is advanced. This kind of disputation has deeper implications, which are advanced later in the book.

Note that the book is concerned with the Canadian polity but not in the ethnocentric sense in which the Canadian polity is unique and different from those of all other places in the world. In a trivial sense, all countries are unique. There are circumstances of life – including geography, weather, and resource endowments – that create different opportunities for citizens in different parts of the world. Indeed, Canada is such a large country in physical terms that Canadians are acutely aware of regional differences and opportunities to engage in politics. A snow-melting machine purchased out of tax revenue by an Ontarian municipality would be considered a bizarre manifestation of 'Eastern' politics by residents of Vancouver Island.

However, some aspects of the basic logic of Canadian politics are similar to the basic logic of the politics of other countries. The combination of a Westminster-type parliamentary system with those of federalism poses immediate parallels with a country like Australia, for example. The theoretical understandings about political life in one country may be compared with that in another country, subject to some unique opportunities and constraints posed by time and place. Readers in countries other than Canada may gain an understanding of the politics within their own communities by reflecting upon the theoretical knowledge advanced in this book. At a minimum, this knowledge provides the possibility of the advance of conjectures and refutations in communities outside Canada.

Finally, attention must be drawn explicitly to the combination of macro generalizations about the workings of the Canadian polity at a constitutional level of analysis and micro generalizations about the operational significance to members of the public of a number of public policies. Books about the Canadian polity rarely trace, in a systematic manner, the policy implications of major constitutional rules. Books about public policies may include some macro inferences, such as those about federalism, but rarely do they reconstruct our knowledge about the 'real' or 'efficient' or constitutional rules-in-use. This book links the macro to the micro by discovering rules-in-use at the three levels of analysis – the operational, the institutional, and the constitutional. It then evaluates their basic logic.

Pathways

Basic understandings of politics are rarely reached in a single experience of perception, rationalization, or revelation. There are few born-again political scientists, as it were. Basic understandings normally represent the product of discussion and experience with others in the many communities of association in which people live. In pure science, the community of association taken as relevant is that of scientific peers by whom refutations may be advanced. In social sciences, the range of peers may be more varied and not simply confined to professional scholars.

This book contains understandings, theories, and evidence accumulated in some twenty years of writing and participation in various communities involved in 'politics.' Conjectures have been advanced, and many have been refuted, some retained, and some corrected. The process has been signalled by previous publications in scholarly journals and monographs. But equally as important have been the unsignalled discussions in classrooms, conferences, clubs, pubs, and boardrooms.

The understandings of this book have progressed and been signalled by previous publications along three pathways. The first and most obvious is the pathway in which an understanding of the institutional rules and constitutional rules in Canada have emerged.

Some early empirical work undertaken in British Columbia (Sproule-Jones and Hart 1973, 1974b) revealed the placid nature of citizen participation, at least outside Quebec, except when formal politics (election times especially) intruded on the daily life and work of a busy and prosperous community That form of participation was in marked contrast, at that time, to the drama and hyperbole associated with the pronouncements of politicians about armed insurrection in Quebec, constitutional reform of the British North America Act, fundamental redistribution of income through the tax system, and new ways to change Canadian cities through citizen participation and neighbourhood associations. An initial attempt to resolve this contrast was signalled by a 1974 publication that, first, explained the stability of the cartel-like constitutional rules of Canadian federalism and, then, explored their consequences (Sproule-Jones 1974a). This early effort was helped to some degree by a previously published and more formal effort to understand constitutional rules (Sproule-Jones 1973).

In 1975, I again explored the basic logic of Canadian federalism, revising my findings in the light of its contrasts and similarities with Australian federalism (Sproule-Jones 1975). While the linkages among the constitutional rules, institutional rules, and operational rules could be advanced by logical analysis, empirical confirmation of these linkages could only be suggested by secondary sources and the reinterpretation of the evidence put forward by other scholars. Since many Canadian political scientists were content with descriptive and inductive analyses, and others were intellectually hostile to liberalism (of which, in a broad sense, this book is a part), it was clear that empirical research on rules and their consequences would have to be pursued.

The late 1970s and 1980s have been marked by largely empirical research on rules and their consequences, especially in the area of natural resources and environmental policies. Before I provide a brief description of this intellectual journey, the second pathway, it is worth noting that the first pathway was not abandoned totally. Previous work on the basic logic of constitutional and institutional rules had focused primarily on federalism and intergovernmental relations. In 1984, I began to explore the logic of parliamentary sovereignty itself, and of some of its consequences for the institutional and operational rules of Canadian public policy (Sproule-Jones 1984a). An explanation of the dominance of executive-centred federalism remains a critical issue to be reasoned through by reflective Canadians. This book returns to this issue, among others.

The second pathway, of empirical research at the institutional and operational levels, was marked by studies of what I termed the 'provision systems,' or what others might call 'the public economies' of water-quality governance in the lower Fraser River and the coastal areas of British Columbia. A rich network of public- and private-sector organizations, interest groups, and economic associations was engaged in the joint production of waste-disposal and water-quality management. In no sense did the system take on the characteristics of a command-and-control hierarchy, nor did the institutional rules facilitate exclusively private-sector negotiations over preferred outcomes, so beloved in formal economic models. The work also revealed how the nature or the attributes of the policy in question created basic constraints and opportunities for joint resolution of preferred outcomes. For example, any study of the rules for the drilling and transportation of oil from the Queen Charlotte Sound–Hecate Straits region of the Northeast Pacific must take into account the fact that waves can sometimes reach 180 feet in foggy winter months (Sproule-Jones and Richards 1984). Finally, this phase of empirical investigation addressed the issue of citizen preferences for the water environment, in part as a possible surrogate for evaluating the present state of and changes to the public policy. A *prima facie* case could be made that, at least at the operational-rule level, citizens were citizen-consumers of the public policy, and their demands (rather than those of regulators or polluters) should form the basis of an evaluation of the value of the operational rules currently in place (Sproule-Jones 1978a, 1978b, 1979, 1981, 1982).

This phase of empirical research revealed the complex dimensions of public policy in so far as they directly affect citizens as 'consumers' or 'users' of that policy. The institutional rules are also complex and interactive in character. They are predicated on multiple constitutional rules, some of which were not domestic in origin. For example, major rivers, estuaries, and harbours are often ports for the transshipment of goods by ship, rail, and road. The ships are frequently registered in one country, owned in a second, insured in a third, chartered in a fourth, captained by someone from a fifth, and crewed by sailors from a sixth. Domestic regulation of these ships, and especially the enforcement of these regulations, must often take into account the multiple systems of constitutional rules in which the regulatory policy is 'nested.' Studies of public policies that base their empirical investigations solely on the product of discussions in the national and provincial capitals are arguably studies of the peripheral in public policy analysis; they study what governments say rather than how people act and react together to make public policies.

Beginning in 1984, this empirical research led to investigations of the multiple uses of Hamilton Harbour in western Lake Ontario. This book presents the major findings in Part II, 'Policy Cases,' although some of this research has been signalled by previous publications (Sproule-Jones 1985, 1986a, 1986b, 1988a, 1989a, 1989b). The thrust of the research was again to understand rule-ordered behaviour at the operational, institutional, and constitutional levels, when public policies interacted and intersected in sometimes complementary and sometimes conflictual ways. The site in question is a micro-level laboratory of Canadian public policies. Many readers living outside the site in question may wonder about its relevance for understanding Canadian politics. The rules, the goods, or the policies under scrutiny, and the character of the individuals involved in collective decision making are sufficiently complex and varied that the understanding of their regularized relationships requires intensive micro-level investigations. Once done, generalizations at a macro level about Canadian politics and its basic logic may then be advanced with more confidence about their empirical manifestations. It is, if one will, a 'bottom-up' rather than a 'top-down' strategy for advancing our understandings of the body politic. However, it is not the only kind of empirical evidence used in this book.

This second phase of empirical investigations into the basic logic of the Canadian governance system employed standard data-collection and -analysis techniques. But it also employed the technique of observer participant, as the author took an active role in the formulation and implementation of policies, in the dissemination of research, and in the negotiating interfaces between governmental agencies, businesses, interest groups, and concerned members of the general public. Observer participation is occasionally used in sociology, rarely used in political science, and often disparaged by scholastics. It is, however, an example of how conjectures may be posed, and refutations advanced, in a community of citizens that wishes to learn about itself and its stock of accumulated wisdom.

It owes some of its inherent value to the genius of a former mayor of the biggest municipality in the site in question.

The third pathway paralleled in time these two previous modes of analysis. This pathway is not usually associated with institutional and constitutional politics, and even less with policy analysis. It is signalled by publications on the methodology of rules and policies, in general, and by the epistemology of rules and policy evaluations, in particular. Early work, already referred to, criticized the narrowness of existing policy evaluations in political economy because of what may be called the 'throat-slitting' characteristics of Occam's razor (Sproule-Jones 1972). More particularly, standard welfare economics used oversimplifying assumptions about the omniscience and omnipotence of political decision makers to make and implement appropriate policy decisions for society. Economic prescriptions for governmental action often ignored the rules under which governmental bodies might take action. Later work reflected on the diverse epistemological foundations for evaluating natural-resources management in general (Sproule-Jones 1981), public policies even more generally (Sproule-Jones 1983), and citizen-based evaluations more particularly (Sproule-Jones 1978b). The difficulties of devising alternatives to standard evaluative techniques, such as benefit-cost criteria, were returned to again in an edited volume of essays explaining the normative basis of rules for interpersonal comparisons of utility (Sproule-Jones 1984b). The strategy in these studies was to generate critical self-awareness on the part of the investigator and the reader as to the fragility of knowledge that underscored social-science generalizations and techniques for verification.

This third pathway and strategy has already been tentatively explored in the opening pages of this book, and will come and go throughout its contents. This strategy recurs because the thrust of the analysis of the basic logic of Canadian politics is evaluative in form. I seek to advance propositions that criticize the rules and outcomes of Canadian politics, and this reasoning must constantly be reinforced by justifications of its epistemological bases. The danger is that the reader may reject the presentation of generalization and evidence as simply one more person's views on the Canadian polity. The book *is* one more person's views, but it is also one more person's views advanced and refined as considered conjectures. The considerations include methodological and epistemological ones.

Progress in the formulation of understandings about political arrangements and their basic logics can proceed with conjectures advanced on the bases of explicit methodological strategies and
epistemological assumptions. Without these bases, scholarship reduces to a series of footnotes citing previous analyses or, even worse,
a matter of acceptance or rejection on the grounds of authority. The
reader as well as the writer of this book share authority for coming
to common agreement about rules and their policy consequences.
Sharing of authority is facilitated by prior appreciation of the modes
of analysis, theoretical and empirical. The question 'Where on earth
is this fellow getting this from?' will be answered in various parts
of the book.

Pedigrees

Any book that discusses the basic logic of government in Canada
must make some reference to previous writings that have influenced
the scholarship in this book. Canadians have long debated the fundamental nature of federalism, not least because of its capacity to
ameliorate, and occasionally amplify, fundamental value differences
between francophones and anglophones. Rival conceptions of the
federal character of Canada have been advanced but not resolved
(Black 1975). Recently, a royal commission was able to take the
current forms of parliamentary government and federalism as
'givens' within which economic-development prospects must be
advanced (Macdonald Commission 1985).

While the influence of these indigenous works will be apparent
throughout the book, the thrust of the book owes its inspiration to
the method and analysis of *Democracy in America* provided by
Alexis de Tocqueville in the first part of the nineteenth century (de
Tocqueville 1960). De Tocqueville rooted the workings of that system in the capacity of individuals possessing sovereign equality to
pursue matters of common concern in concert with each other.
Consequently, 'written laws exist in America, once one sees the daily
execution of them; but although everything moves regularly, the
mover can nowhere be discovered. The hand that directs the social
machine is invisible – In no country of the world does the law hold
so absolute a language as in America; and in no country is the right
of applying it vested in so many hands' (de Tocqueville 1960, I:
73–4). Here, then, are the efficient rather than dignified parts of

the American constitution. There may be a similar basic logic underlying the Canadian constitution, but undoubtedly it will differ from this American experience.

There are three recent books that share this source of inspiration from de Tocqueville. Vincent Ostrom's *The Meaning of American Federalism* (1991), Antoni Kaminski's *An Institutional Theory of Communist Regimes* (1992), and Amos Sawyer's *The Emergence of Autocracy in Liberia* (1992) attempt to describe the basic logic of particular political regimes scattered throughout the world. A Canadian equivalent may be opportune at this time of extended constitutional crisis.

The other intellectual stream of writings on the basic logic of government that will be apparent throughout the book is that most often associated with the term 'public choice.' In particular, the works of James Buchanan on constitutional choice (especially his and G. Tullock's *The Calculus of Consent* [1962]) and Vincent Ostrom on what he calls *Res publica* (see, especially, his *The Intellectual Crisis of American Public Administration* [1989]) have animated the analysis of rules, their logic, and the ways in which they can be discovered.

Other writings have proved to be highly influential in the development of this book. Any discussion of public policy at its operational level must take into account the physical as opposed to the social character of these policies. For example, some principles of hydrology, water chemistry, ecology, and civil engineering may have to be used along with social, economic, and political generalizations to achieve an understanding of environmental policies in any watershed. The policy analyst has to draw upon these principles about the nature of the good in order to understand the limits and opportunities for collective decision making about the environment. This book draws upon a variety of writings about the nature of particular goods or public policies, and especially upon discussions with patient scientists, engineers, and other practitioners of public policies.

Some important writings about the nature of individuals engaged in collective decision making have also proved influential. I refer to studies of coordinated behaviour in markets, such as those by Smith (1937) and Hayek (1948); in hierarchies, such as Ostrom's (1980); and in decision situations more generally, such as those by Axelrod (1984), Oakerson (1988), and E. Ostrom (1989). The thrust of these writings is the search for a basic understanding of individuals in so far as they are engaged in activities with others, without adopting crude and unobservable concepts, like that of utility.

Finally, these writings on the nature of rules, the nature of the good, and the nature of individuals in collective-decision situations have been supplemented by ideas fostered in the philosophy of social science. Paradoxically, it has been the writings of logical positivists such as Hempel (1965) and Nagel (1961) that have persuaded me to treat logical analysis and empirical investigation as contextual in form. Analysis and proof may, indeed, vary in degrees of rigour and sophistication, and should, indeed, be pursued with the highest standards of completeness and accuracy. However, the standards of completeness and accuracy depend on context, on their ability to advance the understanding of those to whom the studies are addressed. I would not go as far as Winch (1958) in suggesting that all understanding is, in turn, rule or culture bounded, nor so far as Ostrom (1980, 1991) in posting that a method of 'empathetic understanding' or *Verstehen* can form the bridge of understanding among scholars, practitioners, and laypeople. I would, however, suggest that multiple methods of analysis pursued in a continual interactive fashion can provide the basis of common agreement between the scholar 'as artist' and the reader 'as social scientist' (Sproule-Jones 1988b).

Contrasts and Comments

Readers who are immersed in current intellectual debates about governments in Canada may find most of this analysis and its findings disconcerting. This book takes a different view on many issues.

First, this book argues that the national and provincial governments act in predictable ways, in accordance with constitutional rules, and that this predictable activity takes the form of *both* cooperation and competition. Constitutional practice is a relatively stable game – a metagame in the light of its role relative to politics as practised in the various parliaments, legislatures, bureaucracies, and other forums in Canada. However, it is a stable metagame, displaying cooperative and competitive strategies on the part of its players. These strategies are irksome to many players at different times and in different policy contexts, and consequently the game is subject to constant demands for renegotiation. The threat of secession is always likely, and is a measure of the desperation produced by adherence to the rules and competitive conduct of the metagame. The emergence of cooperative conduct to contain secessionary impulses is also likely, and has proved sufficient in Canadian history. But strategic errors, fallible players, and a distrust of cooperative manoeuvres may prevent the emergence of cooperative conduct and rend the game asunder. Apart from these contingencies, the emphasis in this book on the concurrency of cooperation and competition in Canadian institutional politics sets the analysis apart from orthodox interpretations alluded to in later chapters.

Second, students of the literature on public policy will recognize herein two important differences from current analysis. First, public policy is treated as public policies, in the plural, because each public policy is defined as having a physical, non-human core that acts as a fundamental technical constraint on human manipulation. Thus, for example, environmental policy includes, at its core, biochemical and biophysical parameters of water, land, or air, or commercial shipping policy includes technical characteristics about cargoes, cargo handling, ships, and docking and related facilities. Second, and as important, public policy is treated as the product of collective action that may or may not include direct governmental regulation or finance. Public policy reflects the public decision making of at least two but, in most cases, a very large number of individuals. Such decision making may, of course, emerge as governmental, but governmental action remains, for the most part, a marginal and alternative form of collective action. These two contrasts with conventional analyses permit us to integrate social and market operations with political and constitutional decisions. The 'state' is thus viewed as neither autonomous from nor representative of society. It is rather a set of arrangements – 'rules' – that is potentially available for public and private manipulation.

Finally, this book offers forms of evaluation of public policies and the rules through which they are provided, produced, and regulated. These forms of evaluation differ from much conventional analysis. The study evaluates three public policies using or extending conventional evaluative techniques. But it goes farther. It evaluates the rules for each policy together – in what we call rule configurations for public policies. We wish to go farther than, say, that policy X – for example, defence policy – is inadequate, but policy Y – for example, environmental policy – is adequate according to our criteria of assessment. We want, rather, to assess the rule configurations and their 'basic logic.' How well does the system work? What seems to drive the system? Is this drive adequate or inadequate? We will be examining 'the constitutive principles' of the Canadian body politic.

The success of these new intellectual thrusts as well as the coherence and clarity of this book rests in part with colleagues who have read and commented on parts of the book at different times. A number of persons have read the entire manuscript and have been of immense help in suggesting improvements. Bill Coleman of McMaster University, Phil Sabetti of McGill University, Tony Scott of the University of British Columbia, and especially Vincent Ostrom of Indiana University have helped immeasurably. A special thanks is due to the Workshop in Political Theory and Policy Analysis at Indiana University for the opportunity to prepare the draft manuscript in a supportive and productive ambience in the autumn of 1989. The people who have endured various bits and pieces of the book in written or seminar form are too numerous to mention by name. Their contributions are, nevertheless, appreciated and acknowledged.

This book is organized in three parts. Part I consists of six chapters in which the emphasis is the discovery of the rules-in-use in Canadian parliamentary federalism. Chapter 1 offers a cursory overview of the content of Parts I and II of the book. It provides a summary model, as it were, of the major concepts and major relationships among concepts that will be used to explain the basic logic of governments at work in Canada. It cannot be more than a summary – the concepts and relationships need to be developed in a gradual and less painful fashion in subsequent chapters. Chapter 2 provides many of the building blocks for analysis. In it, we discuss the characteristics of rules, of goods, and of individuals as they engage in rule-ordered public policies. Chapter 3 extends this analysis by discussing the ways in which rules are designed and the particular meanings that Canadians, in particular, and people in general attach to rules. Chapters 4 and 5 discuss, in turn, the basic logics in Canadian constitutional, institutional, and operational rules-in-use. We examine the constitutional rules and discover that the logic of Canadian federalism creates a 'club' of the federal and provincial governments, and that the logic of parliamentary sovereignty creates a 'club' that is executive centred or Crown dominated. Some consequences of the constitutional logic are revealed in chapter 5 when we analyse the constitutional rules for policy provision, production, and regulation. We show how the institutional rules exhibit instability but within the stable parameters of the constitutional 'super game.' Some conclusions for the operational rules-in-use are also explored in this chapter.

Part II traces the constitutional, institutional, and operational rules for three policy cases in a 'micro site' in Canada. We shift levels of analysis in order to examine and evaluate public policies as they actually occur 'in the field.' The 'micro site' selected is that of Hamilton Harbour, and the methodologies selected draw upon the history and geography of the site (as exogenous variables) and upon the economics, engineering, chemistry, and biology necessary to understand commercial shipping, recreational boating, and water-quality management. These concerns are the contents of chapters 6 through 9. Chapter 10 summarizes the findings of our evaluations of the rules and of governments at work, and of how different configurations of rules result in different policy outcomes. Sometimes good things, like dessert, are better tasted at the end rather than at the beginning of consumption!

Part III is both a conclusion and an evaluation of the 'constitutive principles' of Canadian parliamentary federalism. Here we examine the cumulative effects of rule configurations designed and altered to meet a series of historical exigencies. The evaluation is both pessimistic and optimistic. It is pessimistic because it reveals that the 'constitutive principle' that 'the Crown can do no wrong' is only ameliorated by the competing principles of representative federalism. It is optimistic because the inconsistencies of the 'constitutive principles' permit a series of fundamental contests of ideas to occur within the body politic. And it is the contest of ideas that captures the virtues of Western civilization (Berman 1984). Indeed, this book is offered to contest the prejudgments of the reader. I ask only that the reader suspend his or her prejudgments until the contest is fully engaged at the end of the book. May *each* reader then declare which is the winner.

PART I: Public Policies and Rule Configurations

1

A Framework for Institutional and Policy Analysis

A Time of Turbulence

The late 1980s and early 1990s are proving to be a time of extraordinary political change – in Central and Eastern Europe, in Southern Africa and South America, and in countries and communities, large and small. These changes are most marked at a constitutional level, in terms of a fundamental reordering of the powers of rulers, elected and non-elected. But the changes also reflect a fundamental reordering of political ideas, about the powers of rulers and their relationships with the ruled. The two are related: changes in political ideas are accompanying changes in constitutions and regimes.

The results of all of those changes are uncertain. Political institutions, processes and relationships will change, but in which directions and with what consequences can be only a matter of speculation. What can be said – and this is not merely a truism – is that new and revised public policies will emerge as a consequence. Public policies are the emergent outcomes of structural conditions in different times and places. Political, social, and economic structures provide a framework for policies that evolve in different communities.

Canada is not escaping the worldwide demands for basic structural changes. The effects of such pressure are most marked in the area of constitutional change. A series of constitutional debates has continued for more than sixty years, supplementing the evolution of constitutional conventions and institutional changes. As this book is being written, a set of proposed changes, to replace the proposals of the defeated Meech Lake Accord of 1987, is being vigorously

debated and discarded. Fundamental ideas or agreed-upon conceptions about the constitutional bases of society are being challenged.

But the demands for structural changes are not limited to the
constitutional sphere. Newer processes are being developed for
reordering the relationships in society and the economy. Relationships between men and women, born and unborn, people and an-
imals, humans and the environment, management and labour, foreign
and domestic capital, immigrants and indigenous peoples ... the list
goes on – are being refashioned. The results will be sets of rules
governing these relationships. The end-product will be emergent
public policies that must meet the acceptance of diverse communities or publics.

This book is about the rules or the structures of politics, economics, and society. It is about how the rules for such different
spheres of life fit together. It is also about the public policies that
emerge from such rules. Not least, it is about how well such rules
and public policies work and how governments work within the
rules for Canada. This chapter provides a framework for the analysis
and appraisal of rules, governments, and public policies in Canada.

Basic Ingredients

If eating provides a method for the proof of a pudding, then reading
is the obvious method for proving this book. This is not to say all
readers will share common tastes. To belabour the metaphor a little
longer, the basic ingredients of this book are three concepts – rules,
goods, and individuals. They are explained at length in chapter 3.
Here they are briefly described as the basic ingredients of the framework we use.

Rules

Rules are norms of behaviour that people follow. They include laws
promulgated by parliaments and courts. They also include social
agreements made within and between families, kin, social networks,
formal organizations, and other kinds of collective groupings.

Take the rule of 'fair shares.' This simple rule governs the dividing
up of something of benefit into two or more portions. It is frequently
used as the basis for distributing gifts among siblings, according
road access to converging queues of cars, or providing opportunities

to speak to committee members. It may need to be enforced by an acknowledged referee, who may also have to decide the legitimacy of claims made and the precise fairness of the allotment of shares. This simple rule is not, however, used in all contexts. Assigning unequal shares may be the norm in formal organizations as a method, for example, of dividing benefits according to merit or status. The context or the policy issue may require complex rules.

Typically more than one rule operates in any given context. The school classroom, for example, includes rules of 'good' behaviour, rules about the 'authority' of the teacher, rules about how to learn a subject, and the subject's own internal rules. It may take the students some time to bring all these rules in convergence. Multiple rules, in other words, form a configuration of rules.

A large set of rule configurations applies to governments, those legal institutions for making collective choices about matters that are of value to two or more persons. Rule configurations exist about the selection of government officials, their roles in relation to one another, and the limits on their decision making. Rules about rules also exist in which the institutional arrangements may be codified and changed; these are constitutional rule configurations. But individuals may also make collective choices outside governmental rule configurations.

One example are the choices made about buying and selling in the market-place. Economic transactions take place within rule configurations that may be set and conferred by the traders themselves. These would include rules about contracts, torts, and the security of property. Typically, the rules of the market-place are intermeshed with some rules established and enforced by government institutions, including courts. Of particular concern may be the rules for arbitrating disputes and for ensuring that the rules of the market are fully specified and stable enough for buyers and sellers to make easy comparisons of alternatives.

Acceptance of the rule configurations by individual persons is critical for the rules to influence actual behaviour. Government officials often use the terms 'compliance' and 'enforcement' to refer in broad terms to the acceptance of rules by individuals. The key is whether or not most individuals choose to act in conformity with the rules or choose to substitute alternative and competing rules. Much the same can be said about governmental officials who are charged with the implementation of statutes for the provision, production, and regulation of different governmental policies. When rules actually possess operational relevance – when they are enforced and enforceable – we may refer to them as rules-in-use. In contrast, rules that have no impact on behaviour are rules-in-form. This distinction is critical for understanding how governments in Canada work. We will explore and explain the rules-in-use for public policies and evaluate them in conjunction with rules-in-form. The distinction also imposes methodological demands on the reader (as well as the author). More will be said about these later in the chapter.

One basic ingredient of our analysis is, therefore, rules, which are multiple, configurative, and in use. They span all forms of collective action, some of which takes place with direct governmental involvement. Their role also depends on two other basic ingredients.

Goods

'Goods' and 'public policies' are used interchangeably in this analysis; both include some physical and non-human elements in their composition. Thus abortion policies include, at least, biological matter; environmental goods may involve the chemistry of water; and airline safety policies include metals and energy. Such natural elements are transformed by human ingenuity and marshalled, through rules, into public policies.

Consequently, policies are much more than statements of intent promulgated through legal statutes or other instruments of governmental action. They are assets fashioned by individuals engaged in collective action, and emerge from the constraints and opportunities of the non-human world.

This non-human element in public policies poses considerable demands on the analyst and the reader. It means that an understanding of any public policy requires some understanding of the technologies with which goods are formed and emerge. Thus an understanding of environmental policies requires some understanding of, at a minimum, 'materials balance' analysis for the generation and reuse or disposal of residual wastes from the processing, manufacturing, or consumption of natural resources (as I shall show in chapter 9). Or, to put the point another way, knowledge about a policy field like housing requires some knowledge about how houses are sited, constructed, financed, and sold. One of the most intriguing parts of political analysis is the discovery of how governmental rules and governmental pronouncements percolate into policy outcomes as assets endowed (in part) by nature.

There are times and places in which governments themselves provide and produce their own goods, rather than regulate or help to secure goods established by non-governmental actions. Policies in much of Eastern Europe used to be largely of this sort, as is (to use a Canadian example) electrical-power generation in most provinces. Governmental policies may thus stand apart from collective policies more generally, and be in a monopolistic or competitive relationship with the policies of other 'public' actors. More typically, one finds a mingling of policies, with complex rule configurations developed for each and every policy in a given society.

Individuals

Individuals are the third basic ingredient. We begin with the premiss that individual people – rather than groups such as nations, classes, or policy communities – are the ultimate constituents of the world – but that they combine with others to form a variety of 'publics' from which public policies emerge. Premisses take the analyst and reader only so far; other factors may operate to change the character of individuals. Our other two ingredients operate in this fashion. Consequently, while, in an abstract sense, we may reason that individuals have multiple and adaptive motives, in the context of different rules and different goods certain motives may predominate and certain behaviours become predictable.

For example, in simple competitive markets, where the rules permit repetitive trading and where the good is easily measured, the motives of traders may converge towards the maximization of their own economic advantages. In many of the contexts explored in this book, the rules permit a wider range of behaviours, and policy attributes are much more complex. Less convergence of motives and behaviour is a result, and the policy is much less stable. Such is the nature of environmental-policy making in any urbanized watershed, for example, where the policy is highly complex, the rule configurations are large and ambiguous, and the diverse individuals and their motives are difficult to characterize.

These are all preliminary statements about the people that help to formulate, produce, regulate, experience, and enjoy public policies in Canada. The reader no less than the author is likely a part of these processes.

Decision Situations

Because of the technical character of each public policy, rule configurations are constructed by individuals for each and every good. Decisions made about rules, and decisions made within rules about goods, are 'decision situations.' Decision situations abound and may range from 'street level' matters, such as the decisions reached by teacher and student about a course of study, to matters that engage politicians, senior bureaucrats, and lobbyists in the 'corridors of power.' Much of the drama of politics comes from an intense examination of a few decision situations, such as elections, parliamentary debates, or Supreme Court cases.

I do not attempt to describe, explain, or model decision situations in this book. Rather, I am interested in the rules that set up and structure decision situations and in the rules that flow out of them. Such rules are those, say, under which governments fund and organize schools and those that follow about the scale and conditions of the classrooms. These and other rules result in education as a public policy 'in the field.' It is how the rules-in-use affect public policy outcomes and impacts as they are experienced by members of various communities that is the central concern of this book. It focuses in depth on three public policy cases: commercial shipping, recreational boating, and water-quality management. But, more important, in this book we are engaged in tracing the rules of government from constitutional decision situations through institutional decision situations to common everyday policy decisions that actually affect the public. It is the effects of rules-in-use that provide a major test of how well governments work.

Policy Outcomes and Impacts

Public policies, of course, differ in their intrinsic characteristics, and these have different consequences for the public. We disentangle these characteristics and consequences by emphasizing that policies, when produced (by institutions, government, and/or non-government), have measurable dimensions and that these dimensions affect citizens in measurable ways.

Relatively simple goods, like automobiles or electrical power, can be measured in terms of their physical dimensions of production, for example, the number of cars manufactured or the number of kilowatts generated. They may also have measurable *multiple* dimensions; so, the production of cars and electricity may also be measured in terms of the dollar values of cars sold or kilowatt-hours consumed.

Many goods are more complex, however, including many produced or regulated directly by government. Police patrols may have to be assessed by using multiple measures, none of which is a perfect indicator of the outcomes of the policy of policing. Both miles of streets patrolled and number of sworn officers on the 'beat' may be used as imperfect measures of outcomes. Similarly, environmental regulation may have to be measured by a cluster of indicators, such as changes in the effluent parameters of smokestack or sewer outfall and changes in the violations of permit regulations. The point is that some ingenuity may be necessary to develop valid and reliable measures of policy outcomes as they are experienced by the public.

Much of the same can be said about policy impacts. The size and the socio-economic characteristics of the relevant public will vary from good to good. The development of a commercial shipping port will have multiple impacts, for example, on other competing ports and on competing modes of transport such as rail, road, and air, and these impacts will differ for each community in which a port is located. Some goods, such as national defence, will have a scale greater than or equal to the territorial boundaries of a community. Others will have smaller scales and be diversified in terms of the 'consuming' public. I begin, in chapter 2, to refine these preliminary statements by using and developing the concepts of public goods, common pools, and externalities – concepts that originated in the economics of public finance and are now widely used in political science and other disciplines. The concepts offer a way to help us understand policy outcomes and impacts.

One of our conclusions may be stressed at this time: The dimensions of policy outcomes and impacts will vary with the rule configurations under which they are produced. Public policies are like sculptures; in raw form they consist of a block of material, but they do not take shape and meaning without tools and without the skills of the artist. The rules provide many of the tools, and individuals within various institutions provide the skills. Thus a defence policy, for example, will take shape only when the rule configurations of military organization, alliances, and hostile armies are taken into account and when the skills of politicians and military personnel are applied to the task.

This conclusion means that rule configurations may be changed to alter the outcomes and impacts of a public policy. This is the central hypothesis behind the evaluation of public policies undertaken in this book and in comparable analysis in the evaluation literature. Rule configurations make a difference.

In exploring how the rule configurations for public policies in Canada work and how well they work, policy outcomes and impacts for our three cases are given detailed evaluation and other examples are also examined. These evaluations provide an initial evaluation of how well the current rule configurations work. Thus we will want to specify the basic logic of the rule configurations as found in parliamentary and federal practices, to name only two of the more important sets of constitutional rules.

The analysis also goes deeper: We shall evaluate the basic logic of the rule configurations themselves. We do this for two reasons. First, rule configurations are sets of interacting rules, all of which operate together to affect policy outcomes and impacts. For example, the rules for broadcasting policies interact with the rules for educational and welfare policies. These sets of rules stem from differing institutional rules, some emphasizing federal powers, others provincial powers, and still others the powers associated with so-called private broadcasters, schools and artists under corporate legal rules, and foreign broadcasters and cultures under different political regimes. A multiplicity of different rules and different sources of rules forms any rule configuration. However, a change in one rule may not, in itself, result in an automatic change in policy outcomes and impacts. Other elements in the rule configurations may compensate, overcompensate, or shift in other directions. Thus provincial rules have permitted 'educational' institutions to engage in broadcasting or federal institutions to engage in educational policies under various guises and labels. As a result, we want to evaluate rule configurations together as a cluster of rules.

The second reason is more perplexing, especially to the practical-minded reader. Yet it is essential to gain a full understanding of how governments work. The basic logic of rule configurations will be conducted according to criteria about 'institutional fairness.' The reasons, addressed in depth in chapters 3 and 11, relate to the meanings that different people give to rules. Rules develop an emotional and symbolic significance for many persons. This is most obviously the case for constitutional rules, which one might say, characterize the nation-state, the provincial and local 'homelands,' and traditional transnational arrangements such as alliances. Such significance may also attend more particularized rules such as those of alumnae to a university, of monarchists to the Queen, of new Canadians to immigration rules, or of farmers to 'supply management' rules that 'protect' their way of life. These attachments imply that rules cannot be fully evaluated in instrumental terms, in terms of their effects on policy outcomes and inputs. The criterion of 'institutional fairness' attempts to embrace the instrumental and the symbolic character of rules.

Caution needs to be taken that too much not be read into the term 'symbolic'; as it is used here, it has a slightly different meaning than is customary. I do *not* divide rules into the two categories of real and symbolic. Rather I divide rules into the two categories of rules-in-use and rules-in-form (as previously noted), and each of these types may have symbolic impact. For example, provincial regulatory permits on industrial outfalls may be rules-in-use in most provinces; that is, they may have practical applications in the management of the water-quality environment. However, they may also take on symbolic significance when violations of permits are discovered, symbolizing increasing environmental degradation or industrial priorities for production over the environment. Similarly, the non-compliance of industries with provincial environmental permits may indicate that the permit process is a rule-in-form, as the rules are not being enforced by the agency in question. The non-compliance may be seen as merely symbolic, representing governmental accommodation with the short-run interests of the industrial sectors of the economy. Thus the real and the symbolic are often intertwined. When symbolic significance is attached to rules-in-use or rules-in-form, the value of rules takes on an extra meaning. Rules are not simply instrumental devices for the individual citizen to attain valued ends in collaboration with others, and perhaps through the agency of government. Rules may possess both an instrumental and an intrinsic value. We must consequently employ additional and different criteria of evaluation to those commonly applied in policy analysis.

Time-and-Place Contingencies

Communities of different sizes and scales will face different opportunities and limitations for historical and geographical reasons. Such is obviously the case for natural-resource endowments, which may be in different stages of exploitation or rehabilitation in any locale, if indeed a locale is fortunate to possess an abundancy of resources. Interregional and international rules may have to be developed to permit markets in different locales to trade resources. On a national scale, Canada is fortunate to possess many natural resources, although significant differences exist among regions in terms of abundancies, and of abundancies left from previous generations. The point of these comments is that public policies or goods often are composed, in part, of raw or processed or manufactured resources. The limits or opportunities to provide public policies will be affected by such endowments.

Parallel comments may be made about rule configurations as forms of cultural endowments. Different communities may have developed ways to provide themselves with valued goods, and these ways, expressed in norms and legal instruments, will be inherited by newer generations as they develop newer goods and adapt older ones. Sometimes, these rule bequests will prove adaptable to new circumstances; 'public health' policies, for example, have built successfully upon the learned rules of sanitation developed in Bentham's England. At other times, the rule configurations prove dysfunctional for new generations, such as is the case with the rules for the military-like command of police forces in multicultural communities. The point is that the rules for public policy are never invented *de novo*. Rather they build, particularly at the operational level, on the accumulated wisdoms of previous generations. Canada, like most developed countries, has inherited much 'capital stock' from previous generations in Western Europe and North America.

A close relationship between the cultural endowments in rules and the natural endowments in resources will be found in the stores of ideas and methodologies accumulated by individual persons. It is a truism to state that individuals possess both biological and cultural inheritances. More important for our purposes in a book on Canadian public policies is to remember that individuals are constantly learning and adapting to new circumstances for their own and for their collective advantage. Such is the case even for those persons with power to effect fundamental changes in constitutional rules. These persons have a capital stock of ideas and methodologies about, for example, how parliaments operate, how federal-provincial relations are conducted, or how ministers of the Crown relate to cabinet colleagues. The stock of ideas and methodologies about the basic logic of the rule configurations may be called the 'constitutive principles.' In Canada, the 'constitutive principles' appear to differ from one region to the next, and (historically) fundamental differences exist between French and English Canada over the nature of these principles. We should thus anticipate that 'constitutive principles' will differ from locale to locale and from generation to generation. The turbulence behind the political changes in 1989, 1990, and 1991 is rooted in such differences that exist between communities and generations in Eastern Europe.

These three kinds of issues affect the kinds of generalizations that may be made about the basic logic of rule configurations in Canada. Different time-and-place contingencies exist within Canada and between Canada and other lands. Our generalizations about public policy take into account these contingencies.

The Framework

The basic ingredients of our analysis – rules, goods, and individuals – when combined in multiple decision situations, produce policy outcomes and impacts that vary by time and place. The policy outcomes and impacts, as well as local and historical contingencies, affect, in turn, the rule configurations and the other basic ingredients. This simple framework is presented in figure 1.

The complexities of our analysis will be revealed in subsequent chapters. The basic ingredients and the evaluation of policy outcomes are elaborated upon in various parts of this book. But, most of this book is devoted to an elaboration of the rule configurations to be found in Canada in the late 1980s and early 1990s, rule configurations that demonstrate a basic logic about how and why policies are provided, produced, or regulated. This book is, essentially, a study of rules-in-use.

The framework may be transferable to different times and places. The identification of rules-in-use requires a form of empirical investigation that builds from 'the bottom up,' from policy outcomes and impacts to the rule configurations, many of which have been

Figure 1. Framework for policy analysis

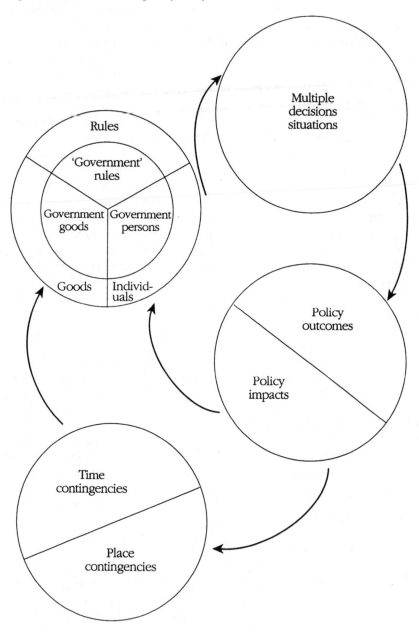

especially constructed to ensure that the technical dimensions of the goods are adapted to the requirements of the individual persons. They are, as it were, 'tailor-made.' Other elements in the rule configurations-in-use make possible this 'tailoring.' These are the adaptable elements of the institutional and constitutional rules. Canada shares many of these adaptable elements with other communities.

The 'bottom-up' methodology may be contrasted with the 'top-down' methodology in which the statements and behaviours of governmental officials are taken as evidence of public policies. Policies exist only at the interface of relationships between goods and individual citizens, and officialdom tends to work only at the margins of this interface. We do not, therefore, examine parliamentary debates or policy reports of ministries in order to discover policy outcomes, impacts, and the rules-in-use that yield such outcomes and impacts. We also do not assume that governments are the sole source of public policies. Policies are often generated by individual persons acting in collaboration, with the aid of rules, and governments supplement, aid, restrict, or diminish the policy process. This is how governments are at work in many policy cases. A 'top-down' view could lead the reader to misjudge how governments work and how well they work.

The ultimate test of the success of the framework must be made by each reader, using his or her own methods of understanding. The framework will now be built again, explicitly in the next two chapters, and in chapter 10. Elsewhere, the success of the framework will be apparent in the analysis of the rules and Canadian public policies. The success of the enterprise we call Canadian parliamentary federalism will be assessed at the end of the book. We begin again by looking at the basic ingredients.

2

Foundations of Understanding

Two Cases

In the beginning, there are two cases ...! Each leads to some useful inductive inferences about rules, the behaviour of persons within rules, and the relationships of persons and rules to policy situations. The identification of the more generic theoretical bases for these inferences is temporarily postponed.

Case One

Consider the simple case of household garbage removal, something most readers will be familiar with. It is a simple case in the sense that the good or policy is technically simple. It has few attributes that have not been understood for many years; there is relatively little uncertainty about its physical/chemical/biological composition and its impact on the natural and social worlds.

A farmer facing the everyday decision about what to do with his garbage has a limited range of choices. He can dig a hole and transport the garbage there once a day or once every few days, and repeat the process when the hole fills up. He could dump the waste in a wood lot. He could separate the garbage into types and compact the wet, easily biodegradable waste. He has few complicated choices to make. For economic reasons, no municipality or private haulage firm is likely to offer its services. There are unlikely to be any institutional rules in the forms of laws and regulations constraining his choices. And his technical constraints may be limited to the availability of wasteland and the availability of such land sufficiently far from the farmhouse (for aesthetic reasons), well water (for health reasons), and stock (for safety reasons).

A city dweller has a much more complicated range of choices. She can transport her own garbage to an unused lot or to a city dump. She could even compact the wet wastes and dig a hole in her garden for the remainder. But she is likely to encounter institutional rules prohibiting the domestic disposal of most trash for public health reasons and for aesthetic reasons. She then must choose either to defy these rules or use municipal or private collection services. She is likely to find that the municipal or private services are cheaper than the next-best alternative, as well as more technically feasible than the continual transport and search for dump sites.

The range of choice paradoxically begins to widen at this stage. The urban dweller must deal with other people in ensuring that relatively safe, cheap, and reliable service is available. The other people can be public work crews, private contractors, elected politicians, and adjacent neighbours. She has a socially interdependent relationship with these persons, and these interdependencies are linked together by rules and norms of conduct about the economic and technical means of safe collection and removal. A community of interests exists.

The community of urban dwellers will have to choose, in concert with their elected representatives, what kinds of collection and disposal services to provide – curbside or back-yard pick ups, weekly or more frequent service – the number of cans and types of permissible wastes that will be hauled away, and the method of payment – in taxes or fees. They may have to go farther (but we typically leave these decisions to politicians and public servants) and determine how to produce (rather than provide) the service – through municipal crews, franchises, or burning rather than burying the waste. Rules will have to be developed, monitored, enforced, and made available for reconsideration and change.

Recently McDavid has provided the scholar and practitioner with a nationwide survey of how Canadian city and town residents have chosen to organize this relatively simple technical public policy (McDavid 1985; McDavid and Schick, 1987; Tickner and McDavid 1986). As one might expect, the choices of these 'communities of interest' have varied considerably, depending on such factors as population density, climate, and rules for provision and production. What is remarkable about the choices that Canadians have made is how costs are only one of many factors they have taken into account. For example, private-sector collection through contracts and franchises is 41 per cent cheaper in terms of costs per household, even when different service-provision levels, scale economies, and environmental factors are considered. Private firms have greater labour productivity, are more technologically advanced, and even pay slightly higher salaries than do public-sector collection agencies. Yet more municipalities prefer to produce their own services rather than contract for them. There are 'rules-in-use' for the provision and production of solid-waste policies that make the mix of choices among similar communities of interest seem different, and seem to differ in the priority they place on economic efficiency.

Case Two

Contrast the simple case of garbage removal with the complex case of environmental policy for a river like the St Lawrence or the Fraser. Ambient water conditions are determined not only by physical characteristics of the river, such as flows, tides, and turbidity, but also by chemical and biological parameters, including dissolved oxygen, nutrients, and concentrations of naturally occurring heavy metals. This natural world is then subject to human intervention, perhaps for water supply for drinking, irrigation, flood control, or industrial cooling. The water may be used for transportation, fishing, recreation, and (typically) waste disposal. It may also be subject to atmospheric depositions and natural or human activities outside the watershed itself. These kinds of interventions may alter the in-stream physical, chemical, and biological conditions. The attributes of ambient water quality as a good may be measured on multiple dimensions, subject to considerable scientific uncertainties as to causes and effects.

This complex web of interdependencies that characterizes the good in question may be partially captured by the concept of a 'public good,' in which ambient-water-quality conditions are jointly produced (by multiple human and non-human 'uses') and jointly consumed (by human and other biological 'users'). The concept of a 'public good,' which is discussed in greater detail later, directs our attention to the fact that any *one* person's contributions to and requirements for the water-quality environment are not noticeable in comparison with every *other* person's contributions and requirements. It is therefore possible to conceive of a world in which no one bothers to take account of his or her environmental interdependencies with other persons, and, at the limit, the river becomes severely polluted because of this 'beggar thy neighbour' attitude.

Fortunately, rules have been developed to take account, at least partially, of these environmental interdependencies. Canada inherited the rules developed in common law, such as the rule regarding 'nuisances,' to regulate individual behaviour and environmental pollution. It also inherited the customs of indigenous and immigrant populations, and has supplemented (and sometimes replaced) these rules with federal, provincial, and local laws and regulations.

This does not mean, of course, that the 'rules-in-use' are always appropriate. They may be inadequate to deal with changing social activities, as are the rules governing the use and disposal of persistent organic chemicals by households and industry. They may be inadequate to deal with pollution that crosses political boundaries, as is the case with international transfers of sulphur dioxide, which can be deposited in watersheds in the form of acid rain. They may also contain inherent contradictions in the sense that some regulated uses of a riverine environment, such as the construction of docks, wharves, and marinas, may destroy other regulated uses, such as the preservation of wetlands for the nurturing of fish and lower forms of biological life.

Resolution of contradictions and conflicts at this, the operational-rule, level of the direct production or regulation of a policy can be resolved at 'a higher level,' the institutional-rule level. Agencies, in conjunction with corporate persons, and individual persons are granted institutional authority to resolve contradictions and conflicts. The solutions enforced at this level may again be technically and operationally defective – at a minimum, they may be in the interests of only some uses and users – and appeals are often made for rejigging the institutional rules-in-use.

Frequently, complaints are made at the operational-rule level that the multiple uses of a river are not coordinated and that conflicts among uses are amplified by the institutional rules. In the late 1970s, my investigations of these complaints on the Fraser River suggested they were unfounded. At the operational level, 54 agencies and organizations were centrally involved with environmental water policy. These 'units' had worked out 781 coordinative arrangements, more than 400 of which were frequently instituted and were planned between two or more organizations. Regular and integrated co-ordination took place, irrespective of level of government (local, provincial, federal) and of public or private ownership of the organization (Sproule-Jones 1981: 651–79). These data do not imply that multiple-use conflicts did not occur or were not resolved in a 'technically effective' way; they do imply, however, that the institutional rules were functionally related for operational-rule co-ordination.

Implications of the Two Cases for Public Policy Analysis

The two cases provide some useful lessons as we begin to formulate a more rigorous analysis of Canadian public policies, the rules through which they are manifested, and the roles of government in the process.

First, the cases illustrate how public policies differ in their technical attributes. Solid-waste collection involves simple mechanical technologies, and can be produced and provided in a variety of ways. There are few uncertainties involved in the production of the good, and the production outputs may be relatively easily measured in terms of tonnes collected or households serviced. (Solid-waste disposal, as opposed to mere collection, has more complex technologies because of environmental hazards and uncertainties.)

Water-quality management, in contrast, has complex technical attributes. Traditional forms of waste disposal rely on relatively simple mechanical, chemical, and biological treatments at point-source sewage outfalls, allied principally to the natural assimilative capacities of the water-body. These technologies have often proved technically ineffective in dealing with discharges of nutrients, heavy metals, and toxic chemicals from both point and non-point sources. The 'cushion' of the assimilative capacities of the water-body has often proved inadequate or has been questioned in relation to these forms of wastes. As a consequence, rules regarding controls at sources, land- and air-based treatments, land- and water-use plans, preconstruction assessments, and recycling of residuals exist for many watersheds. Overlying all these technologies are the scientific uncertainties of causes and effects, in the long and short run. In many cases, new scientific knowledge increases rather than reduces the uncertainties. As a result, it is difficult to measure the effectiveness of the technologies and regulations, the cost-effectiveness of alter-

native technologies and regulations, and the monitoring and enforcement of these interventionist strategies.

In more generic terms, the nature of the good makes it difficult
to apply public policy analyses for one good to another. Generalizations about rules, behaviour, and governmental activities in one
public policy field may not be easily transferable to another. In
particular, we should expect that the relevant communities of interest will vary from one public policy to the next. The community
of individuals that seek to solve problems of solid-waste collection
on environmental water quality or some other policy will vary in
size and territorial scale (Dewey 1927; Ostrom, Tiebout, and Warren
1961; Olson 1969). And the rules we should expect to find regarding
the provision and production of the policy will also vary – in number
and complexities – from one good to the next.

The second lesson to be learned from these cases concerns the
role of individuals in relation to different goods and rules. Individuals share common attributes, as genetic biological beings, and are
thus able to engage with others in matters of mutual concern. They
may do so in markets, in the form of economic transactions. They
may do so in non-market situations, in the form of tangible and
intangible exchange relationships. The patterns that these exchanges exemplify can be destructive of community interests, as in
the 'beggar thy neighbour' or 'free ride' strategy, or they may be
supportive of community interests, as in the reciprocity strategy of
'tit for tat' or the Golden Rule of 'do unto others as you would have
them do unto you.' Much depends on whether individuals share
interests on the basis of the technical nature of goods, in which case
they may jointly produce and/or jointly consume those goods. As
in the case of water quality, they may be bound into commonality
by virtue of jointly producing and jointly consuming the good. But
much also depends on whether individuals share commonalities by
virtue of rules. Individuals may be involved in mutually productive
or mutually destructive situations because of the 'rules-in-use' for
any public policy.

The third lesson is that the rules-in-use for any public policy
create incentive systems, with predictable consequences. At the operational level, rules-in-use need to be distinguished from rules-in-
form. One's friendly garbage collector may decide to ignore the rule
for curbside pick-up only for an elderly resident, or a garage me-
chanic may pour used engine oil down a storm drain in contra-

vention of a municipal by-law. These rules-in-use have been converted to rules-in-form. Also, the rules-in-use may have to be carefully distinguished in order to trace their respective consequences. For example, the common law of 'nuisances' has proved inadequate as a rule for assessing liability from non-point sources, and hence for reducing certain kinds of pollutant loadings. However, it provided riparians with direct legal means to reduce traceable contaminants from point-source dischargers. Its replacement in most Canadian provinces with inconsistently enforced statutes and regulations governing permissible dilution rates from point sources of pollution has removed the potential liability of dischargers from 'downstream' riparians. The consequences are readily apparent for the potential outfall owner.

Finally, it is worth noting how individual citizens are frequently involved in the production and provision of public policies, irrespective of governmental involvement. They may be involved in co-production through simple means such as placing their garbage cans at the curbside, or composting vegetable wastes and thus storing nutrients in their gardens. They may also be involved in co-provision – minimally through elections and maximally through volunteer efforts. Thus the rescue of swimmers and boaters in rivers and bays may be undertaken by privately organized boating groups with little reference to governmental authorities. In the light of this lesson, studies that attempt to measure the relative size of the public and private sectors may be studies of an intellectual artefact and political ideology rather than of a situation involving rules, goods, and individuals.

We are now be in a position to move from preliminary inferences from two hypothetical cases of public policy to a more considered analysis of the rule-based nature of public policies. We begin with the building blocks or hard-core concepts of goods, individuals, and rules.

The Hard Core

Our basic concepts may be called the 'hard core' of our explanation of how government works in Canada. The 'hard core' refers to the basic assumptions and auxiliary hypotheses that are accepted by scholars working in a particular research program (Lakatos 1974). The hard-core concepts do need, however, to be discussed in detail.

One of these hard-core concepts, the nature of rules, forms the basis for much of our understanding of Canadian politics.

The Nature of the Good

Different policies or goods have different technical attributes. That is apparent from our previous discussion. The differences may be captured along a number of different dimensions. Two of them I call 'first-order dimensions.' The remainder I call 'second-order dimensions,' in the sense that they are especially (if not exclusively) significant in any situation in so far as they may affect the first-order dimensions. In other words, they are variables that may be analytically held constant in order to discuss the first-order dimensions. It must also be emphasized that the nature of individuals and the nature of rules may affect, as variables, the first-order dimensions. Again, they are held analytically constant for purposes of clear explication.

First-Order Dimensions of a Good
A useful way to describe the first-order dimensions of any good has been developed in welfare economics during the last thirty or so years. The first of these two first-order dimensions of a good refers to its divisibility or availability. (The terms 'subtractability,' 'rivalness,' and 'joint consumability' are also sometimes used in referring to this dimension.) Some goods, like a loaf of bread, are highly divisible; if one person takes an extra slice, another gets one fewer. Other goods, like clean air, are indivisible for people living within an airshed; if one person takes a breath more, no other person takes one fewer breath.

Some goods possess the characteristic of excludability. It is technically easy to exclude some people from consuming a loaf of bread or cashing an old-age pension cheque, whereas it is technically difficult (or costly) to exclude some people from listening to radio frequencies.

Thus we may construct a simple two-by-two matrix to describe these alternative categorizations of the nature of a good. In figure 2, the two dimensions are displayed, with examples. It may be worth noting that economists sometimes fold the dimensions into one, and refer to public goods as those possessing low degrees of divisibility and exclusivity, and private goods as those possessing high degrees

Figure 2. Two dimensions of goods

Divisibility

	High	Low
High	Bicycles	Bus system
Low	Freeways	Safe streets

Exclusivity

of divisibility and exclusivity. The terminology of such a simple dimension is confusing, however. We may expect public goods to be provided by the public sector, and private goods to be provided by the private sector, yet there is nothing about the technical characteristics of goods per se that would lead us to anticipate these outcomes.

The lack of exclusivity and divisibility of a good establishes a degree of technical interdependence between users and/or producers of that good. Technical interdependencies can also exist between goods, in the sense that production and/or use of one good can create positive or negative consequences for another good. These are normally labelled in welfare economics 'positive' or 'negative' externalities. Thus, orchards create positive externalities for honey production, and pop-radio broadcasts can create negative externalities for beachcombing. In the natural-resources field, many goods have positive and negative externalities for each other, as lands, airsheds, and watercourses are typically used for multiple purposes. The degree of publicness and privateness of each of these externalities or third-party effects varies from good to good and from site to site.

Second-Order Dimensions of a Good
The second-order dimensions of a good are important as they may affect the divisibility and exclusivity of a good over time. They may turn our matrix from a static to a dynamic model as goods change positions on the dimensions as a result of these second-order factors. One set of factors relates to the abundance or scarcity of the good,

either in its natural state (a natural resource) or in a production state (a produced good or service). When goods or services are in abundant supply, there is no 'congestion' over their use and enjoyment, and there is thus no significant divisibility or subtractability problem. Thus a swiftly flowing large river like the Fraser that possesses its own large re-aeration capabilities may easily assimilate oxygen-consuming wastes pumped into its flow without reducing that available for other dischargers. A municipal swimming pool may easily accommodate a large number of swimmers before congestion sets in and one person's enjoyment reduces that of others. Few if any goods are like gravity, where divisibility is never a concern to users. (Remember that institutional factors such as property rights may change the degree of divisibility, but we are looking at technical factors at this stage of our analysis.) Similarly, technical factors may change the degree of exclusivity of a good. For example, the invention of satellites has changed the scarcity of television programs that can be relatively easily watched at home. The size of an aerial and such factors as climate, atmosphere, and land mass are no longer technical factors affecting the exclusivity of television broadcasts.

Three variables affect the technical abundance or scarcity of a good or service. Durability of a good or a service can affect its abundance, as bridges, fire trucks, and even labour-intensive social services can begin to 'wear out' with use. Some goods and services perish with time rather than with use. Still other goods and services may be easily renewable, whereas others may be exhausted and cannot renew themselves easily, as is true of many natural resources.[1]

Finally, one other variable related to divisibility is an important technical attribute of a good, and will prove to be important in subsequent chapters of this book – the measurability of the good. Some goods have easily measurable attributes, related, in part, to their divisibility. Garbage collection can be easily measured in terms of tonnes collected or households serviced. It is easy to partition the goods into such units. Indivisible goods tend to be more difficult to measure and tend to have overlapping technical attributes. Thus

---

1 This discussion has benefited from reference to Kiser and Ostrom's (1987) analysis of the nature of a good. In their discussion of technical characteristics, they suggest a more elaborate scheme, including such additional first-order dimensions as extractability, sensory appeal, and consumability.

water quality may be measured by dissolved oxygen levels in a litre of water, but such a measure captures only one aspect of water quality, and dissolved oxygen levels are related to some other attributes of water quality, such as nutrient loadings.

In sum we must be alert to the first-order and second-order dimensions that describe most of the technical features of a good. They provide, in a static sense, a set of constraints and opportunities that individuals and rules have to take into account in determining the range and diversity of policies available to communities of interest. In a dynamic sense, they provide complexities behind which individual knowledge and rules often lag.

The Nature of Individuals

Our analysis is rooted in the concept of methodological individualism, which has both metaphysical and substantive implications. At the metaphysical level, individuals are taken as the ultimate constituents of the social world. Such is the case whether individuals act independently (for example, reading or burning this book), in concert in institutional settings (such as bureaucracies, markets, or sports clubs), or in concert in informal settings (such as parades or social classes). To put the matter another way, all group concepts – such as the nation-state, social norms, or the genetic endowments of the human species – can be disaggregated into relationships between and among individuals.

It may be important to note that these claims are not made about the methodologies of social science or about the nature of the experiential world. In terms of methodologies, the claim is not being made that all analysis must be made at the micro level about how, for example, individuals choose to vote, exchange goods in markets, or coalesce into political parties or fisheries cooperatives to attain chosen ends. Analysis can proceed at various levels, from the micro situation to the middle range, to the macro analysis of nation-states and the conditions of international war. Decisions about the level of analysis are strategic on the part of the analyst and are based on what best explains the social world.

That claim makes no statement about the nature of the experiential world either. Analysts may disagree about appropriate and valid operationalizations of such social facts as national governments or political parties, and may disagree further about the appropriate theoretical significance of such facts. Resolution of the disagreements can be made only at a metaphysical level and with a common understanding about the meaning that may be assigned to the word 'person.' We adopt the posture that individual human beings are persons and thus similar in many, but not all, observable dimensions. The posture has ethical implications that have been consistent with the mainstream of Western civilization for at least two millennia.

The substantive implications of methodological individualism may be more interesting to the reader who expects this book to illuminate his or her understanding of how government works in Canada. The explanation of Canadian government developed here includes statements and inferences about individual motivations in the light of situations structured by both the nature of the good and the rules of the society. Explanations are developed that imply that individuals have a privileged causal status. The moving agents in society are individuals acting independently or collectively, although the strategic importance of differing individuals in differing situations is recognized. In a banal sense, the prime minister is of more strategic importance to Canadian society than the adolescent growing up in Baie Comeau, Quebec. However, institutions, collectivities, and groups do not possess motivations comparable to those of individuals. This feature sometimes causes analytical difficulties when common-law rules treat corporations as legal persons. Rules and goods are simply elements of a situation in a static sense, or factors that may induce some preference change on the part of individuals in the longer run.

We postulate that individuals have different motivations, and these are revealed in situations structured by rules and goods. Individuals also have mixed motives, different degrees of information, and different capabilities for thinking through the consequences of actions within situations. They may also differ in their abilities to learn from successes and failures in different situations. Thus, in simple repetitive situations, where the good is technically simple and easily measured and where the rules permit comparisons between goods, such as in competitive market situations, individuals are motivated by their narrow self-interest to maximize their economic gains (Kiser and Ostrom 1987). Most situations are not of this kind. Economists, nevertheless, find this model useful for understanding most market situations.

The policy and political situations we deal with in this book often differ radically from those where: a / they are repeated regularly so that individuals may learn from their mutual errors; b / the policy or good is technically simple and easily measured; c / the rules are fully specified and stable enough to permit easy comparisons of alternatives; and d / maximization of a single preference is the dominant strategy. One or more of these conditions is often violated in decision situations, and consequently we can predict only with some inaccuracy the consequences of individuals making decisions about goods within different rule-based opportunities and constraints. Despite this handicap, some generalizations may be usefully made. Individual adults, whether private citizens, elected officials, or appointed officials of government, appear to respond to their own rule arrangements and seek more rather than less of some good in order to satisfy their diverse preferences.

The Nature of Rules

Rules consist of the laws, regulations, and norms of a given society that are enforced against deviant behaviour. They may consist of the constitutional laws and statute laws that are normally associated with government. They may also consist of the statutory instruments (regulations) that are made pursuant to statutes and have become a major feature of parliamentary government in many countries in the twentieth century. They can also consist of parliamentary conventions, such as those of collective and ministerial responsibility, and policy manuals used by many bureaucracies to enlarge upon statutory instruments, provided these conventions of subparts of government are routinely enforced. They may also consist of 'court made' rules, such as the common law, derived from the resolution of conflicts between persons over contractual and damage claims. The enforcement mechanisms can consist of courts, tribunals, politicians, or senior officials, and we witness the existence of relatively stable judicial, administrative, legislative, or bureaucratic cultures in most societies as rules are formulated and enforced in relation to individual members of these cultures as they carry out tasks associated with the provision and production of goods.

Other rules also exist to bind individuals in society in a variety of communities of interest. One of the smallest units, the nuclear family, is bound largely by mutually agreed-upon conventions and defined in more traditional communities by a designated 'head of household.' It is also subject to rules formulated in common, canon, and statute law, with the last having more operational relevance in modern societies. Larger units may also be subject to regular, enforceable norms, perhaps along lines of linguistic, religious, or ethnic cleavage. In these respects, Canada is sometimes termed a 'consociational' society.

One class of rules is especially important for providing and producing policies in Canada – the class known as 'property rights.' Property rights are bundles of rules determining the rights, duties, liberties, and exposures (Commons 1924) to relationships in market and non-market situations. For example, most forest land in Canada is owned by the provincial governments as Crown land, which vests in them the rights to authorize the use of the forests by logging companies subject to certain correlative duties (such as preserving Indian burial grounds) that may be imposed by the constraints of constitutional authority. The logging companies, in turn, possess the property rights to market the wood and wood fibres under laws of contract and tort that are enforceable in the courts.

Different rules have different consequences for the provision, production, and regulation of similar goods. Such is the case because they create different incentive systems for individuals to pursue their own and their common concerns. And, in turn, they create different levels and distributions of transaction costs for individuals to negotiate, implement, monitor, and enforce agreements. For example, rules that prescribe that municipalities seek the prior approval of riparians before they pump wastes into a river will impose different levels and transaction costs than will rules when prior approval is not necessary. Or rules of a municipal hierarchy that are frequently used to produce garbage collection in a community will have different consequences than will rules of contractual provision with an 'outside' producer.

A wide range of different rules exist to deal with the technical characteristics of goods. At the operational level of policy delivery or of policy regulation, we may have, in the case of garbage collection, myriad trivial rules about the number, size, composition, and contents of garbage cans. A more complex policy like that of outdoor recreation will include rules on acreage, on acreage subject to different kinds of possible developments and intensities of usage, on hours or seasons of usage, and so on. And a highly complex policy like that of the atmospheric environment will include rules about levels and rules of emission of gaseous materials and suspended particulates, technologies of reduction and emission, outright bans varying with airshed conditions, and so on.

Any of these kinds of rules will impinge on individuals within a community in different ways, and one or more individuals may well seek remedies from and changes to these operational rules. These remedies and changes are sought at the institutional level, though altering the composition of collective-choice decisions in courts, bureaucracies, legislatures, tribunals, and intergovernmental and interorganizational agreements. It may also be possible to shift the levels of remedies and alternatives to the constitutional level to alter the rules for collective-choice situations. Rules may thus be 'stacked' in different configurations for different policies.

Policies may also 'nest' within more than one stack of operational, institutional, and constitutional rules. Many aspects of environmental or defence or trade policies 'nest' within operational, institutional, and constitutional rules that are also 'stacked' by national origin. We may thus have multiple kinds and sources of rules at all three levels, depending on the nature of the good, and it may be only a convenient fiction to talk of Canadian agricultural policy, or Albertan energy policy, or nuclear-waste disposal policies at Darlington, Ontario.

Rules at the operational, institutional, and constitutional levels may create interdependencies in the production and/or consumption of any single good, or externalities between goods, irrespective of the technical characteristics of those goods. These rules are most visible at the operational level in the phenomenon of cross-subsidization. Thus the government of British Columbia used to have an operational rule requiring apartment owners to rent 10 per cent of their units to persons on social welfare assistance. More generally, rent controls cross-subsidize renters' income out of the current income of landlords. The deregulation movement in Western countries, including Canada, is designed to reduce these operational interdependencies, irrespective of the nature of the good.

At the institutional level, the rules may be constructed to create interdependencies. Legislative assemblies within any level of government (local, provincial, or federal) frequently use rules based on simple majority or plurality voting, and decisions made on these grounds are then binding upon the whole legislative assembly. The convention of collective responsibility is a rule adopted by cabinets to ensure that ministers remain as bonded interdependent actors in legislative deliberations.

As another example, which has direct relevance for public policy analysis, the courts in Western societies create or confirm legal rights, but normally in conjunction with legal duties. The right of a land-owner to withdraw water from a river for domestic, agricultural, or industrial purposes under either the common law or statutory water-rights legislation is attached to a duty to return this water to the river in a condition beneficial to downstream users. Or a tenant may have a legal right to demand of a landlord that he or she give notice of rent increases, of inspections, or of evictions, but subject to the duty to keep the apartment in a condition reasonably free of wear and tear. One recurring problem in Canadian law as it affects the interdependencies within or between goods is that governments may not have correlative duties associated with their legal rights. For example, the Crown may possess sovereign immunity under common law from civil liability for many of the actions of its agents (bureaucracies, Crown corporations, or individual public servants). It may pass statutory legislation absolving its instrumentalities from specific duties, like the duty of a hydro electric Crown corporation to pay market-value compensation for compulsory purchase of lands or the duty of a municipality to compensate landowners for changes in zoning regulations. In these cases, the rule-based interdependencies are disassembled.

Constitutional rules may also create interdependencies. Thus provincial and federal governments in Canada may share concurrent jurisdiction in a policy field like agriculture or immigration. Or the federal government may be constitutionally required to provide equalization payments to certain provincial governments that have tax revenues below a particular standard negotiated between governments on a five-year basis. The phenomenon of multiple constitutions may also create interdependencies for public policies and their production or consumption. The absence of stable constitutional arrangements in many countries of the world is currently creating demands for changes in the institutional and operational rules for Canadian immigration and refugee policies.

One final feature of rules must be noted at this stage of our analysis. The number and variety of rules at all three levels of analysis can be confusing for the new student of politics or for the citizen who is operating outside his or her normal routines. A policy like that of recreational boating involves rules about property and the markets for boats, marinas, tackle shops, restaurants, and equipment; it involves rules about boating traffic, safety, vessel pollution, rescue, and the uses of waterfront lands; it involves rules about legislative assemblies and bureaucracies at more than one level of government, as well as about rules of boating associations and conflict resolvers (like courts); it involves constitutional rules about boating opportunities provided in different government territories, including those in adjacent countries.

One way to simplify these numbers and varieties of rules is to adopt a conceptual scheme describing the salient characteristics of rules. Elinor Ostrom and Larry Kiser have provided such a scheme when the focus of attention is placed on the strategies and outcomes of strategies of individuals who find themselves in decision-making situations (Kiser and Ostrom 1982, 1987; E. Ostrom 1986, 1989). Thus they depict action situations in terms of a minimal set of seven rules:

POSITION RULES specify the positions that people may assume as they interact with one another. The rules may specify as many different positions as there are participants or as few as a single position

BOUNDARY RULES specify conditions that people must meet in order to occupy each position and the conditions required for people to leave those positions. Boundary rules are often called entry and exit rules.

AUTHORITY RULES specify actions allowed for each position in the situation. If actions occur in a series, the rules specify the allowable sequences.

SCOPE RULES specify the outcomes that participants in each position may, must, or must not affect in the situation.

AGGREGATION RULES specify the process through which actions taken by individuals finally result in outcomes. Technology may make a number of alternative procedures possible, from which aggregation rules select one or more procedures.

INFORMATION RULES specify channels of communication that may be established among participants in the situation and the language or form of that communication.

PAYOFF RULES assign payments and payoffs (including cost and sanctions) to the allowable actions and outcomes distributing the payments and payoffs among participants in the situation. (Kiser and Ostrom 1987: 20)

The empirical parts of this book address the apparent complexities of rules involved in public policies with a *different* analytical strategy. The focus is on the outcomes and impacts of public policies, as these outcomes and impacts are commonly understood in evaluation studies of administrative effectiveness and economic, social, and environmental impact assessments. The rules-in-use that lead to these outcomes and impacts are traced, and then disaggregated according to levels and sources. The analytical tool of rules-in-use is the central concept in this book. Thus, its central concern is not any particular decision situation, but the consequences that flow from multiple decision situations for different public policies.

Combining the Hard-Core Concepts

The hard-core concepts come together with auxiliary concepts to form a network of propositions about public policies.[2] The key to understanding the generalizations in this book is comprehending the relationships among the hard-core concepts. One must consider the nature of the good before one can draw conclusions about the associations between institutional arrangements and individuals. Further, one must consider institutional arrangements to understand the relationship between individuals and goods, and one cannot understand this relationship without considering citizen preferences.

The interlocking nature of the hard-core concepts is manifested in policy outcomes and impacts. In this section, the interlocking nature of the hard-core concepts is demonstrated by the kinds of conclusions about natural-resources policies that would be reached if each of the hard-core concepts were missing in turn. Were the hard core to delete the nature of the good, the conclusions would tend to fit 'mainstream' political science. Were individual preferences to be deleted, 'mainstream' public administration would ensue. Were institutional arrangements to be deleted, 'mainstream' economics would be the result. This interdependence of the three concepts justifies their selection as the hard core of our analysis.

2 The following paragraphs are based on Sproule-Jones (1982).

Without the Nature of the Good: Mainstream Political Science

A river basin typically has multiple uses. In-stream uses may include shipping and navigation, recreational boating and swimming, commercial and recreational fisheries, and waste disposal. On-the-land uses may include water supply for irrigation, industrial cooling, and domestic consumption. Other possible uses include shoreline sites for docking, marinas, recreation, wild fowl, fishery feeding, and houses and cottages. Positive and negative externalities may exist between two or more of these uses, and some uses may display the characteristics of exclusiveness and/or divisibility. The water quality of the river, for example, may be diminished by some uses, such as the disposal of toxic wastes, but undisturbed by others, such as pristine forms of outdoor recreation.

A critical difference between our analysis and a political science analysis of the multiple uses of a river basin is in the scale or unit of analysis chosen for scrutiny. One of our basic units of analysis is a provision system that consists of all of the individual, corporate, and governmental users as well as the regulators of users of the resource (Gregg 1974; Sproule-Jones 1978b, 1981). The boundaries of a provision system may or may not correspond with the legal territorial boundaries of a single government. Indeed, a provision system is most unlikely to coincide with a single jurisdiction (Kneese and Bower 1968; Klevonick and Kramer 1973), owing to the nature of the good and the number of and interdependencies among its uses. One *expects* to find a large number of individuals and a large number of locally, regionally, nationally, and internationally owned corporations and groups jointly involved in the production and consumption of one or more uses of the basin. One also *expects* to find agencies of government (organized at the local, regional, national, and international levels) jointly involved in one or more uses, either as direct users or as regulators of other users. In the 'water-quality provision system' of the Fraser River, for example, there are more than one hundred policy actors from some fifty-four agencies and organizations, including local, provincial, federal, and international agencies of government, plus local, provincial, federal, and international corporations and groups (Sproule-Jones 1981). In addition, one expects this organizational network to be changing in complexity over time, as new marketable and non-marketable uses of the basin are enhanced or diminished.

An analysis based on the territorial legal boundaries of governments reaches differing conclusions about water-resource decision making and the role of institutional rules, as well as about more generic policy topics (e.g., Ackerman et al. 1974; Golembiewski 1977; Dye 1979). Citizen preference for one or more uses of a river basin may be articulated (or sometimes remain latent, in the case of public goods) through private market and group action, but it may be voiced through electoral behaviour and traditional forms of representation. Elected and appointed officials of a level of government may have a severely constrained impact on resource decision making; variables designed to indicate the policy outputs of a level of government are likely to exclude some river-basin uses, such as private marketable ones, and include some water uses from more than one basin.

Analysing a resource like wheat production and processing, we would predict a different kind of provision system, varying in complexity and in the nature of policy decisions. Water resources and wheat production have different kinds of technologies for exploitation and interdependencies with other agricultural and land-use resources. Generalizations about citizen and governmental behaviour would be correspondingly different. It would be unlikely that generalizations about citizen and governmental behaviour within a particular system of government could be transferred from one resource area to the other. Only a careful analysis that takes into account the nature of the good can unravel the extent and significance of political behaviour.

Without Individual Preferences: Mainstream Public Administration

The multiple uses of a river basin, or of any other 'bundle' of resources found in a well-defined geographic space, provide an apt example of the differences between our analysis of resource policies and what might be called 'mainstream public administration.'

Mainstream public administration recognizes the problems associated with public goods and externalities. Mainstream public administration, however, tends to emphasize that the expertise necessary to solve such problems is ineffectively applied, that organizational conflicts may amplify resource interdependencies, and that governmental agencies with the power to make and implement resource decisions are not accountable to the general public. A provision system, with its multiple organizations and authority fragmented among its governmental agencies, is a case in point. A number of public agencies, each responsible for a particular resource use – for example, waste disposal, navigation, or fishing – may ignore the positive and negative externalities among resource uses without necessarily ensuring that functional specializations are effectively coordinated. The public, too, is often left confused because it does not know which level of government or which agencies at which level of government are responsible for managing different resource uses, and government levels and agencies can abjure responsibility for overall management.

The solution often posed is to move to a set of hierarchical institutional arrangements. A single river-basin authority should have the powers delegated to it to eliminate the overlap and fragmentation among agencies, and to coordinate effectively resource use in the light of public values. The model found on the Ruhr should be imitated elsewhere (Kneese and Bower 1968).

Our analysis of river-basin management suggests that comparisons should be made between alternative institutional arrangements. A fragmented provision system is costly, but single hierarchies tend to be more costly in a number of ways. First, they place a river-basin authority in a monopoly position, and public monopolies can be successfully captured by one resource user or a subset of them, because of the distribution of benefits and costs associated with demand articulation. Second, a monopoly of expertise contained within a single authority implies that elected officials cannot estimate the real value of governmental activities, with the consequence of inflated budgets and overregulation, the so-called Niskanen hypothesis (Niskanen 1971). Third, the number and complexity of resource interdependencies may ensure that any river-basin authority is of such size that control from the top of the hierarchy is dissipated, and that managerial diseconomies of scale will usher in a lack of coordination and agency 'free enterprise' (Tullock 1965).

The fragmented authority found in typical provision systems does not, by definition, contain such disadvantages of monopoly, and our previously cited empirical evidence on the Fraser River indicates that a / there is substantial coordination within the provision system; b / this coordination is not sporadic and unplanned; and c / it takes place both across *and* within government and the privately owned sectors (Sproule-Jones 1981). Citizen preferences for different resource uses may be better articulated and aggregated through a multiplicity of political access points combined with market prices rather than through concentrated political authority. The Fraser model is more appropriate than the Ruhr (Sproule-Jones 1978b).

Without Institutional Arrangements: Mainstream Economics

Mainstream economics recognizes market failure when prices fail to signal, or signal inadequately, the value that citizen consumers may place on certain resource uses, and the value that producers of commodities (involving resources) may place on their form of production and processing rather than on another form. Market failures and weaknesses include private-sector monopolies, public goods, externalities, and so-called equity or income-distribution concerns. The role of rules is to correct for such market failures and weaknesses. In this regard, mainstream economics does not appear to differ greatly from our analysis, except in so far as we see markets as one of a number of ways in which coordination is possible through different rule configurations.

The case of the multiple use of resources, however, illustrates the differences between the two kinds of analyses. Mainstream economic analysis of multiple use is based on the premiss that the costs to any single class of resource users should be balanced against the benefits to those users. For short-run pricing decisions, it means that a variety of market-like mechanisms should be introduced by the private- or public-sector proprietors of a land, air, or water site. The mechanisms include user fees, transferable licences and permits, and bonus bids. Any user will then have an incentive to use a resource only to the degree that his or her satisfaction is equal to or greater than the satisfaction his or her use forces others to forgo (Walter 1978). For a long-run investment decisions, public- or private-sector facilities should be introduced only if the aggregate benefits to all resource users exceed the aggregate costs over a specified time horizon. The criterion of evaluation is utilitarian; net benefits should be maximized over all uses.

The implication of such an analysis for the nature of rules is that the public sector is both an 'ethical observer' in that it can estimate and aggregate non-market values with marketable ones and a monopolist in that it can implement the appropriate pricing and investment decisions (Sproule-Jones 1972).

In contrast, our analysis would argue that the rules in any society will create benefits and costs for different resource uses (marketable and non-marketable) with differing consequences, depending on the nature of the good. Moreover, the property-right structure for resource users is also a dependent variable of constitutional rules governing the operation of the 'state.' One would anticipate, for example, a different distribution of benefits and costs and a different mix of resource uses if commercial fishermen were given a statutory property right for the protection of fish habitat rather than if such rights were the exclusive preserve of the riparian or tenant. Also, such a change in property rights would indicate that commercial fishermen and their allies were more successful than riparians and tenants in exploiting the institutional arrangements under which statutory changes are enacted. In other words, rules make a difference.

Understanding Public Policies

Our previous arguments are intended to demonstrate that any satisfactory public policy analysis must draw upon the hard-core concepts about the nature of the good, the nature of individuals, and the nature of rules in order to make satisfactory explanations about public policies. They help to simplify the complexities of understanding the operation of all of the many variables that can constitute public policies. These hard-core concepts distinguish our form of policy analysis from traditional disciplines like political science, public administration, and economics.

One would expect that any nation-state like Canada will have developed its own particular rules (at constitutional, institutional, and operational levels) to take account of different preferences for different goods, given the circumstances of life under which the country has evolved. Before we turn to the rules-in-use for the communities of interests in Canada, we will take another look at the nature of rules in the next chapter. Because rules have been constructed by people as artefacts and are not given in nature, they are more easily refashioned in the light of changing circumstances, and may provide – if properly understood – the strategic means by which Canadians can improve their lots.

Some readers may prefer to skip to chapter 4 in order to see more immediately how the hard-core concepts explain the workings of governments in Canada. They can then return to ponder the kinds of philosophical implications of rules-in-use and rules-in-form that are discussed in chapter 3.

3

The Design and Meaning of Rules-in-Use

Context

The central thrust of this book is the examination the rules-in-use in Canadian government and politics and their consequences for the provision, production, and regulation of public policies. Rules-in-use are those subsets of decision-making processes that are involved in situations about the level, quality, and distribution of a public policy (the operational level); about the forums, participants, and agendas involved in constructing these situations (the institutional level); and about the terms and conditions for adopting and enforcing one or more of the institutional rules (the constitutional level). Rules-in-use are one of the hard-core concepts, which, intermingled with technical characteristics of the nature of goods and with our ontological and empirical generalizations about the nature of individual people, provide the foundations of an explanation of 'how government works.'

The previous paragraph was intended as a reminder to the reader of what chapter 2 contained, and with this reminder to begin to alert the reader to the content of this chapter. But reader beware! We will be discussing some ontological, epistemological, and ethical issues related to rules-in-use. These issues usually do not enter the frames of reference of readers of books on Canadian government and public policies, and they might appear difficult to comprehend in the sense of being easily relatable to the stored knowledge and experience of the reader. An attempt will be made, again, to create a common understanding between text and reader with the use of empirical examples, hypothetical scenarios, and references to literature in the field.

An attempt will be made to demonstrate that rules and rule configurations are much more than devices to help the collective actions of individuals. People infuse rules with a variety of meanings about their roles and significance. Rules thus come to represent difficult cognitive and emotional realities for different persons. They are much more than instruments for the provision, production, or regulation of public policies.

This characteristic of rules and rule configurations poses immediate difficulties for policy analysis. The prevailing paradigm for evaluating public policies, including the well-developed methods of economic evaluation, fails to grasp the complexity of this characteristic. Political science as well tends to simplify this aspect of rules and rule configurations with unfortunate results for those who wish to grasp the constitutional and institutional bases of Canadian public policies. A preliminary resolution in favour of an empiricist epistemology is made in this chapter; a fuller resolution is left until chapter 11. However, the basic riddle of policy analysis – namely, that understanding rules by using an empiricist epistemology that cannot itself reveal the full meanings of these rules – is posed here. Readers are simply alerted, at this stage, to the possibilities of further ontological and ethical issues embedded in institutional and policy analysis.

The argument proceeds as follows: first, rules are discussed as human artefacts, in the sense that they are instruments consciously designed by human communities to codify and enforce regular patterns of social interaction. Then, an assessment is made of how they may be used by these human communities as ways to change and alter the circumstances of life within these communities. Some fundamental ontological considerations about rules are then analysed and the riddle posed for the analyst of Canadian rules is introduced in terms of the knowledge requirements for assessment and evaluation. Only a tentative and preliminary solution to the riddle is presented at this stage.

Rule Design

Rules are deliberately designed human artefacts that are established or modified in response to situations of time, place, and the opportunities and constraints of the non-human world. Their artefactual character implies that they are not given in nature; they are fashioned by sets of the current, and frequently the previous generation. They are deliberately designed in the sense that they are the product of human intentionality, which does not imply that no rules are the product of conscious errors. The situations of time and place and the parameters of the non-human world imply that different rules are established and modified for different communities; the fact that many rules appear to evolve or to be culture bound or to be inappropriate for the current state of technologies reflects these contingent characteristics of rules.

Some examples at the constitutional, institutional, and operational levels illustrate these features of rules. First, let us take the example of constitutional rules in Canada. The most visible set of constitutional rules in Canada is those codified in the Constitution Act of 1867 (as amended). These are the product of the intentions of a number of human actors of the present generation, including:

- the prime minister and provincial premiers (excluding the premier of Quebec) who met in deliberations on constitutional reforms in 1981;
- the justices of the Supreme Court who ruled in 1981 that many constitutional amendments did not require the consent of all eleven governments; and
- British parliamentarians who passed the Canada Act of 1981, ratifying the constitutional changes at that time.

Previous generations also played significant roles, in the sense that actors in Canadian, British, French, and even other communities fashioned one or more of the Canadian constitutional rules. The following examples indicate how wide reaching was the realm of actors of previous generations:

- the minister of the British Colonial Office who, among others, agreed to the Statute of Westminster of 1931, removing British veto power on the foreign affairs of the Canadian government;
- the participants at the Westminster Conference of 1866 who wanted to unite the provinces of Canada, Nova Scotia, and New Brunswick into a confederation 'with a constitution similar in principle to that of the United Kingdom';
- the signers of the Treaty of Paris of 1763, which granted international recognition of the conquest of Quebec four years earlier.

These and other constitutional rules were formulated in response to time, place, and natural circumstances. For example, the early years of government for Newfoundland were dictated as much by demands of seasonal climates and the abundancies of fishing stocks as by a desire for permanent settlement, British Columbia's early settlement patterns reflected as much the exigencies of physical barriers of ocean and mountains and the abundance of gold deposits as did military considerations.

Errors would occasionally be made in the formulation of constitutional rules in the sense that their predicted consequences did not automatically follow and persist. Few Fathers of Confederation could have predicted that provinces would emerge as coequal governments with that of the Dominion along many dimensions of legislative powers. They failed to predict the consequences of another (unchanged) constitutional rule that gave the Judicial Committee of the Privy Council authority to resolve conflicts over the division of legislative powers.

The evolution of Canadian constitutional rules and the changing sets of actors with authority to devise rule changes has meant that there is no coherent 'cosmology' that articulates the design principles of these rules. The Canadian rules embody the political ideas of different times, places, and actions, and the mixture of ideas often gives rise to a mixture of inconsistent design principles. The political theory of 'sovereignty,' for example, which articulates the design of unicentred political authority, fits uneasily with the political theory of 'federalism,' which articulates the design of dispersed political authority. In this respect, Canada differs from the cosmology provided by Confucian thought for Imperial China (Yang 1987) or by Leninist thought for the Soviet Union (Kaminski 1989). Smiley (1969) characterizes the Canadian political culture as a noncreedal culture. In this respect, Canada remains in the centre of the traditional ways for constitutional design in Western civilization. Constitutional design and redesign in Western countries have been characterized by contests between political ideas and cosmologies (Berman 1985).

Both institutional and operational rules are similar to constitutional rules in the bases for their design, as the following examples illustrate. A government bureaucracy consists of an institutional rule configuration consisting of:

– rules of hierarchical structure, such as unity of command, spans of control, specialization in work process by person or subunit,

and organization of units according to purpose, process, place, or clientele. These so-called proverbs of administration are an incomplete set of rules as Simon (1948) and other organizational theorists have pointed out;
- rules regarding the recruitment and deployment of personnel, land, and capital for bureaucratic tasks;
- rules regarding the legality of their operations in relation to legislative requirements (statutes and statutory instruments), cabinet requirements (Crown prerogatives), court requirements (common-law principles such as 'natural justice' as well as enforcement of statutes and statutory instruments), central-agency requirements (rules of resource deployment), and constitutional requirements (especially concerning federal arrangements); and
- conventions and enforceable norms of bureaucratic conduct, particularly those of responsiveness to the dictates of a minister from whom, in a reciprocal relationship, bureaucrats may expect conformity with the convention of 'ministerial responsibility.'

These and other elements of the institutional rule configuration for a bureaucracy make up the concept of bureaucratic accountability, and the rule configuration is often changed for the production or regulation of designated goods. Even corporations and 'quangos' (quasi-autonomous non-governmental organizations) with varying degrees of bureaucratic accountability have been established ostensibly to design a rule configuration appropriate for diverse goods.

Bureaucracies themselves typically design operational rules, often called 'service-delivery rules' or 'standard operating procedures.' Some codify these rules in policy manuals, but their codification is frequently difficult when bureaucratic tasks require the exercise of judgment and discretion on the part of individual public servants as they apply general procedures to individual cases. Service-delivery rules are thus often variables rather than constraints as they enter the decision-making calculuses of public servants.

For example, a prime service-delivery rule in bureaucracies designed to regulate market and social behaviour is to establish workloads on the basis of complaints. Thus human rights commissions will operate largely on the basis of complaints from citizens in specified target groups (such as women, visible minorities, immigrants, and the handicapped) that they have suffered from discrimination in one of three designated areas (employment, housing, and public facilities). Or egg-marketing boards will find much of their work-loads set in response to claims of some chicken farmers that other chicken farmers are selling eggs directly to the general public rather than to the monopoly agency. Such agencies, in turn, must either resort to the queuing of cases or, more frequently, adopt other rules to act as 'gates' through which only a reduced number of complaints may pass. 'Gatekeepers' in the form of intake officers may be granted the discretionary authority to reject certain kinds of complaints and accept others. Cases of alleged discrimination against minors may be thus discouraged, as may cases against farmers who sell eggs only on the farm property. If, in turn, complainants are disappointed with these responses and seek redress from the minister directly, new operational codes of conduct may be imposed through policy directives set near the apex of the bureaucratic hierarchy.

Many service-delivery rules are formulated by bureaucracies according to professional 'standards' in the light of the technical characteristics of the goods being produced or regulated. For example, public-works departments at all levels of government employ engineers, architects, draughtspersons, surveyors, and purchasing agents whose expertise in dealing with the built environment is certified by professional associations. A key service-delivery rule may not be one that is established by or changeable by institutional rules within the bureaucracy itself. Nevertheless, the certification process embodies rules of expertise, consciously designed by humans in the light of experience in other times and places. They represent, as do all rules, enforceable norms as human artefacts. One big question remains – how can we evaluate such rules?

Evaluative Rules

Public policy evaluations subscribe in different degrees to a standard paradigm or model of evaluation. In this model, policy outputs (outcomes) like the number of complaints processed or the number of complaints successfully resolved before or at determining tribunals, are taken as the consequence of operational rules. Inputs in the form of the costs of or the non-financial measures of factors of production are controlled along with 'environmental' circumstances of time and place. The capital costs associated with regulatory agencies are typically small, for example, but these are controlled along with 'environmental' factors, such as many aspects of the demography of the population, as these can affect the number and type of complaint. Some studies will go farther and assess the natural environmental impacts, the social impacts, and the macro-economic impacts of policy output changes. Some may even assess the feedback among outcomes, impacts, and rule changes. Figure 3 presents these relationships among variables in terms of a flow dia-gram.

The thrust of the model is to suggest that, other things being equal, rule changes will alter policy outputs. Consequently, rules may be manipulated to produce desired policy outputs, albeit in light of the uncertainties of accurate and precise data analysis. 'Unsatisfac-tory' rules, at least at the operational level, may thus be evaluated and changed in the light of their policy outcomes and impacts.

This basic paradigm is adopted in different degrees by policy analysts. They assume that rules are human artefacts subject to change in the light of their revealed consequences. Thus if, to use a trivial example, a regulatory agency redeploys staff and resources to re-gional offices, and the number of processed complaints (and other measures of outputs) increases, other things being equal (for ex-ample, budgets), rules should be adopted for the regional process-ing of complaints and (perhaps) their investigation.

The basic paradigm is relatively easy to apply to evaluations of measurable operational rules and policy outputs. It is difficult to apply at the institutional- and especially the constitutional-rule lev-els as the effects of changes in one or more of these variables may not be automatically correlated with policy output changes. For example, the monopsony and monopoly powers of an agricultural commodity marketing agency imply substantial discretion on the part of the agency to trade off the economic advantages of this market power with other preferred outcomes, such as maintaining the number of producers, increasing the production opportunities of younger farmers, changing the quality attributes of the product, and other measures of 'discrimination.' A change in one institutional rule, such as requiring the agency to engage in collective bargaining with its employees, may or may not be reflected in prices of products bought and sold by the agency. Other elements in their operational-rule configurations may compensate for this one institutional-rule change.

The difficulties are compounded when one or more constitu-tional-rule changes occur. For example, a hypothetical Canadian

Figure 3. Standard evaluation models

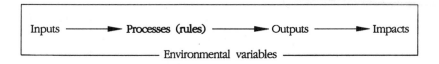

constitutional-rule change that would permit provincial marketing boards to sell products into other provinces might lead to institutional changes that responded directly to this incentive in terms of changed operational rules facilitating interprovincial competition. However, they may not lead to these policy changes if marketing boards engaged in institutional changes facilitating collusion and market sharing. Rules are configurative in form (and may be both 'stacked' and 'nested'), and a change in one rule may reshuffle the configuration of rules associated with a policy, and without measurable changes in policy outputs.

The basic paradigm may therefore imply complex methodological assumptions and techniques of empirical analysis. More fundamentally, they imply that all rules have the same ontological status and may be compared and manipulated according to their revealed consequences. All rules may be human artefacts, but artefactual knowledge may be contingent upon a shared ontology or belief system about the realities of facts among rule changers. A constitutional rule that grants a human foetus the same constitutional rights of protection and non-discrimination as a born Canadian is making a fundamental ontological statement about the concept of a person. This ontological statement is different in kind from an ontology embodied in an institutional rule that permits any farmer to complain to an agricultural marketing board. Before this issue is explained in more depth, a digression on the character of economic policy evaluations is in order, as economic policy evaluations have developed farther than those in other disciplines, and are frequently posed as an important model for government officials to follow.

Economic Policy Evaluations

Economists tend to adopt a partial view of the standard evaluation paradigm. They are concerned with public policies in terms of outputs or benefits and inputs or costs. They assume away rules at the operational, institutional, and constitutional levels, and the complex rule configurations associated with different goods. Thus outputs or benefits become aggregate global benefits rather than benefits associated with particular institutional and operational rules, and inputs or costs become aggregate economic costs rather than particular expenditures associated with different rules.

The technique of benefit-cost analysis is not a simple one. Judgments must be made about a wide range of potentially measurable benefits and costs, about discount rates, and, in some studies, about macro-economic interactions with the measured variables and about distributional impacts of current and proposed policy changes. The thrust of the conclusions of benefit-cost studies is to recommend to some set of decision makers that policy changes be adopted if, at a minimum, the ratio of benefits to costs of any change is positive or, ideally, that alternative policy changes should be ranked according to the size of their comparable benefit-cost ratios.

It is now widely understood that the process of placing 'shadow prices' on benefits and (perhaps) costs that are not bought and sold in a market-place involves using an economic calculus as a common yardstick of measurement. Thus a hydro-electric reservoir project would involve benefits of both increased electricity sales and downstream flood control, and these two, as well as other benefits, would be converted into the common currency of money.

It is also now widely appreciated that the decision-making criterion of choosing between alternative projects on the basis of their benefit-cost ratios is utilitarian. Benefits, costs, and alternative benefits and costs are measurable on a single scale that reflects the utilities or preferences commonly shared among the community of interest in question. Benefit-cost analyses are criticized because of the ontological assumptions that all benefits and costs are comparable on a currency scale, and that utilitarianism is an appropriate standard against which to evaluate public policies. Benefit-cost analyses may also be criticized because they assume away the existing rule configurations in any society. As was suggested earlier, they assume that the decision makers in any situation possess omniscient and omnipotent powers enabling them to calculate, weigh, and implement the recommended policies, at least within the broad parameters of uncertain 'environmental' flux. Policy evaluations also rest, it is assumed, on an independent objective basis and are not influenced by the incentives of rules and the preferences of decision makers.

It is partly as a result of these criticisms that some economists adopt the standard of Pareto optimality as a substitute for utilitarianism. Since utilities cannot be measured directly and must be inferred from revealed preferences, some economists substitute the Paretian criterion that states that, at a minimum, policy changes are to be chosen if they make at least one person better off and no one worse off. The criterion implies that the willing consent of all parties to any transaction is required if a change from the status quo is to be implemented. The status quo is thus preferable to changes from the status quo. In our terminology, the existing rule configuration is ontologically prior to alternative rule configurations. This assumption is at best arguable. In terms of purely market-based transactions, for example, it reifies the current property-right arrangements.

Economic evaluations of public policies and public policy changes are therefore bound up with assumptions about rules, about objective truths that exist independent of rules, and about criteria of evaluation that may be commonly used to discriminate between policies as preferred states of community affairs. Rules cannot be ignored. These assumptions and others common to the basic paradigm of evaluation must now be dissected. The design of rules as human artefacts may succeed only if the design principles are understood. Three issues of design are now discussed.

Rules and Realities

The first design issue concerns the causal relationships between individuals and rules. If artefactual rules are to be designed, monitored, enforced, and revised by human ingenuity, there is a sense in which human beings may be considered as existing prior to rules. Such is a possible implication of the treatment of individuals as existing in a state of nature, as envisaged by classical political theorists, or as existing behind a veil of ignorance, as envisaged by some modern rational-choice theorists (for example, Buchanan and Tullock 1962; Rawls 1971). The inference would be imprecise, however. First, we know that even in primitive societies some patterns of regular behaviour are accepted and enforced as rules, behind which individuals may artfully construct other artefactual rules for social choice. There always appear to be fall-back rules in existence in modern societies, even if they are treated by some people as dysfunctional for the attainment of their ends. Some public policies never appear to fully 'fit' the preferences of individuals, especially policies of a more public-good nature that may require coordinated collective action if they are to be implemented in large groups (Olson 1965).

Second, we know that rules can affect individual conceptions of possible and desired outcomes, and hence their revealed preferences for public policies. Socialization experiences in hierarchical situations, such as a family with a head of household, a schoolroom with a single teacher, a factory floor with a boss, or a political system with a single sovereign, may limit the range of rules and preferred outcomes contemplated in a society. For example, the community participation movement in Canada, which has grown and evolved since the 1960s, has always operated within the context of institutional and constitutional rules and has viewed participation as a means to improving the informational bases of governmental decision making rather than a means to dispersing power and creating newer community collective actions. Today, there are widespread opportunities for public participation in the formulation and implementation of service-delivery and other operational rules, but few opportunities for setting agendas at the institutional- and constitutional-rule levels (L.G. Smith 1983, 1987; Sproule-Jones 1975).

A better interpretation of the ontological status of the relationships between individuals and rules is to treat individuals as enjoying some degree of personal autonomy distinct from the collective autonomy of rules. Thus rules may or may not be functional for the preference satisfaction of all individuals. Some rules, obvious examples being those of criminal and those rules of tax law, are coercive and perhaps oppressive in character. Other rules may facilitate the liberation of individuals directly through the provision of public policies (such as health care for the sick) or indirectly through expanding the range of human artefacts for a collective solution to common problems (such as rules encouraging the volunteer production of some kinds of health care for the handicapped).

Two further ontological issues are those involved in rule design and the provision and evaluation of public policies. The first concerns the possibilities of a social and existential basis for rules. It would appear from the basic paradigm of evaluation and from our distinction between rules-in-use and rules-in-form that rules have an exclusively instrumental character; that is, rules are understood as leading to particular consequences for the welfare of individual citizens, and thus, if rules do not lead to these consequences, they should be modified or discarded in favour of alternative rules. Indeed, I have previously written that rules which may favour only the interest of some citizens acting in a non-citizen capacity, such as bureaucrats, judges, politicians, or corporation executives, should be redesigned (Sproule-Jones 1982). This is now, I believe, a mistaken conclusion. Rules do, indeed, have an instrumental character, but they also have intrinsic value in any community. Rules-in-use may have been carefully crafted in the light of known experiences, but only over time have the full range of their consequences been revealed. For example, those Canadian constitutional rules crafted and modified in Victorian times may well have represented a 'compact' between the English- and French-speaking populations, a covenantal basis for the fulfilment of the aspirations of the two founding populations of Canada (Sabetti 1980, 1982). Over time, these rules proved less adequate to deal with the full range of circumstances in Canada. Settlement, self-government, and federal arrangements for the prairie populations also seemed to require a valuable adaptation of the constitutional rules. Some measure of personal autonomy for individual English and French Canadians in the light of the dominance of collective majorities in central Canada also seemed to require some basic constitutional-rule changes. The covenantal basis of the original constitutional rules began to erode, and the claims today of a 'distinct society' for Quebec, in the light of any original 'compact' of peoples, is barely understood by pan-Canadian nationalists and multiculturalists.

This example suggests that there may be a social and existential basis for rules-in-use. They may not simply be instrumental representations of a natural level of reality. It may be more difficult to appreciate these ontological connotations in the context of more institutional and operational rules, but they may be crafted and carefully modified as part of a common social and perhaps existential set of experiences. For example, an institutional-rule change amalgamating the Army, Navy, and Air Force into a single force under a Department of National Defence in 1967 represented, for many Canadians, a destruction of shared social and existential meanings about the conduct of two world wars rather than the organization of national defence. Similar rule changes in the 1960s and 1970s, which political scientists would call 'symbolic politics,' represented the contestation between alternative meanings associated with such terms as 'Dominion,' 'Red Ensign,' 'Royal Mail,' and 'Ministry.' At the operational-rule level, supporters of particular rules may be treated at one time as vested interests and, at the same time, as beneficiaries of valued entitlements. Dairy farmers may be both successful rent seekers and 'spear-carriers' for an agricultural way of life. Tenants may be rent-control lobbyists and, at the same time, guardians of affordable shelter for the less well-to-do. Rules appear to have more fundamental meanings than their instrumental character would suggest. As well, there is a suggestion that changes in rules and in rule configurations may be more difficult to accomplish than any amendment process would imply. The possibilities for redesign of rules that may be infused with natural, social, and existential meanings will be addressed after we discuss a final ontological connotation of our analysis of rules as artefacts.

The final issue concerns the historical role of rules. James Buchanan once wrote: 'For my purposes, I shall call my dog a "natural" animal, and I shall call anyone of us a "natural and artifactual" animal, or, perhaps preferably, an artifactual animal bounded by natural constraints. We are, and will be, at least in part, that which we make ourselves to be. We construct our own beings, again within limits' (1979: 94). Buchanan is calling attention to the ontological status of individuals, rules, *and* the revealed consequences of rules. Public policies, as they emanate from communities of interest and the rules for the aggregation of interests, may only partially reflect the intentions of the actors and the rule designers. The conservation of South Moresby may reflect, in part, the federal government's environmental policies and the British Columbia government's forest policies, but it may represent other meanings that individuals attach to a 'preferred state of community affairs.' Standard economic theory may well try to grasp these meaning with such concepts as 'option demands' for the use of a resource in the future or apply low discount rates for a benefit-cost analysis of the elimination of 'irreversibles.' But, again to use Buchanan's words, 'choices made in becoming a different person are irrevocable, regardless of their productivity, when viewed *ex post*. We move through time, constructing ourselves as artifactual persons. We are not, and cannot be, the "same person" in any utility maximization sense' (1979: 100). Individuals do not simply have an 'it-status,' they have a 'being-status' (Laing 1965, cited in Schumacher 1984: 214). And thus the policies that are the product of rules always represent what we may call the 'been-status' of past human endeavours. So, Canadian public policies will always have some meaning that reflects the 'been-status' of individual Canadian actors and the rules within which they operated. But we cannot expect to give full meaning to our analysis of Canadian rules and public policies in terms of the evolution of understandings about the world held by you, the reader, and others who may participate in the Canadian political process. This third ontological issue raises further questions about the nature and kinds of evidence appropriate to an understanding of 'governments at work.' To these questions we now turn, examining how political science smuggles into its policy evaluations assumptions about rules and methods of analysis that may be as suspect as those assumptions made in economics. First, however, some discussion of how to explain rules to the reader – what I call 'contextual explanations' – is required.

Understanding Rules and Policies

Contextual explanations foster shared understandings between the theorist and his or her audience. The effectiveness of contextual explanations depends on two factors. First, a common language must exist between the author and reader in the sense that concepts – which are, after all, merely descriptive words that characterize the attributes of phenomena – have a shared meaning, and sentences – which relate concepts to each other – convey agreed-upon signals to both parties (Ostrom 1980). Second, contextual explanations are effective to the degree that both parties treat concepts and sentences as plausible conjectures that may or may not reveal accurate insights into the subject-matter of the discussion. The emphasis must be placed on the plausibility of the conjectures rather than on a pre-judgment of the conjectures.

These two features of contextual explanation do not imply that the reader is an 'empty' person without his or her own presuppositions about the meaning of, say, rules or about the standards of adequate analysis and proof. They merely imply that contextual explanations about the rules-in-use in Canada or the dimensions of public policies and their evaluations rest on some preconceptions about the nature of discovery and justification. Canadian political scientists bring their own preconceptions to their studies, as must the readers of this book. Let me illustrate three sorts of preconceptions that many Canadian political scientists seem to share about the rules embodied in modern government.[1] Political scientists, too, make ontological assumptions because of the ways in which they understand (in their epistemologies) the nature of rules. This digression may help our own contextual explanation. It further illustrates the complex character of rules and their appropriate assessment.

Three Examples

Our first example is the stream of writing about government in Canada that may be called 'power resides somewhere' studies. The assumption is that one person or a group of persons possesses supreme authority in government. Scholars recognize that legislative supremacy, in the context of disciplined party government, means executive domination of parliaments and provincial legislatures. But the unarticulated premiss is that if parliaments and legislatures, consisting of an identifiable group of persons, no longer possess supreme authority, then such authority must be possessed by an alternative group of identifiable persons. Traditional thinking would have it that the cabinet (on either plane of government) is the centre of power in parliamentary systems, in part because ministers have executive responsibilities, but also because they have influence on party caucuses, legislative agendas, and the procedures and conventions of Parliament. Cabinet, as has been flatly stated by one thinker, is 'the policy-making organ of government' (Mallory 1971: 96).

Most recent writings find that this cabinet power is transferred. Some authors find power located in the office of the prime minister. The most extreme comment is perhaps that 'we seem to have created in Canada a presidential system without its congressional advantages' (Smith 1969: 358). Other commentators suggest that the prime minister (or premier) and his ministers share power with senior civil servants: 'Under the present constitution, [the royal] prerogative permits ... the creation of executive-bureaucratic extensions to the cabinet system outside of parliamentary supervision or sanction'

1 The examples are drawn from Sproule-Jones (1984a).

(Campbell and Szablowski 1979: 238). Writers also suggest that power resides in the meetings of federal and provincial officials, certainly the elected ones and possibly also the appointed ones: 'The underlying assumption of [British parliamentary] tradition is that the legislature is sovereign. ... This assumption is challenged when the actual locus of decision-making is transferred from the cabinet, which is collectively responsible to the elected chamber, to intergovernmental bodies' (Smiley 1977: 259).

These examples of writings on government in Canada assume that 'power resides somewhere,' although the candidates for the locus of power vary in place and size. The subsidiary concern then becomes one of ensuring that the locus is accountable and responsible. Government, one might infer, is but a large chain of command, with Parliament or a provincial legislature or even the 'sovereign people' at the apex of this hierarchy. One text even contains an organizational chart depicting such a hierarchy (Wilson 1982: 200).

Studies of Canadian federalism often reveal comparable preconceptions about the rule configurations at the constitutional and institutional levels of analysis. The governments of Canada and the ten provinces are treated accurately as sovereign governmental bodies within the (somewhat flexible) constraints of a constitutional division of powers. But the difficulties of Canadian federalism are interpreted as ones of either centralization of political authority in Ottawa or decentralization of authority to provincial governments. Centralization or decentralization (or sometimes development of administrative and political procedures to ensure flexibility over time in the degree of centralization or decentralization) are seen as major prescriptive reforms necessary to alter an apparent problem in federation. The problems vary from one work to the next. They may be of a more sociological character, as are those of maintaining the linguistic, ethnic, and cultural bases of English- and French-Canadian societies. They may be of a more pragmatic character, as are those of responding to threats of secession. They may also be of an economic and administrative nature, as are those of reducing interprovincial spillovers, producing collective goods to exploit economies or diseconomies of scale, minimizing the transaction costs within and between governments, and redistributing tax revenues between governments to ensure equity.

It is assumed that the rules for Parliament must correspond to the modern concentrated power system of legislative supremacy: 'In general terms, Canadians throughout their history have shown a pronounced disposition to adhere to a version of the Westminster model which provides for executive dominance. Even the more thoroughgoing plans for the reform of the institutions of Canadian government brought forward in recent years suggest, for the most part, that these patterns be perpetuated at least in some modified form' (Smiley 1980; 15). The purposes of legislative supremacy receive little scrutiny. The dispersal and deconcentration of political authority, for example, with the aim of promoting political liberties and limiting the arbitrary powers of governments, do not appear to enter seriously the preconceptions and assumptions of many writings on Canadian federalism.

A third and final illustrative example of the preconceptions about rules is the writings on political culture in Canada. Political culture or the modal attitudes of Canadians are usually described as deferential, ascriptive, particularistic, and statist or collectivity oriented (Lipset 1965). Such attitudes are shown to vary by region, linguistic group, ethnic group, or some other demographic correlate. Moreover, variations in political attitudes, such as alienation or efficacy, are interpreted as the consequence of the culture(s) of Canada, when they are not completely determined by demographic correlates (Simeon and Elkins 1974). Culture is, in other words, a set of residual factors that are usually seen as having some impact on government and public policy. Government and policy decisions are in some sense a response to cultural deference or some other cultural value. This usual interpretation of Canadian political culture reveals two unarticulated assumptions about government that are not juxtaposed. First, deference, ascriptiveness, and particularistic and collectivity orientations are the types of attitudes one would expect to exist in a 'colonial' type of political system when the rights and liberties of citizens are determined by governmental elites concentrated in executive positions. Second, the assumption that cultural factors have some causal impact on government and public policy reflects the secondary normative assumption about modern parliamentary government, namely, that the values of preferences of citizens are represented in legislatures and parliaments. In sum, much of the content and method of studies of political culture in Canada reflect twin assumptions that appear to justify some current constitutional rules, namely, legislative (in practice, executive) supremacy and political representation.

All three examples are presented to illustrate an inevitable feature of our understandings about rules and political behaviour. The understandings – in these three cases, the understandings of Canadian political scientists – are based on preconceptions or the rudiments of an epistemology of the artefactual world. The epistemology allows the analyst to make assumptions about the character of rules. Authors and readers can form a shared understanding, it is suggested, if such preconceptions of their epistemologies are treated as mere conjectures, subject to refutation, revision, or revolution. They will not reach any shared understandings if the preconceptions are used to explain away or rationalize inconsistencies and anomalies in the presentation (Lakatos 1974). We must now make some conjectures about the epistemological foundations for the analysis of this book, and present it in a way that the reader may use to address his or her own preconceptions as mere conjectures. Unless the reader's preconceptions are so viewed, the character of rules and their evaluation will remain confusing for him or her.

Alternative Preconceptions

In the previous chapter, the hard-core concepts of rules, individuals, and goods (policies) were described and illustrated at length. All three concepts were given empirical referents, or ways in which they were manifested by observable phenomena. Their combination in the form of conjectural hypotheses and deductive arguments are thus made amenable to treatment with an empiricist epistemology. The bulk of this book consists of generalizations that are confirmed by such 'factual' data of both a statistical and a non-statistical kind.

The choice of empirical referents for our concepts, and the selection and interpretation of the 'factual' data are infused with theoretical significance, in the sense that the primitive terms and axioms in our deductive arguments would logically suggest they are valid. For example, our selection of the rules-in-use in Canada and also their policy consequences are logically based on the premises that such rules and consequences enter into the decision-making calculuses of different individuals in differing policy situations. The theory as a whole, as well as its particular hypotheses, are thus advanced as conjectures for reflection and interpretation.

This particular version of an empiricist epistemology is now generally accepted in philosophy of science as a 'mainstream' version

(Chalmers 1981). It does imply, however, that there can be no 'objective' analysis of public policy that stands apart from its theoretical roots. Theories and hypotheses are not fictional devices that can be revised if they do not 'fit' the so-called 'real' world (cf. Friedman 1953; Davis 1969). The cognitive and experiential worlds are integrated in any analysis.

It is at this level of analysis that our study deviates from much of the orthodox economic analysis of public policy. Our theory treats rules as a hard-core concept, and it builds the rule-bound nature of human choice into its theory. The empirical dimensions of any public policy, as well as the normative dimensions intermingled with them are impregnated with this theoretical perspective. Benefit-cost analysis, Paretian evaluations, and concepts of a social-welfare function are understood as the outcomes of the rules under which the set of policy actors, including the analyst, operate.

There is always a danger that the conjectures of an analysis may be explained away by the theoretical underpinnings of a rival epistemology. That is why the analysis of this book is posed in terms of a contextual explanation. In a sense, any theory has an 'outer' as well as an 'inner' rationality. It makes connections to the experiential and other epistemological worlds of the reader, as well as 'inner' connections to the worlds of policy actors. These 'outer' connections take a variety of forms; they may appeal to the logical capabilities of the reader, to his or her empathetic understandings for individuals in rule-bound situations, and also to their values as innate sensibilities. We ask only that the reader approaches the analysis as a benevolent sceptic.

We must readdress the fundamental riddle in our analysis and evaluation of rules. The epistemology just outlined must allow the reader an understanding of the full character of rules. No empirical methods can, it is suggested, deal satisfactorily with the range of meanings that have been identified as being associated with rules. An empiricist methodology can offer a reasonable approximation of the artefactual design of rules, of their instrumental character, and of the personal autonomy and change in individuals in relation to rules and other individuals. But the approximation is in terms of the natural and, to a lesser degree, social meanings of reality that the author and the reader bring to the analysis. To go farther, and to step outside the bounds of an empiricist epistemology, in order to understand the existential meanings of rules, goods, and their relationships to individuals, would require a form of investigation that an academic observer wishing to explain in any succinct way the design and policy consequences of current Canadian rules-in-use is precluded from undertaking. We will nevertheless proceed by examining the constitutional, institutional, and operational rules-in-use, as rule configurations for public policies, in largely analytical/empirical terms. The fuller meaning of rules must be tentatively suspended by the reader. When the analytical/empirical parts of the book are completed, an attempt to deal with the fuller meaning will be made.

Conclusions

The Canadian political system is characterized by sets of rules that have developed and evolved over time. At the constitutional level, rules have been devised as human artefacts by a range of policy actors in response to historical situations and problematic circumstances of time and place. No single cosmology or creed appears to justify the variety of constitutional rules, and many have fallen into disuse as the intensity of problematic circumstances has eroded.

Similar conclusions may be made about the institutional and operational rules, except that the speed of change appears to increase as one shifts attention to lower levels of rules. Indeed, for rule design, the problems posed – first, at the institutional and, then, at the constitutional level – are frequently the product of inconsistencies and anomalies in the rule configurations as they result in public policies 'in the field.'

Whatever the causes of rule design and rule change, rules will have policy consequences that are evaluated by individual Canadians in their various situations as citizens, bureaucrats, farmers, or priests. Over time, a basic paradigm has emerged in which the relationships between rules and their policy consequences are posed as hypotheses for examination by policy actors, including those professionally employed to devote serious attention to these relationships. Disputations still remain, however, about how to evaluate policies and about what, if any, are the precise contributions of rules to these policy consequences. The disputations are especially exemplified in the analyses of economists.

A fuller understanding of the appropriate design of rules requires that some basic presuppositions about the nature of rules and their policy consequences are made explicit. Constitutional, institutional, and operational rules in Canada have meanings for individuals that go beyond a causal-natural level of reality. They cannot be simply changed, as one would a pair of shoes. Various ontological preconceptions, at the natural, social, and existential levels of reality, attach themselves to the rule configurations in which individual Canadians deal with others for the enjoyment of preferred states of community affairs.

An experiential epistemology can provide only partial understanding of rules and their policy consequences, when rules and other features of the socio-political world have a variety of ontological meanings for individuals, including the readers of this book. None the less, this book now attempts to explain the rules-in-use and their configurations in ways, it is hoped, that the reader will accept as a helpful preliminary understanding. A fuller evaluation of rules will be postponed until the last chapter. We begin again, as it were, with constitutional rules.

4

Constitutional Rules

Basic Logic

Constitutional rules for any community or country are many in number and varied in predictive effects on the authority of institutions to provide, produce, and regulate public policies. The key ones pose incentives for the exercise of institutional choice. Others may have become part of the 'dignified' constitution, and still others are of minor significance. Examples of key or 'efficient' parts, 'dignified' parts, and those of minor significance occur in the Canadian Constitution Act, 1867 (formerly called the British North America Act, 1867, as amended):

- The Preamble to Section 91, which enumerates the powers of the national government, grants to Parliament the power 'to make Laws for the Peace, Order, and good Government of Canada.' This rule is still invoked by the national government as a legal rule granting it authority to legislate in specified policy matters.
- Section 90 extends to the provincial lieutenant-governors the authority to reserve provincial bills for periods up to one year, pending disallowance by the governor general, acting in the Queen's name. This national government power has not been part of the efficient set of constitutional rules since 1938, and has been publicly repudiated by a succession of national governments.
- Section 23(1) prescribes that a senator 'shall be of the Full Age

of Thirty Years,' which is hardly a major constitutional variable affecting the operation of the Dominion Parliament.[1]

The key constitutional rules form a rule configuration. Certain rules can be understood, in terms of their significance for institutional authority, only with reference to other rules. Thus, the legislative powers of the federal government in section 91 of the Constitution Act must be read in conjunction with both section 92, which deals with the 'Exclusive Powers of the Provincial Legislatives,' and with other rules pertaining to the powers of the executive government.

While many Canadian constitutional rules are contained in the Constitution Act, 1867, as amended, many are common-law rules associated with the prerogatives of the Crown, and still further constitutional rules are conventions of Canadian parliamentary government. One of the more visible examples of Crown prerogative powers is the authority granted to the governors general and lieutenant-governors to prorogue and dissolve their respective parliaments. By another constitutional rule – in this case, a convention – these representatives of the monarchy exercise this authority only on the advice of the prime ministers.

The constitutional rules contained in the Constitution Acts as and the Crown prerogatives are enforceable in court. Since 1947, the highest court for judicial determination of these constitutional rules has been the Supreme Court of Canada. Other constitutional rules – conventions – are not enforceable in court. Conventions are customary rules that regulate the workings of political institutions both separately and collectively. They are thus subject to contests of power by, typically, coalitions of elected officials themselves. Thus, it is often difficult to distinguish between conventional authority and operational authority granted in, for example, the statutes of a parliament. It is arguably the existence of conventional constitutional rules that make possible the diversity of metaphysical understandings about the nature of Canadian confederation.

1 The terms 'national,' 'federal,' and 'Dominion' are used interchangeably in the text, even though some Canadians believe that each term connotes different meanings about the status of the federal government. Similarly, the terms 'Legislature' and 'Parliament' are used interchangeably, regardless of the level of government, as are the terms 'prime minister' and 'premier.' This is the older, if not more popular, use of these words.

The importance of non-domestic constitutional rules in establishing the basic logic for Canadian public policies cannot be estimated apart from an examination of the policies themselves. We limit ourselves, in this instance, to the constitutional rules that are amendable in Canada.

Canadian Constitutional Rule Configurations

The constitutional rules affecting the authority of Canadian political institutions fall into three major and overlapping sets of rule configurations. The first set, which is written mainly within the Constitution Act, sets out the legislative authority of the eleven Canadian governments, national and provincial. The second set concerns the legislative supremacy of the federal and provincial parliaments and the sources of executive authority at both levels of government. All eleven governments are granted legislative supremacy subject only to the common-law rules of *ultra vires* (including its application to the constitutional division of legislative powers), natural justice (except when a statutory rule discloses a contrary intention), and the Charter of Rights and Freedoms (incorporated as constitutional rules in 1982 and including a rule guaranteeing natural justice in matters of criminal and civil law). Because of the conventional rules that the Crown will not exercise its prerogative rights except under local cabinet advice and that cabinet ministries must enjoy the confidence of parliaments – rules that are enforced by political party discipline – legislative and executive authority are fused at both levels of government.

The third set of rules concerns the aforementioned charter. The charter elevated, entrenched, and extended various statutory rules concerning the liberties of citizens in relation to the authority of political institutions. However, the scope of the charter, including its interaction with the legislative authority of the eleven governments, is currently limited. Those aspects of the charter that fit with the two other rules of parliamentary federalism (such as the confessionality of schools) are treated as constitutional rules in use. Those that conflict are generally treated by the Supreme Court as rules-in-form. That is not to deny that the charter has attained significant symbolic and 'dignified' status as rules-of-form. Contests of power between and among governments and interest groups are increasingly framed in the language of charter 'rights.' As a result, the precise role of the charter in the constitutional-rule configurations can be overestimated. The continuing uncertainties about the charter and how it fits into constitutional rule configurations are discussed below.

The basic logic of these three sets of rule configurations may now be briefly stated before they are explicated and then their consequent incentive systems described. The basic logic of Canadian constitutional rules is to grant both levels of government concurrent authority to affect the provision, production, and regulation of public policies.

Constitutional Concurrency

Courts are often called upon to make determinations as to whether the plaintiff or the respondent is the winner in a dispute. When the plaintiff or the respondent is a government, and the dispute invokes a constitutional rule, then the court establishes a precedent as to which party in which instances will be a likely winner in similar future disputes. These precedents can accumulate into a constitutional rule for judging future disputes. For example, the Canadian courts use the rule called the 'pith and substance test' or 'the aspect doctrine' to settle disputes arising from the conflict of legislative authority between the two levels of government. As a result of such determinations, it would appear to any casual observer that the legislative authority of both levels of government is carefully zoned by the courts. A listing of constitutionally enumerated powers, such as in sections 91 and 92 of the Constitution Act, can reinforce this view.

This view can be beguiling; it seems to fit an easily comprehensible ordering of rules and authoritative institutions. A fuller story would have to deal with disputes resolved in different ways, in non-disputatious dealings between governments, and in the character of constitutional rules as rule configurations. If one considers, by analogy, a marriage as a set of rule configurations, it is as if one judged the roles of husband and wife, as well as the institution of marriage, by the property settlement imposed in a divorce court.

Concurrency is a feature of the basic logic of Canadian constitutional-rule configurations because the operational rules (established at the institutional level, for the provision, production, and regulation of public policies) do not flow exclusively from those constitutional rules enumerating the legislative powers of both levels of government. This conclusion needs 'unpackaging' to make it understandable.

In the first place, public policies at an operational level require the supply and transformation of 'inputs' for the production of goods as 'outputs.' For purposes of analysis at this juncture, it does not matter whether the policies are produced by one or more organizations, or whether the organizations are privately or governmentally owned. Nor does it matter whether the institutional rules are about governmental provision, production, or regulation of these public policies. What does matter for our analysis is that one or more 'inputs' may fall within the political authority of one level of government and that one or more of the 'outputs' of this policy may fall within the political authority of another level of government. For example, the so-called exclusive legislative power of the federal government to provide national defence (section 91[7] of the Constitution Act) requires the supply and transformation of land, labour, and capital, land and labour being subject to the concurrent authority of both levels of government. The existence of private-sector military-equipment producers amplifies this concurrency.

Second, public policies often display technical as well as institutional interdependencies. For example, the provision of policing services is largely an exclusive authority of the Canadian provinces (section 92[14]). But policing is technically interdependent with public policies about education, social welfare, and economic 'stability,' as well as other aspects of the administration of justice, such as penal services. These other public policies are the product, in part, of the constitutional authority of the other level of government.

Third, the Constitution Act makes explicit rules for concurrent legislative powers in some policy areas. Thus section 95 makes agricultural and immigration policies subject to concurrent federal and provincial legislation, as does section 92A, added in 1982 to 'preserve' the natural-resources powers of the provinces.

As a result of the fact that public policies in some respects derive their operational rules from the political authority of both levels of government, both levels have some opportunity to affect the provision, production, or regulation of these policies. This does not mean that the opportunities of both levels are equal and symmetrical; the bargaining powers of both levels of government differ, depending on the policy in question (we return to these matters in chapter 5).

Among the constitutional rules that provide leverage for federal-government influence on ostensibly provincial-governmental authority has been the rule permitting the federal government to spend on any object out of general revenues, providing the legislation authorizing the expenditures does not amount to a regulatory scheme falling within provincial powers. A major rule providing provincial leverage has been the power to legislate in questions of property and civil rights (section 92[13]).

The major institutional rules for joint federal and provincial activities are diverse. They include:

- parallel legislative enactment and/or administrative regulation;
- delegation of legislative powers by one government to an administrative body or private association (such as a medical association) created and recognized by another government;
- fiscal transfers and grants, and associated 'contracting-out' options for such transfers and grants; and
- forums for consultation on matters of common interest to both levels of government, most visibly the Conferences of First Ministers.

In short, the constitutional-rule configurations are sufficiently flexible to afford the opportunity for any level of government to affect the provision, production, or regulation of a public policy. Thus it appears as if Canadian political institutions are 'living,' in the sense of changing and evolving to meet new circumstances (Cairns 1970).

Concurrency and Cartel

When political institutions possess joint, if not equal, opportunities to affect the provision, production, or regulation of a public policy, they are simultaneously potential collaborators and potential competitors. Moreover, when *all* governments collectively possess the constitutional authority to exclude others from joining as collaborators/competitors, and when *each* government cannot be excluded by the collaboration of other governments, then the constitutional-rule configurations fit the model of a 'cartel' or of a 'club.' This statement needs to be unpackaged, in part because the terms 'cartel' and 'club' are sometimes pejorative terms, and in part because the stability of the 'cartel' or 'club' was threatened during the 1980s.

Until 1982, any change in the Constitution act required the passage of an act of Parliament in Westminster. Following a series of agreements between the British government and those of the older Dominions in the British Empire in 1926 and 1927, each Dominion was granted autonomy for constitutional amendment, provided a domestic amending procedure could be agreed upon. The British government was essentially codifying into law a convention for constitutional change under which it formally ratified requests for constitutional amendments from such countries as Australia, Canada, New Zealand, and South Africa. However, in the Canadian case, the Dominion and provincial governments could not agree on a domestic amending formula, nor could they do so in later years. The British government carried on with conventional practice and formally approved requests for constitutional change on the petition of the Dominion government.

The Dominion government generally sought unanimous provincial consent to constitutional changes, especially those affecting the legislative powers of the provinces. The BNA Act was actually amended in 1949 by the British Parliament, on the petition of the Dominion, to retain its sole authority to amend the act, but only in six classes of subject-matter or sets of rules, including the legislative powers of both levels of government. Both levels of government engaged in unilateral actions to amend, without challenge, their legislative and administrative procedures. A number of Dominion and provincial statutes became constitutional rules, in effect, in so far as they altered the political authority of their own legislative and the executive powers (Sharman 1983).[2] But the key constitutional rules affecting intergovernmental relations became amendable, by convention, only with the unanimous consent of all eleven govern-

---

2 An exception was ultimately to be found in the ability of the federal Parliament to alter unilaterally the method of appointment of senators and the structure of the Senate. In 1980, the Supreme Court held that since this upper house was designed to protect provincial interests, it could be altered only by the British Parliament. Meanwhile, the last of the provinces that possessed an upper house took unilateral action to abolish it by the Act respecting the Legislative Council of Quebec, 1968.

ments. Each of the governments secured its status as a sovereign government, and any joint actions between governments became subject to unanimous consent of all governments. The 'club' or 'cartel' became solidified. None of the eleven governments could be excluded without its own consent, and all governments had to consent to the entry of new competitors. These are the rules that characterize a club or a cartel, whether it is the Organization of Petroleum Exporting Countries or the Toronto Cricket and Curling Club. Canadian parliamentary federalism has at its centre of rule configurations comparable rules to those of OPEC and the TCCC.

Before the predictable consequences of club behaviour are traced, the potential destruction of the club in 1981 merits a brief comment. While threats to the club still remain, the 1982 constitutional amendments, the defeated 1987 amendments (the Meech Lake Accord), and the various proposals advanced in 1992 (the Charlottetown Accord) have re-established the viability of the club.

In 1981, the Supreme Court held that the proposed changes to the constitutional rules that the Dominion was requesting of the British Parliament did not require either the Court's approval or the unanimous consent approval of all provinces. The domestic amending procedures prior to British parliamentary ratification were, it was held, conventional constitutional rules rather than legally enforced constitutional rules. Further, while there was a convention for the Dominion to seek the approval of provinces, this convention required only the substantial and not the unanimous approval of all provinces. With this justification, the Dominion government forwarded to the British government the constitutional amendments that had been approved by only ten of the eleven governments, the political consequences in Quebec notwithstanding.

The 1982 changes, in so far as they affect the status of the club, were, and are, modest in scope. Some uncertain threats remain, largely in the form of the Supreme Court and its political theory about federalism and the rights of individuals. We address these uncertainties below. Five amendment procedures were adopted, their application varying with the particular sets of constitutional rules under scrutiny.

First, each province retains its sovereign status in relation to the unilateral amendment of its own constitution (its own executive and legislative processes) and its veto over any changes in its legislative power, and proprietary and other rights (sections 45 and 38[2]). Second, the Dominion also retains its comparable status, ex-

cept with regard to some aspects of the composition of the Commons, the Senate, and the Supreme Court (sections 44, 41, and 42).
Third, some constitutional rules explicitly retain unanimous consent procedures (section 41), and in those cases including one or
more, but not all, provinces, both the Dominion and the provinces
in question retain a right of veto (section 43). Fourth, only those
residual constitutional rules not covered by the rules noted above
are now amendable by less than majority rules (the Dominion and
at least seven provinces containing at least 50 per cent of the national
population). Finally, most of the charter rights, interpreted and
amendable by the Supreme Court, are subject to legislative override
provisions (section 33[1]). In other words, the potential for the break-
up of the cartel implicit in the Supreme Court's decision in 1981
disappeared in the 1982 amendments. The changes envisaged in the
amendment formulas since 1982 would strengthen the role of the
cartel. In particular, securing various provincial approvals of constitutional amendments is made more difficult by the provisions'
requiring both Crown and majority referendum agreements to
change.

Thus the cartel remains intact. It can exclude existing or potential
rivals, and it cannot exclude any one of its own. The logic of such
a group is predictable. Two consequences of this logic are apparent
at an institutional level. First, the dominance of the executive
branches over the national and provincial parliaments is increased.
In the words of one perceptive commentator:

> It has long been recognized that shared jurisdiction and federal-provincial
> collaboration in matters of joint concern is to a greater or lesser degree
> incompatible with the effective accountability of governments to Parlia-
> ment and the provincial legislatives; in such instances the legislature is
> reduced to *post hoc* debate on decisions already negotiated in the in-
> tergovernmental context, but ... [e]ven in circumstances where only one
> jurisdiction is involved, the House of Commons and the provincial leg-
> islatures have not as yet developed ways to make governments effectively
> accountable. A more important consideration here is that federal-provin-
> cial cooperation contributes to secrecy in the governmental process and
> to the frustration of public debate about important aspects of our common
> affairs. (Smiley 1980: 98)

In other words, the agenda and deliberations of parliaments are
dominated not only by their respective governments of the day, but

also, to some degree, by their non-respective allies in the federation. Some modest reforms of parliamentary procedures have been implemented in the current and previous national parliaments, in particular in relation to the role of parliamentary committees. These reforms have increased the scope of public debate on legislative issues (Pross 1986). However, these reforms have generally not been mirrored at a provincial level (except perhaps by the active role of parliamentary committees in Quebec since the 1970s), and the concept of 'executive federalism' is now an acknowledged term for describing the importance of federal-provincial relations for the exercise of political authority.

The second consequence of the logic of cartel behaviour occurs when governments attempt formal or even tacit coordinated behaviour. This consequence is not part of our current knowledge of the workings of 'executive federalism.' It is, however, an expected consequence of cartel behaviour. Each government has an incentive to be the sole provider or regulator of public policies within its jurisdiction, and each has an incentive to enlist the other level of government in the sharing of the costs of policy provision or regulation. In this way, a government would, from its own position, maximize its benefits (tangible and intangible) while minimizing its costs (tangible and intangible). In contrast, each government has an incentive to prevent another government from raiding its treasury to defray the tangible costs of policy provision and regulation in its territory, or to shift the blame for the intangible costs onto the other level of government. As a result, each government has to ensure that programs undertaken by the other level of government meet with its own willing consent. There must be unanimous agreement between the federal and provincial government or governments or no coordinated action is possible. Note that the number of provincial governments involved in any single mutually agreed-upon decision between levels may vary. However, sometimes the size of the unanimous coalition is eleven governments.

Three further aspects of the logic of unanimous consent merit discussion. First, the logic grants any hold-out government in a coalition extraordinary bargaining power. Such a government may be able to extract a larger than proportionate share of the pay-off from group activity. Quebec has historically used this strategy with effect in constitutional amendment discussions since 1927, a strategy emulated in recent years by the federal (Trudeau) government insistence on an entrenched charter and an Albertan insistence on further entrenchment of provincial legislative powers over natural resources. Occasionally, the threat of secession has been used as a hold-out strategy. At least four provinces threatened secession prior to 1901 and received Dominion grants *in lieu*, while more recent threats have been voiced by politicians in Quebec, the Western provinces, the Maritimes, and Newfoundland (Dupré 1965: 85). One result of such hold-out and similar strategies has been the series of complex tax- and revenue-sharing agreements, discussed in more detail in chapter 5. The strategy has now been elevated to the status of a constitutional rule in section 36 of the 1982 amendments.

A second feature of the logic of unanimous consent is the size of the transaction costs borne by each government in intergovernmental negotiations. Documentary evidence can give only a partial indication of the range of formal and informal meetings of First Ministers, other ministers, and civil servants on matters involving institutional and operational policy rules. Between 1906 and 1987, sixty-one official First Ministers' Conferences were held, and since the so-called Regina Accord of 1985 annual meetings have been institutionalized (MacKinnon 1988). The Meech Lake constitutional amendment proposals of 1987 recommend the elevation of this institutional agreement to a constitutional rule (section 50), already anticipated in the limited provisions of the 1982 constitutional changes (sections 50 and 51). More than four hundred politicians and senior civil servants now attend these official meetings.

The process is partly paralleled in official meetings of provincial premiers now held on an annual basis. Premiers also meet officially in regional groupings (the council of Maritime premiers, for example, meets four times a year) and irregularly on a bilateral basis, as do, of course, the federal prime minister and any of his provincial counterparts. The Canadian Intergovernmental Conference Secretariat alone services more than one hundred intergovernmental conferences annually, 40 per cent of which are interprovincial (MacKinnon 1988: 19). Further, and more extensive, are the contacts between public servants in different jurisdictions on a multilateral and bilateral basis (McRoberts 1985). Most governments now have a permanent agency and a designated minister of the Crown with the responsibility, *inter alia*, of monitoring and assessing the status of intergovernmental relations at a constitutional, institutional, and operational policy level.

A third feature of unanimous consent is that the incentives of the constitutional rules-in-use in Canada give rise to exchange relationships between governments that, in a static sense, resemble horse-trading ('principled compromise'), and in a dynamic sense resemble log-rolling ('shared accommodations'). The 1982 constitutional changes represented in large measure a 'principled compromise,' although the horse was not big enough for Quebec to mount. After the original package of federal government proposals for changes in the rules for amendment, entrenched rights, and fiscal equalization were announced in 1980, measures that were designed to attract the interests of Ontario, Quebec, and the poorer provinces, further modifications were made to secure the support of Newfoundland (section 6[4]), Manitoba and British Columbia (section 33), Alberta (sections 50 and 51, pertaining to section 92A of the 1867 act), and the minuscule hint of the exercise of British trusteeship for aboriginal peoples (section 37[2]). Seen in the light of thirteen years of intensive negotiations on the constitutional amendment procedures alone, the 1982 reforms could also be interpreted as log-rolling. Ontario, for example, gave up its absolute rights of veto over many constitutional rules in exchange for a virtual veto (because of its population size) and the perceived appeal among its citizens for patriation of the Constitution.

Similar examples to these kinds of exchange relationships can be found at a constitutional, institutional, and operational policy level. Some will be elaborated in due course. The cartel is however, no longer as secure as it once was. We must examine the potential threats it faces.

Threats to the Cartel

As is true of all cartels and clubs, periodic threats occur to the basic logic implied by concurrency and unanimity. Some of these threats are a result of the changing composition of parliaments and governments at both levels, as well as of the changing composition of the 'referee' of club 'games,' the Supreme Court. Provincial politicians, at least outside Ontario, are often elected and re-elected on the basis of claims about undue federal intrusions or intransigence. Federal politicians are often elected and re-elected on the basis of claims about new policies necessary for Canada/the national interest/the whole population. The claims of politicians at both levels are often, as we shall see in the next chapter, a strategic exploitation of the logic of concurrency and unanimity, rather than a fundamental challenge to the stability of the cartel. The Parti Québécois is an obvious counter-example. New Supreme Court justices, unlike politicians, are often unpredictable, as their political theory about federalism rarely receives full public scrutiny prior to their appointment.

More basic threats to the constitutional metagame have occurred during the 1980s. Two of these threats have come from the Supreme Court. The third has come from other collectivities that have wished to join the club and the game, or have wished to secede from the constitutional arrangements.

The first of the threats from the Supreme Court has come in the form of new judicial rulings about seemingly settled constitutional rules-in-use. As noted earlier, in 1980 the Court created the potential for the 'liquidation' of the cartel in its rulings on unanimous consent for constitutional amendments affecting the division of legislative powers. The potential was effectively eliminated with the actual changes adopted in 1982. In other rulings the Supreme Court has taken a constitutional rule-in-form (at least since the decision of the Judicial Committee of the Privy Council, the Court's predecessor as referee, in the *Local Prohibition* case of 1896) and turned it into a rule-in-use. This rule is the plenary power or residual clause in section 91, permitting the Dominion 'to make laws for the Peace, Order, and good government of Canada.' While we still await the full implications of the judicial incentives set for an expansionary and centralizing role for the federal government, it is worth quoting the dissenting opinion of Mr Justice La Forest in the *Crown Zellerbach* case of 1988 (1 SCR 401). After citing three cases dealing with the interpretation of the 'POGG' clause since the 1930s, he opines:

[The cases] do not fit comfortably within Provincial power. Both in their rulings and in their practical implications they have predominantly national dimensions. Many of these subjects are new and are obviously of extra-provincial concern. They are thus appropriate to the general legislative power. They are often related to matters intricately tied to federal jurisdiction ... [but] It is ... fallacious to ... [take] a number of quite separate areas of activity, some under accepted constitutional values within federal, and some within provincial legislative capacity, [and] consider them to be a single *indivisible matter* of national interest and concern lying outside the specific heads of power assigned under the Constitution ... To allocate the broad subject matter of environmental control to the federal government under its general power would effectively gut provincial legislative jurisdiction [my emphasis].

The Supreme Court is also changing its interpretation of the standing of individuals in relation to intergovernmental relations. The charter itself changed a fundamental relationship of individual citizens to the constitution when it expressly granted judicial standing to individuals to enforce the rights enumerated in the charter (section 24[1]). The Supreme Court itself reversed its own formulation of a constitutional rule when it held, in 1981, that individuals could possess constitutional standing to challenge constitutional rules if a / there is a serious issue as to the validity of legislation; b / the plaintiff has a 'genuine interest as a citizen' in the validity; and c / there is no other reasonable and effective manner for judicial review (*Borowski* v. *The Queen*, 1981, 2 SCR 575). As a result, a welfare recipient with 'a genuine interest as a citizen' in the federal conditional grant to Manitoba under the Canada Assistance Plan was granted standing to sue the federal Crown rather than the Manitoba Crown, which had administrative authority over the disbursement of all welfare expenditures in the province (*Finlay* v. *Canada*, 1987, 1 WWR 603, 71 NR 338, SCC). In other words, individual citizens now possess some constitutional grounds, albeit limited, for challenges to the institutional rules formulated in the club for fiscal transfers. This decision, if sustained over a period of time, is a major threat to the scope and nature of political authority in Canada.

The Supreme Court in its interpretation of charter cases poses a second threat to club stability. The charter is sometimes viewed as one of three subsets of the major constitutional rules in Canada, the others being the parliamentary and the federal arrangements. However, the charter as a set of rules-in-use rather than rules-in-form depends on Court interpretations of its relationships with other rules. The Court determines the role of the charter and how it fits with the logic of the club. Charter cases can override the statutory powers of both levels of government, for example, unless a government invokes section 33, as has been done by the governments of Quebec and Saskatchewan. The scope of this threat is a matter of judicial determination alone, and legal scholars appear to indicate that, at least since 1986, the Court is exercising judicial restraint in setting limits to the political authority of the eleven governments (Weinrib 1987; Russell, Knopff, and Morton 1989). Thus, section 1 of the charter, which 'guarantees the rights and freedoms set out in its subject only to such reasonable limits prescribed by law as can be demonstrably justified in a free and democratic society,' is now read in terms of a reasonable *balance* between the political authority of governments and the rights of individuals in a free and democratic society, rather than in terms of the *effects* of the exercise of political authority on the fundamental rights and freedoms of individuals (*Regina* v. *Oakes*, 1986, 1 SRC 103). Further, the charter applies only to the exercise of political authority by a government when sanctioned by statutory or common law; it does not apply to disputes between private parties under common law, even when governments enforce Court resolutions of such disputes (*Retail, Wholesale, and Department Store Union* v. *Dolphin Delivery Ltd.*, 1986, 2 SCR 573). In other words, the threats to club stability posed by the Supreme Court do not appear to come from its interpretation of the charter. The charter is integrated within the other rule configurations at the constitutional level. Rather the threats, as we have seen, come from new interpretations of the residual powers of the federal government and from new interpretations of the standing of citizens in constitutional cases.

A third source of instability to the political cartel of governments fashioned under concurrency and unanimity comes from the attempts of other collectivities to join the club as coequal members. Canadian municipalities orchestrated two major campaigns, in 1972 and 1981, to be included in the club. Both unsuccessful campaigns met with the vigorous resistance of provincial governments. It appeared between 1980 and 1987 that the Yukon and Northwest Territories might become coequal members. The 1982 amendments explicitly called for their participation in the first constitutional conference subsequent to the passage of the act (section 37[3]). Moreover, the general (residual) amending procedures adopted in 1982 guaranteed that no province could extend its jurisdiction into any territory, as had been envisaged by some Western provinces (section 42[1E]). Changes proposed in the accords of 1987 and 1992 were ultimately not adopted. As of 1992, the two Territories remain legal creatures of the federal government.

More serious assertions of coequal status have been advanced by a number of aboriginal peoples, in part as a consequence of the legal recognition of Indian land claims not freely negotiated with the Crown by Native bands and tribes (*Calder et al.* v. *Attorney General of British Columbia*, 1973, SCR 313). As a result, the 1982 amendments to the Constitution 'recognized and affirmed' the 'existing aboriginal and treaty rights of the aboriginal peoples,' including the application of charter rights to these peoples (sections 25 and 35). The threats to the club or cartel represent the empirical manifestation of fundamentally different conceptions of political authority held by 'immigrant peoples' compared with 'Native peoples.' First, the authority of existing governments in relation to citizens is linked to territory rather than to ethnic origin, regardless of place. Second, the authority of existing governments in relation to citizens is seen as bounded by enforceable constitutional rules rather than mutually enforced rules of custom, even when more than one government exercises authority in relation to citizens, as is the case in federal countries. Because of these differing cosmologies, the eleven prime ministers and the leaders of the aboriginal peoples were unable to reach agreement on the status of aboriginal peoples in constitutional conferences held between 1982 and 1992. Unanimous agreement reached in 1992 was, in turn, rejected in the national referendum of October 1992. The existing visions of the nature of political authority and the existing cartel of governments remain in place. Before we examine, in the next chapter, the basic forms of institutional arrangements worked out by the constitutional club or cartel, we turn again (briefly) to visions of the Canadian constitutional regime.

Canadian Constitutional Rules and Meanings

Constitutional rules, like all rules of design, can take on a variety of meanings for the builders and users of such rules. The construction and change of constitutional rules are as much art as science in that the texture of the rules is subject to people's aesthetic sensibilities. Such sensibilities can be articulated in a coherent fashion, depending on the range of ontological meanings – natural, social, and existential – associated by people with the texture of rules.

In this respect, constitutional politics is like those two other subjects never discussed in polite conversation – religion and sex. People attribute a variety of meanings, sometimes several simultaneously, to religious and sexual experiences. These meanings can form a coherent creed or philosophy that articulates the aesthetic sensibilities of a particular person. It remains an empirical question as to how far other people share these creeds or philosophies.

A distinguishing feature of the meanings associated with constitutional rules in Canada is the plurality of coherent statements associated with their design. The plurality persists because of the distinction between constitutional rules-in-use and constitutional rules-in-form. The rules-in-form offer an opportunity for symbols to enter the meanings about rules. And symbols, by their very definition, do not translate into operational rules for the provision, production, and regulation of public policies.

Take, for example, the place of the monarchy in the Canadian Constitution. Many attributes of the monarchy are purely symbolic. They are constitutional rules-in-form, such as the ceremonial openings of parliaments. They exercise the meanings of government, however, for those persons possessing monarchical or republican sensibilities. The same might be said of the Royal assent to legislation. However, this attribute of the monarchy is part of a rule configuration that indicates, by convention, that assent is exercised only upon the local advice of the privy councils. The convention itself, as a rule-in-use, may take on special significance for those persons who attach ontological significance to the nature of representative and responsible government in Canada.

A plurality of meanings may give rise to the articulation of a plurality of design principles for the Canadian polity. Some of these principles may appear to be mixed and incompatible in terms of their empirical significance for the basic logic of Canadian confederation. Others may be mixed and compatible.

Ed Black, in an important volume on Canadian federalism (1975), has reconstructed five different meanings given to the constitutional and institutional rules for federalism. In my words rather than Black's, these are:

1 / The Centralist Concept: In this view, Canadian federalism represents, or should represent, a hierarchy of authority, with the national government at its apex. The constitutional rules-in-form that granted the national government a trustee relationship

with the provinces (such as the rules for reservation, disallow-ance, declaration, residual powers, and spending powers) should be exercised in accordance with both the intentions of some of the framers of the 1867 act (Smith 1984) and the policy re-quirements of national economic planning (Thorburn 1984).

2 / The Administrative Concept: In this second view, the basic logic for federalism is, or should be, one of close collaboration and cooperation between coequal governments. The newer struc-tures of executive federalism are to be welcomed and strength-ened so that governments may proceed with devising effective institutional and operational rules for policy provision, pro-duction, and regulation.

3 / The Coordinate Concept: This view seeks a clarification of the jurisdictions of both levels to enhance, simultaneously, both province building and nation building. It would also reduce the transaction costs of intergovernmental arrangements (Breton and Scott 1978). It implies a reduction in the exercise of the federal spending power and a greater reliance on the enumer-ated legislative powers as the major constitutional rules in the rule configurations at the constitutional level.

4 / The Compact Concept: This interpretation of the 'proper' form of federalism views the Canadian state as a pact between prov-inces that have agreed to the delegation of powers to the central government. It accords with the regional diversities of the coun-try and the thrust of the constitutional decisions made by the Judicial Committee of the Privy Council after 1890. It finds expression in modern times in constitutional rules about amend-ments, legislative overrides of the charter, and proposals for provincial nominations to the Supreme Court and the Senate.

5 / The Dualist Concept: Federalism in this view was and is a con-stitutional arrangement for harmonizing relationships between two coequal founding cultures. It requires separate decentral-ized structures for the protection of both languages, education and culture, and bilingualism and biculturalism, in the national government especially. Different constitutional rules should be adopted for federal arrangements in English Canada and in French Canada to recognize the existence of 'a distinct society' based in Quebec. The exercise of federal authority in its enumerated fields of jurisdiction as well as in its spending power must re-flect this cultural dualism.

Since the publication of Black's book, a sixth concept has attained a modest popularity. This may be called:

6 / The Competitive Concept. In this view, governments are rivals among themselves and with private institutions in seeking to supply policies to meet the preferences of citizens (Breton 1985). The objective of constitutional rules is to limit collusive (co-operative) agreements within governments, such as party discipline; between governments, such as unconditional grants other than those to strengthen small provinces; and between governments and the private sector, such as through strengthened charter 'rights.' The enforcement of rules for competition between governments is best left to a Senate elected on the basis of provincial constituencies (Breton 1987) – a Canadianized version of the Connecticut compromise.

All six concepts reflect alternative visions and meanings given to the Canadian state in general, and intergovernmental relations in particular. All six versions can find some empirical justification in some elements of the constitutional rules, and some observations of the operation of the basic logic of these rules. Most of the first five versions listed are, to a large degree, mutually compatible. They imply that constitutional and institutional rules can be fashioned to minimize conflicts between governments and, thus, by a series of unarticulated assumptions, promote the responsiveness of government. The competitive concept also postulates that responsiveness is the goal of good government, but it sees virtue in competitive arrangements as means to this end.

Two conclusions may be made about these alternative visions in the light of our analysis of the basic logic of constitutional rules. First, cartel behaviour is both cooperative and competitive, often *at the same time*. It is cooperative because each level of government has an incentive, resulting from the concurrency and unanimity features of the rules, to enlist the contributions of the other level in providing, producing, and regulating public policies as well as in reducing the transaction costs of governance. It is competitive because each government has an incentive to capture the full range of benefits (tangible and intangible), while avoiding the full range of costs (tangible and intangible) for these public policies. This dual nature of cartel behaviour manifests itself at the institutional and operational levels, which we address in broad terms in the next chapter.

The second conclusion is that these visions are generally agnostic towards a rationale for constitutional rules other than those which promote responsiveness, in the two senses of being representative of all interests in society and effective in policy delivery. Weinrib, in her pessimistic account of Supreme Court decision making in charter cases, articulates a different vision for constitutional rules *in relation to* the natural, social, and existential meanings that *any individual* may wish to grant to these rules:

> An alternative model of constitutionalism pivots not simply on the democratic process but on the idea that political ordering must respect certain substantive values ... Each individual must be able to espouse and follow his or her own conception of the good and to change that conception as desired. These deeply held views may be religious, political, philosophical or rooted in other commitments; they may involve espousal of existing belief systems or development of new ones; they may mandate individual commitment, entry into community, or detachment from community. The important feature is that the premise of collective life is the creation and continuity of a structure in which these commitments may be pursued to an equal extent by all. Other values are left to the give and take of the political process. The constitution ensconces these principles as pre-political rather than pro-political. (1987: 11)

A similar conclusion may be reached about another part of the constitutional rules-in-use, namely, those regarding parliamentary sovereignty. Canadian conceptions of parliamentary sovereignty as another example of a missing vision for constitutional-rule configurations are briefly discussed below.

Parliamentary Sovereignty: A Case for Scrutiny

The concept of parliamentary sovereignty emerged over a period of centuries in the English-speaking world. As a theoretical concept, it played two roles. First, it granted legitimacy to the series of political and constitutional changes that took place in England, especially from the sixteenth century onward. Second, it set the agenda for thinking about constitutional design, its weaknesses and reform. As important, it reflected the normative assumptions among political thinkers about the purpose of the state and the design of its institutions, for it was not a doctrine about governmental authority, or about legislative supremacy. Rather, was a doctrine about the promotion of political liberties and the devices necessary to limit the exercise of arbitrary power.

What were the main elements in this doctrine? By the eighteenth century, three streams of political thought coalesced into a conception of constitutional design (Vile 1967). First, Parliament was seen as a representative institution. In the anachronistic politics of England at that time, 'representative' meant the representation of the three interests in society. The monarchy, the aristocracy, and the democracy were to be represented in, and to be a part of Parliament. But Parliament was to represent and reflect the claimants in a secular society.

Second, government was meant to be an effective instrument. It should embody the three necessary functions of political rule – a law-making function of promulgating general rules, a magisterial (judicial) function of applying these rules to particular circumstances, and an executive function of carrying on the daily routine of government. The three functions were not to be exercised by separate agencies; in a practical sense, such separation could lead to deadlock and perhaps resolution of deadlock by violence. Instead, Parliament was to embody all three functions, and all three functions were to be shared by the King in Parliament, by the Lords in Parliament, and by the Commons in Parliament.

There was also a crucial third element of parliamentary sovereignty. Parliament was to be balanced and mixed. The danger was that one of the interests represented in Parliament would dominate the others. For this reason, constitutional curbs were to be placed on the King. He would share legislative authority. His budget would be subject to an annual scrutiny, and controls were to be placed on his civil list. Parliament as a whole would determine succession, and impeachment would be institutionalized. Finally, fundamental liberties would be established through statutes, such as a bill of rights, that would guard against executive power.

Curbs were also to be placed on the power of both the Commons and the Lords. The Commons was to share legislative authority with the Lords and with the veto powers of the King. The Commons was to be limited both by fundamental liberties placed beyond the power of this one house and by the exercise of judicial power by the Lords acting as the final court of justice. The Lords themselves would only share legislative authority, so that the judicial function was to be subordinate to the laws of Parliament. It would be the King, not the Lords, who would appoint judges subject to life tenure; but the Commons would initiate money bills. The task in constructing a mixed and balanced government was to ensure that curbs were placed on the power of any one function and interest represented in Parliament. The task was neither to divide the functions of government into separate powers, nor to give any one interest supremacy within its sphere.

Parliamentary sovereignty was thus, by the eighteenth century, a concept used to describe a representative, functionally effective, and mixed and balanced institution. The assumptions underlying its definition were normative in cast, and arose from a number of 'practical problems': curbing the financial appetite of the Crown; limiting the legislative excesses of the monarchy, the Protectorate, and Parliament; and ensuring that the exercise of judicial power was responsible to the interests of society. After the Glorious Revolution, the system of government began to approximate the theoretical concept of parliamentary sovereignty. The changes were codified in a series of statutes, such as the Appropriation Act, the Bill of Rights, the Triennial Act, the Act of Settlement, and the Toleration Act.

The impetus for further constitutional and institutional changes of the eighteenth and much of the nineteenth century came from this concept of parliamentary sovereignty. One task was to eliminate the corruption of the Commons by the spoils system of the Crown or by the operations of party and faction. Another task was to reform and extend the franchise to correct for the undue influence of the King and the Lords in Parliament through the use of bribery and the maintenance of rotten boroughs. A later task was to reform and extend the franchise to widen the representation of interests in the Commons.

During the nineteenth and twentieth centuries, this concept of parliamentary sovereignty gradually disappeared. Concurrently, the normative assumptions underlying the theory and practice of Parliament waned. The institutional focus became that of ministerial and collective responsibility of a supreme lower house. The normative concerns behind this shift were ones of popular representation and administrative efficiency. The older concerns with political liberties and the limits to arbitrary powers were gradually eroded.

Parliamentary sovereignty as a representative, functionally effective, and mixed and balanced system of government became trivial and archaic in party-dominated modern Britain.

The mixed and balanced nature of parliamentary sovereignty had insufficient time to emerge as a practice and doctrine in Canada. At the time of its greatest flowering in Britain, Canada enjoyed a fundamentally different system of government. Some examples of these different constitutional rules may be usefully reiterated.

For example, in Nova Scotia after 1713, the executive functions were never part of a mixed and representative legislative assembly. The governor was always responsible to the imperial Parliament, even after 1758, when the legislature was popularly elected. The governor always possessed independent sources of revenue – customs, Crown lands, and military grants. The upper house was merely an appointed oligarchy; it had no judicial function. The courts were ultimately responsible to the House of Lords.

In Quebec, and later Upper and Lower Canada, as well as in New Brunswick and Cape Breton, executive authority remained similarly and substantially independent. Even as late as 1871, in British Columbia, the governor appointed more persons to the single legislative house than were popularly elected. But the major constitutional change – the introduction of ministerial and collective responsibility of the Dominion cabinets – did not take place in 1848, and this constitutional convention was, in a few decades, as in Britain, inimical both in form and in substance to the older concept of parliamentary sovereignty. Legislative supremacy became the crux of the new institutional system.

Some odd and inconsistent quirks of the older concept of parliamentary sovereignty did remain after the passage of the British North America Act of 1867 (Resnick 1987). The most notable were the dissolution, prerogative, and veto powers of the governor general and lieutenant-governors, the appointed Senate with its shared powers, and the bicameral experience of three provinces. But Canada passed from a colonial system in which responsibility was vested in the British Crown and imperial Parliament, to a 'colonial system' in which responsibility is theoretically vested in popularly elected single or lower houses in the provincial or federal governments. What makes this transition viable is the dominance of provincial legislatures and parliaments by the disciplined mass parties that evolved in the late nineteenth century, for the disciplined parties enable executive considerations to dominate legislative ones. The mixed and balanced nature of parliamentary sovereignty did not have time to emerge as a practice and doctrine for government in Canada.

Canada, therefore, lost the imperially appointed élites who ran its executive-centred system of government. It replaced them with indigenous élites, periodically elected but operating within the matrix of the same kinds of constitutional arrangements about the internal arrangements of each government within a federal system. The modern state has grafted some newer constitutional devices onto the older colonial system; but the intent seems to be to improve the popular representation and administrative efficiency of government rather than to deconcentrate or otherwise limit the abuses of political power.

These two rationales for the parliamentary constitutional rules (mostly in the form of conventions of legislative supremacy) in many ways parallel the alternative conceptions about the rules for federalism detailed previously. They are both about the authority of government and of governments in relation to each other. They are not fundamentally about governments and their relationships to individual citizens, who seek some measure of autonomy from rules in order to construct their own meanings about community and freedom. This conclusion is still valid in the light of the first decade of experience with the charter.

Conclusion

The major constitutional rules-in-use in Canada form a rule configuration about 'government' and set incentives for the exercise of political authority. The exercise of this authority is a basic logic that drives the formulation of institutional and operational rules for policy provision, production, and regulation. Of particular importance are the rules for concurrency and unanimity between governments at both levels, federal and provincial.

The basic logic of Canadian federalism structurally models that of a cartel or a club. Competitive and cooperative behaviour among governments, as in a cartel, occurs sequentially and even simultaneously in their mutual interactions. The club remains currently viable despite threats posed largely by the Supreme Court in its new interpretations of the Constitution Act. In this last regard, the charter is currently interpreted so as to fit within the rule configurations for the club. Uncertainty does still remain, however.

The constitutional rules-in-form and rules-in-use make possible a variety of meanings regarding the Canadian polity in general and parliamentary federalism in particular. Many of these meanings are compatible with the basic logic of the constitutional club. The meanings, however, address the values of representative and effective collective (governmental) action. Curiously absent are the values of freedom and community. The symbolic value of the new charter may possibly develop a newer meaning, in future years, about the relations between rulers and the ruled. Nevertheless the rules-in-use are currently about the authority of government and of governments in relation to each other; they are largely silent about the authority of government in relation to individual citizens. We now examine how, in general, these constitutional rules-in-use are exemplified at institutional and operational levels.

5

Institutional and Operational Rules

Constitutional rules determine, for any community, who can exercise political authority, under what conditions this authority may be sanctioned, and what limits to and remedies from this exercise of authority are available. We have seen that the basic logic of the rules-in-use in Canada grant major political authority to the executives (prime ministers and cabinets) of eleven governments. These governments exercise authority under conditions of concurrency and unanimity. The limits to their collective authority are set by procedural requirements of the constitutional rule of law, and by the procedural requirements of representative government set by both laws and conventions. The major remedies themselves are contained in the rules for representation and in judicial scrutiny of these and other constitutional rules.

We must now explore, in general terms, how the institutions of government face the situations and opportunities posed by the constitutional rules-in-use. We shall be looking mainly at cartel behaviour, to use the term introduced in chapter 4, and the rules formulated jointly and individually by members of this cartel for the provision, production, and regulation of public policies.

The technical characteristics of different public policies become of immediate analytical importance at the institutional and operational levels. Institutional and, more obviously, operational rules may have to be accurately synchronized with the technical characteristics of each good if they are to contribute to the welfare of individual citizens. For example, a combination of federal and provincial taxes on crude oil and petroleum producers that exceed 100 per cent of profits is at least likely to dissuade most entrepreneurs from reinvesting their capital in those activities! The institutional-rules of taxation of natural resources, as well as the operational rules affecting the incidence of taxation on petroleum production, may well have to be 'rejigged' in the light of such consequences.

The precise operational rule configurations for each public policy will have to be discovered through a micro-analysis of such policies. That is one of the thrusts of Part II of this book. Only their general character can be discussed at this stage.

One may be more precise about institutional-rule configurations and their importance for understanding how governments work. Institutional rules are normally designed with the purpose of permitting their applicability to a range of policy circumstances. They are bounded only by the basic logic of constitutional rules.

We will discuss the institutional rules affecting, in turn, the provision, production, and regulation of public policies, as well as the rules affecting non-governmental collective action. In our discussion of provision and production, we will discuss the characteristics of delegated authority, as formal legal authority of collective-choice institutions is frequently transferred to other decision-making forums. In our discussion of regulation we must also discuss the institutional bases of commercial and other voluntary transactions, as the establishment and enforcement of different property-rights regimes makes possible a wide range of social and economic policy choices. Throughout the discussion of institutional rules, we witness the pervasive influences of executive federalism on the character of Canadian 'provision systems' or 'public economies.'

Institutional Rules for Policy Provision

Executive Government

Reference was made in chapter 4 to the executive-centred characteristics of modern parliaments at both levels of government. The scope accorded to parliamentary discussions of policy provision, production, and regulation by the executive of the government in question is a matter of degree rather than of kind. In crucial debates on the continued viability of the executive, such as votes on supply, on confidence, and on the Speech from the Throne, the executive

2

will impose a three-line whip on its party members. Similarly, the Crown prerogatives of prorogation and dissolution of parliaments are exercised, necessarily, with ruthless executive self-interest.

There are situations of time and place when the prime minister and major party strategists must modify their approaches to legislative deliberations. Most obviously this occurs in situations of minority government, which, empirically, occur more often at a federal than a provincial level. Similarly some contentious policy issues can stimulate the formation of back-bench coalitions, and government leaders must be alert to the implications of back-bench 'revolts' and their exploitation by opposition leaders for electoral purposes. Bargaining and negotiation, while never absent within party ranks, become more visible in these circumstances. What is remarkable is not that government leaders make errors of calculation in these circumstances, but that they make so few.

Bargaining and negotiations are never absent within the government executive itself. They are bounded, however, by the conventions of ministerial responsibility and collective responsibility, and structured by a range of institutional arrangements affecting the bargaining power of members of the executive. The 'residual' power, as it were, of the prime ministers consist of the convention that ministers, ministers of state, and other members of the Privy Councils are appointed and dismissed by the Crown solely on the advice of First Ministers. Further, the prime ministers can determine the rules for the size, composition, and agendas of the cabinet, of cabinet committees (including inner cabinets), and of central policy-making agencies such as (at the federal level) the Privy Council Office, the Treasury Board, and the Prime Minister's Office. Prime ministers also set the rules for determining the selection of deputy ministers and increasingly (since the personnel-appointment function now rests with ministers and central agencies rather than with a more independent civil service commission) senior public servants as well. No prime minister who wishes to avoid serious errors will avoid consultations with key members of his or her party and with key members of the appointed officialdom before exercising rule-making powers. However, bargaining and negotiations will occur, and occur simultaneously with policy deliberations, within the context of the institutional rules devised by prime ministers. Public scrutiny of these processes for policy provision are precluded by oaths of secrecy.

The processes of executive federalism are also often secret. Parts of the Meetings of First Ministers are held in public, and the product of deliberations is often exposed to intense public scrutiny in parliaments and the media. Confidentiality remains a norm of much of executive federalism, however. It is enforced by group solidarity within the cartel, and its persistence is attributable to the logic of cartel behaviour in which no one member can afford to be excluded from a long-run series of decisions. Again this is an incentive rather than a necessary imperative of cartel behaviour; occasionally members of a government will reject the incentive, regardless of the costly consequences.

Reference has already been made, in chapter 4, to the logic of cartel behaviour when each government operates interdependently with the other level of government in the provision of concurrent public policies. Any single government would prefer to maximize its benefits (tangible and intangible) and minimize its costs (tangible and intangible) in dealing with the other level of government. Thus, in terms of policy provision, a government has an incentive to enlist the other government level in bearing the costs of a tangible policy or bearing the blame for an intangible policy, as well as an incentive to capture the tangible and intangible benefits for itself. Elected and appointed officials are thus continually involved in joint decision making about the formulation and financing of public policies.

Four types of institutional solutions emerge as a result of intergovernmental policy provision. A government may be the sole or joint policy provider and the sole or joint policy financier. This situation is depicted in figure 4.

The provision of post-secondary university education provides examples of three of the four possible solutions. Prior to 1951, university education was provided solely by the provinces and financed solely by the provinces, with the exceptions of some private universities subsidized by provincial funds. This was also the solution in Quebec between 1952 and 1959. Thus, university education in these years is an example of Box A in figure 4.

Between 1960 and the present in Quebec, and between 1967 and the present in the rest of Canada, university education would fall into Box B of figure 4. Federal funds for university education are allocated to universities via the consolidated revenue funds of the provincial governments. (Since 1977, these funds are raised through

Figure 4. Matrix of institutional possibilities

Financing authority

		Single	Joint
Policy provider	Single	A	B
	Joint	C	D

mutual adjustment of tax revenues plus some smaller cash grants from the federal government to the provinces.)

University education fell into Box C of figure 4 between 1951 and 1967 (excepting the Province of Quebec after 1952). The Canadian government was involved by making annual grants to recognized universities. These national funds were distributed among universities by the National Conference of Canadian Universities.

A Canadian case that falls into Box D of figure 4 is the collection of personal income taxes for nine provinces (the exception being Quebec) and corporate income taxes for seven provinces (the exceptions being Alberta, Ontario, and Quebec) undertaken by the Dominion government. Since 1947, the Dominion has alone financed the collection of these taxes for the provincial governments concerned, although the tax rates on a jointly agreed-upon tax base are set by each government alone.

Although the provision of policies can be predicted to fall into one of the four institutional solutions illustrated in figure 4, the precise institutional solution cannot be predicted theoretically. It is empirically set by the bargaining powers of the governments. This issue is discussed in the next section of this chapter. However, we must first examine two further consequences of the institutional solutions to policy provision established in the processes of executive federalism. Both consequences imply that, in the long run, any particular institutional solution is unstable.

First, if a policy is jointly provided, its subsequent modification carries with it the inevitable consequence of another round of bargaining with the other governments involved in joint provision (at a maximum, eleven governments; at a minimum, two). Bargaining with one or more governments involves transaction costs plus any side payments to take account of holdout strategies. Given constant perceived benefits from an existing institutional solution, governments will be inclined to avoid such costs, either by the short-run solution of making no modifications in the existing policy or by the longer-run solution of adopting a single institutional-provider rule. The short-run solution is rarely feasible since modifications in existing policies are usually pressed by new personnel and party shifts in one or more governments.

The longer-run solution is more feasible and is often reached by rhetoric about cooperative federalism. Herein lies the Canadian preference for 'equalization' and other unconditional grants, block grants, subsidies, and tax abatements rather than conditional revenue transfers with their attendant jurisdictional 'intrusions.'

Prior to the Second World War, only seven conditional grants were ever offered *in toto* by the federal government to the provinces, at the height of this granting period, in which a grant was provided for unemployment relief during the Depression, federal grants constituted, on average, only about one-fifth of provincial revenues. Since the Second World War, the number of conditional grants has grown, but at their postwar height, in 1963, they still constituted only about one-quarter of provincial revenues (Gettys 1938: 15; Carter 1971).

In contrast, unconditional transfers were used widely before the Second World War, and, at their height, in 1868, they constituted more than one-half of provincial revenues. Since 1945 unconditional transfers have continued to grow in absolute terms. Currently, unconditional transfers, including tax abatements, represent approximately three times the dollar value in revenues to the provincial treasuries of that of revenues from conditional transfers.[1]

Unfortunately, the single-policy-provider solution is also unstable. It creates incentives to revert to joint provision. First, interjurisdictional spillovers often feed back into the political process at

---

1 Most public accounts in Canada classify block grants and tax abatements as conditional rather than unconditional transfers. This practice is, I believe, misleading. Under the granting procedure, no legal constraints are placed on the recipient governments since their revenues are 'mixed' in a common budget pool. The figures cited in the text are based on data from the Canadian Tax Foundation (1987). The continuing debate concerning federal established-programs financing is fundamentally over whether recipient governments have a non-legal obligation to spend bloc grants and tax abatements in accordance with the preferences of the donor government.

either or both of the two levels of government, and a government may respond to these spillovers by reopening the terms and conditions under which the existing institutional solution has been settled. Second, citizens, groups, corporations, and other interests within a given jurisdiction may press one level of government to enter a policy field occupied by the other level of government. In both cases, of course, the response is not automatic; it depends, among other factors, on the perceived costs of renegotiating existing agreements. Both incentives may, on occasion, operate and lead to a change in the institutional solutions for policy provision.

Thus, the making of institutional solutions for public policy in Canada is based on interactions *within* and *between* the members of the federal-provincial cartel. As might be expected, no government will always act as a team in the sense of possessing a single and consistent vector of preferences. Also, no intergovernmental arrangements will always perfectly balance the preferences of member governments. But the relatively stable constitutional metagame drives the processes of executive federalism to predictable rounds of institutional subgames for the provision of policies.

Delegated Powers

Two sets of factors are also influential in establishing the rules for policy provision in Canada. Both influence the conduct and agenda of negotiations within and between governments in executive federalism. The first is an outcome of delegated authority by the elected officials who make up a government. The second is the set of constitutional rules affecting the *relative* bargaining powers of members of the club of eleven governments. The first will be discussed here; the second in the next section of this chapter.

Modern governments, partly in response to the scale of their policy provisions and partly in response to the need for technical expertise in understanding the nature of the goods they provide, have delegated legislative powers to public bureaucracies, local governments, Crown corporations, 'quangos,'[2] administrative tribunals, marketing boards, and chartered professional societies. The delegated authority will have a statutory basis, but the scope of delegated authority tends to vary with the nature of the good in question as

2 Quasi-autonomous non-governmental organizations

well as with circumstances of time and place in the establishment of the organization in question. Thus the federal government preferred to delegate Crown corporate status when it desired to engage in the production and sale of petroleum products, in part in response to the relative efficiency of decentralized operations for a marketable resource and in part in response to the perceived need in 1975 to compete with foreign-owned production 'majors' (Doern 1978). In all such cases, there is some loss of control by elected officials over governmentally owned organizations. The loss is signalled by newer understandings of the convention of ministerial responsibility. A minister is no longer responsible to a Parliament for the actions of public servants, unless he or she knew of these actions and the actions were contrary to explicit government rules for bureaucratic accountability, such as the rules for budgetary revenues and expenditures.

This phenomenon of modern government is amplified in the context of executive federalism. Members of the privy councils at both levels of government incur substantial transaction costs in establishing, implementing, and monitoring public policies. These politicians are confronted with 'political overload,' to a large degree of intergovernmental making. We shall briefly examine the range of response of politicians to this overload and then reformulate the responses in the language of transaction-costs theory. The overall conclusion is that the responses enable production values – those of professional public servants within and without government organizations – to be paramount over consumption values – those of citizens and communities of individual citizens. A first response to the overload in executive federalism is the priority accorded in intergovernmental coordination between bureaucracies and individual bureaucrats. Politicians have an incentive to conserve their time and energy in resolving conflicts between bureaucracies, and between bureaucracies and their respective clienteles. We have already noted that regular and coordinated planning exists between governmental agencies of different levels of government, and between these agencies and clientele organizations. This interaction is marked by a network of contractual relationships, referral systems, protocol agreements, interorganizational committee decisions, and informal agreements. Governments have also, we noted previously, established entire agencies with the function of intergovernmental coordination. But, while this response may be simply interpreted as one of adding to the economic costs of bureaucracy, it is much more. It takes a large part of the agenda of politics away from the elected officials or providers of services, and transfers this agenda to the decision-making venue of appointed officials or the producers of services. Moreover, through the use of statutory instruments and similar legislative powers, bureaucrats have been granted the legal authority to determine what items should be placed on the agenda, who should discuss these items, and what rights should be distributed to the interests of the participants. Empirical studies confirm the role played by bureaucratic discretion in setting, resolving, and implementing the policy agendas of government (Langford 1976; Lucas 1976; Sproule-Jones 1981; Sproule-Jones and Richards 1984).

Second, the delegation of legislative powers to chartered professional societies and (largely) 'self-governing' organizations such as municipalities, Crown corporations, marketing boards, and regulatory agencies is often used by these organizations to redistribute economic wealth away from citizens as consumers to other citizens as producers (Stanbury and Lermer 1983). This is the phenomenon of 'rent-seeking,' and while it is not a necessary consequence of delegation of legislative powers, it is sufficiently pervasive in Canada to suggest that many organizations respond to the incentives of these institutional rules to reinforce the primacy of producer values.

Finally, the systems of bureaucratic accountability alluded to earlier are framed in terms of their functional effectiveness for cabinets and politicians. While this might appear to aid the control of elected officials over the producers of services, its effect can be perverse. Centralized standards of accountability, such as those incorporated in program budgeting, comprehensive auditing, personnel appraisals, 'person year' establishments, and collective-bargaining 'exclusions,' require some central-agency rules for implementation. Depending on the nature of the good, such centrally established rules can increase political and producer accountability at the expense of consumer accountability. The major constraint on the domination of producer values appears to be the degrees of competition in the product and input markets for governmentally produced goods and services that can be bought and sold in economic market-places. It is an empirical matter, in this third response, as to whether the bureaucratic rules of accountability promote or limit citizen-consumer values in the policy-provision processes.

This analysis suggests a number of features about the public sector that distinguish it from the private sector. The comparison is made by using the concepts and language of transaction-costs theory.

First, rules and hierarchies adopted to constrain 'shirking' on the part of public employees (Alchian and Demsetz 1972) may not correlate well with efficiency considerations in producing goods and services in the public sector. They may help constrain the economic costs of production, but the apparatus of accountability in place in Canadian governments (as well as in other governments) may or may not correlate well, as is argued above, with both supply *and* demand considerations.

Second, the delegation of authority to professional bureaucrats and licensed professionals can be interpreted as a rational response to the transaction costs of 'bounded rationality' (March and Simon 1958). But, in the absence of an easily measurable output for bureaucratic and professional services, this delegation represents a form of 'contracting' in which the 'buyer' of services is at a disadvantage in the bilateral exchange process. Elected politicians may have lost their abilities to monitor the production of many services, and the resulting managerial discretion can lead to a variety of responses in terms of efficiency, all of which are consistent with the Niskanen hypothesis and its rivals (Niskanen 1971; Breton and Wintrobe 1979, 1982). It is the managerial discretion in relation to the non-measurability of outputs that permits some services to be efficiently delivered and others inefficiently delivered. Professional values dominate ultimately because of the constitutional design of executive federalism.

Finally, the separation of ownership from control that is a feature of the transaction-costs theory of the firm takes on a different character in the public sector. The loss of control for elected cabinets as the legal owners of public corporate bodies is associated less with the transaction costs of organizing disparate interests than with limited time and energy of the owners to monitor the formulation and implementation of public policies. The roots again are traceable to the constitutional arrangements that sanction these institutional rules.

The net impact of the delegation of authority by elected officials operating within the constitutional rules of executive federalism may now be suggested. First, it becomes highly unlikely that any one of the eleven governments can operate over time in a consistent way to implement a well-defined set of preferences. There are limits to the way each member of the cartel can negotiate as a team within the logic of executive federalism and in the face of 'bureaucratic pluralism' (Pross 1986). This introduces further instability at an institutional-rule level into the consequences of the relatively stable constitutional metagame.

Second, the delegation of authority introduces further degrees of complexity into the formulation of institutional rules for joint and separate policy provision. While elected officials may have negotiated an understanding about which government does what, when, and how for different public policies, appointed officials may well work out alternative understandings in the light of their own organizational concerns. Appointed officials may be 'working around' the institutional rules established within the cartel, rather than working through these rules to implement a public policy. In other words, a rule configuration exists at the institutional level that is more complex than the image of a club (like a club for playing dominoes or for supporting muscular dystrophy) would suggest. Before we examine some of these rules of production in the institutional-rule configurations of executive federalism, we must first address another aspect of policy provision.

Asymmetrical Federalism

The constitutional rules-in-use set up the basic logic of executive federalism in Canada as a grand metagame for policy provision, production, and regulation. Relations between members of the club are not always symmetrical; however, one should anticipate asymmetrical bargaining power.

The asymmetries are part of the language of constitutional and institutional politics in Canada. Western political leaders constantly perceive their provinces as possessing unequal bargaining power in negotiations with both the federal government and the central Canadian provinces of Ontario and Quebec. The Maritime provinces share similar sentiments, at least in terms of what economists call 'horizontal equity,' the relative bargaining power of their provinces compared with those of Ontario and Quebec.[3] Quebec governments also constantly perceive unequal bargaining power with the federal

3 Strictly speaking, 'horizontal equity' refers to equal governmental tax revenue per capita and is not a generalized term referring to bargaining relationships in a federation.

government as the 'representative' of majoritarian English Canada. Ontario politicians also carry a general perception that they possess greater than average degrees of 'horizontal equity,' if not 'vertical equity,' in their relations with the federal government.

Once the conditions of asymmetry are acknowledged, institutional rules for policy provision may not correspond in a one-to-one sense with the internal rules of an economic cartel or exclusive group. Thus institutional rules for the joint provision of environmental policies in the Maritimes may imply federal domination in so far as these institutional rules are subject to the decision making of public bureaucracies organized on a quite different scale. Conversely, joint provision for the water environment of the Great Lakes Basin implies asymmetries that favour the Province of Ontario over the federal ministries.

Three sets of rule configurations appear to account for the relative bargaining powers of the governments over joint and single provision of public policies. First, the more that any government acts as a team, the greater its bargaining power within the cartel. Thus, minority governments, which have occurred more frequently in the federal government than in any provincial government, can tilt bargaining power towards provincial concerns. The federal government, in these circumstances, has to maintain a parliamentary coalition, and this incentive may strengthen its willingness to agree to provincial demands.

Second, the degrees to which any governmental level possesses a monopoly of constitutional authority on either the input (land, labour, capital) or output sides, or both, of policy provision will increase their bargaining powers vis-à-vis other governments. For example, the exclusive constitutional authority granted to the provinces to provide educational policies confers near monopoly powers on the output side of education, which the provinces have then used as a bargaining tool for fashioning the institutional rules of labour policies, social welfare policies, and even broadcasting policies.

Third, the tax bases and potential tax revenues of each government (as well as its debts and legislated entitlement rules) will influence its bargaining power. Thus, the rules for the exercise of the federal spending power are a subject of contentious intergovernmental relations as they signal 'vertical inequities' in relation to the 'poorer' provincial governments in Confederation.

These three factors lead to asymmetries in bargaining powers of the club members. The institutional-rule configurations for any policy provision will reflect this dynamic within the context of the processes of executive federalism.

Policy Production

Policy provision and policy production are frequently melded together in institutional configurations for public policies. It is in the nature of public bureaucracies to integrate the two or to combine 'policy' and 'administration.' Delegated legislative authority legitimates, in a legal sense, the fusion of policy provision and production.

However, rarely will any public organization operate in isolation relative to other public and private organizations; thus, 'public service industries,' 'public economies,' and 'provision systems' are a characteristic of policy production. As indicated previously, the relations between organizations within a public economy are often formalized in terms of contracts, referral systems, and other kinds of agreements, enforced usually under institutional rules of unanimity, but subject to appeal to the elected officials who devise the provision rules. These elected officials, as members of the cartel, operate within the unanimous consent and concurrency principles of executive federalism, albeit without perfect symmetry in bargaining powers.

Institutional rules for policy production are critical for tailoring the operational rules to the nature of the good. This tailoring is exemplified by the rules through which some attributes of a good may be purchased by a providing government from a producing organization, *whether publicly or privately owned*. Well-written contracts enable providing governments to capture the economic advantages of scale economies, internalize technological and institutional externalities, and exploit the efficiencies of competitive tendering . In contrast, institutional rules may rig the tendering processes, produce badly written contracts, or augment the profits of the monopoly producer. Thus institutional rules for contractual production of attributes of goods as diverse as jails, family counselling, employment training, or water-chemistry laboratories may promote efficiencies in some time-and-place circumstances and inefficiencies in others. In the aggregate, it appears that the frequency of efficiencies exceeds the frequency of inefficiencies in the contractual production of goods compared with 'in-house' production (Bish 1985).

Deficiencies in the operational rules for policy production create a major incentive for changing the institutional rules for policy production. Thus deficiencies in the operational rules for producing elementary and secondary education have led most provinces in recent years to revise the institutional rules for assessing curricula, teacher quality and quantity, and capital and operating expenditures of both public and private school systems. Unfortunately, bureaucracies are highly imperfect error-correcting mechanisms, and operational-rule deficiencies do not immediately produce required institutional-rule changes.

One of the advantages of federalism, whether the variant practised in Canada or that of other democratic regimes, is that it provides alternative models of institutional rules for public production that may be copied in the light of perceived deficiencies experienced by citizens and their elected and appointed representatives. These alternative models may help to compensate for the imperfect error-correcting mechanisms of bureaucratic production in both unitary and federal regimes. There is thus a competitive (as well as a collusive) element to executive federalism in Canada.

Finally, it is worth reiterating again that the institutional rules for policy production are highly influenced by the nature of each good or policy. The institutional and operational rules-in-use will vary, depending in part on the nature of the good, and their analysis will, in turn, depend on a 'bottom-up' methodology of investigation of different public policies. Before we begin to use such a methodology (in chapter 6), we must first address the character of the institutional rules for the regulation of public policies and for the non-governmental varieties of policy provision and production.

Policy Regulation

Public policies in liberal democracies are often based not on explicit governmental provision and production, but on institutional rules established and enforced by courts. These institutional rules in English-speaking countries and provinces form the corpus of common law. Modifications in the institutional rules are then not made exclusively by courts but also by governments, in the form of statute laws. Governance thus consists of rules, including institutional rules, through which individuals engage in collective actions such as the purchase and sale of automobiles, or the acquisition and deployment of defence forces, or the formulation and enforcement of sanctions against pollution. In this sense, all collective action is regulated. The critical issues concern the ways and means (the institutional rules) by which regulation is established and enforced, and the consequences of alternative ways and means for differing citizens. There is no such thing as deregulation, only re-regulation (Samuels and Shaffir 1981–2; J.C. Smith 1983; Buchanan and Vanberg 1989).

Viewed in this way, much collective action takes place within institutional rules devised by the parties to collective action and made public and enforced by judges in civil court. The processes of executive federalism in Canada would then seem to operate at the margin in redesigning the institutional rules for market and other types of collective behaviour. *Three important caveats* must be made to this generalization. *First*, the Crown-in-the-right-of-the-Dominion and the Crown-in-the-right-of-[a Province] are often direct parties to the common-law processes, as they own legal title to approximately 90 per cent of the land and its resources, as well as to most of the water and its resources (except in those eastern provinces where riparian rights are still enforced) (Feldman and Goldberg 1987; LaForest 1969). Governments are thus legal persons exercising Crown prerogative rights in collective actions enforced by the courts as common law (or civil law in Quebec). When these common (civil) law rights are added to the institutional rules of direct regulation (made possible under section 92 of the Constitutional Act), provincial governments can dominate resource markets. To the degree that Canada remains a resource-based economy, therefore, the rules for commerce remain 'politicized.'

'Politicization' of the institutional rules for resources extraction and processing means, in the context of the rule of law, that their formulation, monitoring, and implementation must not be 'arbitrary and capricious' on pain of judicial remedies. The corpus of administrative law, therefore, is critical for understanding how government works in resource markets. For example, administrative law defines at least five different elements that constitute the bundles of legal rights accruing to resource users (Schlager and Ostrom 1987):

– Access: the right to enter a defined physical property, including the right to discharge wastes

– Withdrawal: the right to obtain the products of the resource
– Management: the right to regulate use patterns and to enhance the resource
– Exclusion: the right to determine who will have access or a share thereof
– Transfer: the right to sell, lease, or bequeath all of the above rights in whole or in part.

As provincial governments are the major owners of resources, they retain all five legal rights specified above, and when resources have been 'alienated' or transferred to private parties, they frequently retain proprietary rights associated with the first four of these five. Typically, individuals and corporate persons are merely authorized users of resources in which they are granted rights of access and withdrawal only.

The retention of ownership or proprietary rights by the Crown carries with it the burden of monitoring and enforcing these legal rights as well as the rights of lease and permit holders. There is much evidence to suggest that provincial Crowns are unwilling to bear these transaction costs, and that, as a result, there has been substantial rent dissipation and resource degradation of Canadian lands and waters (Copithorne 1979; Gunton and Richards 1987; Webb 1987; Sproule-Jones 1989b). There appears, therefore, to be a break in the linkage between the institutional rules and the operational rules for resources management and implementation. The efficient rather than dignified institutional rules-in-use may have to be revealed by a 'bottom-up' methodological investigation.

Second, a similar conclusion appears necessary for the understanding of the institutional-rule configurations for policy regulation outside resource markets. Governments are involved in regulating commercial and social behaviour on a vast scale. Institutional rules have been established to change the conduct of social interactions in families, child care, education, housing, the consumption of food and drink, the production of a range of goods and service industries, the disposal and wastes and unwanted products – even the growth of dandelions on one's front lawn! Were governments at all levels to monitor and enforce these regulations, the entire national population might have to be conscripted to carry out the tasks. Governments have thus devised a range of service-delivery rules for public officials to employ at their discretion and for citizens to mobilize at their discretion to 'trigger' the regulatory processes. Typically, regulatory rules are triggered by complaints to a public bureaucracy or tribunal and then both screened and processed by public officials for disposition, or the public officials will themselves schedule investigations and enforcement according to bureaucratic 'standards' (perhaps codified in policy manuals). The impact of these service-delivery rules on the actual conduct of social affairs is difficult to estimate. It seems likely that many social relationships in a community will remain outside the domain of these institutional (service-delivery) rules-in-use. Further investigations are called for, as academics always seem to say.

Third, in some cases institutional rules as regulations are explicitly designed, monitored, and enforced to redistribute the benefits and burdens of social life in favour of one section of the community at the expense of another section. In these cases, a policy that is a 'public good' for some persons becomes a 'public bad' for other persons. Figure 5 illustrates these possibilities of redistribution between producers and consumers of different public policies.

Redistribution – in the cases of tangible wealth – can take place between and among producers and consumers of goods and services. When redistribution takes place between producers or between consumers, cross-subsidization exists between, for example, less-skilled workers and more skilled workers in labour markets or between long-distance and local service customers of telephone companies. When redistribution takes place between producers and consumers, sometimes consumers benefit at the expense of producers (for example, tenants at the expense of landlords) or vice versa (dairy farmers at the expense of milk drinkers).

These kinds of regulations often persist for long periods of time. Redistribution back to the original position may be as costly for the beneficiaries of the current rules as it was for the beneficiaries under the older rules. One of a number of feasible solutions for governments is to limit the enforcement of such regulatory rules.[4] Again

4 The set of feasible solutions may include the outcomes of the strategies used by political parties in electoral situations or by elected and appointed officials in lobbying situations. The size of the set of feasible solutions appears, in the last instance, to be determined by the constitutional arrangements of strong executive governments within federalism and the discretion afforded by these arrangements to the policy-provision actors to adopt any of a variety of behaviours, depending on their own perception of what constitutes a winning strategy.

Figure 5. Matrix of redistributional possibilities

Redistribution from

		Producer	Consumer
Redistribution to	Producer	e.g., minimum-wage rules	e.g., milk-production rules
	Consumer	e.g., rent controls	e.g., long-distance telephone rates

a gap may appear between the institutional rules 'on the books' and the institutional rules-in-use.

In sum, public policies may be influenced by governments as much in terms of the formulation, monitoring, and enforcement of regulatory institutional rules as by policy production. Much of the regulations are devised, monitored, and enforced by common-law processes in the settlement of disputes among private parties. Governments intrude on social affairs in Canada through explicit redistributions, through rules ameliorated by the transaction costs of monitoring and enforcing regulation, and through direct ownership of resources. These intrusions, in scope and methods, are made possible by the strong executive-government features of the constitutional arrangements. The impact of other cartel members on the regulatory processes themselves takes place in a manner similar to that discussed in the policy-provision and -production processes. The range of institutional solutions discussed previously holds in the context of policy regulation as it did in the processes of provision and production. Strong executive federalism remains in operation.

Voluntary Collective Action

It is easy to forget that the strong executive-government nature of Canadian federalism may have some limits to its policy-provision, production, and regulation processes. As noted above, social and commercial authority may have their own rules formulated, in the latter case especially, in the corpus of common law (or civil law in Quebec). Social activities including voluntary collective action may also take place within the norms of reciprocity, as a major rule enforced by social disdain and social rewards. There are few cases in which a 'free rider' strategy can be successfully pursued by individuals in collective actions. Repeated reiterations of the strategy are punished and rewarded by the enforcement of social norms.

Governmentally produced policies and regulations commingle with the institutional rules and social norms generated in voluntary collective actions. Indeed, very few governmentally produced policies and regulations can have operative effects without the willing cooperation of individual citizens. Garbage cannot be removed from households unless the residents set it outside the door or at curbside. Education cannot be provided unless the student is minimally interested in schooling. Social-welfare policies cannot be delivered if clients elope from government offices. Pollution regulations cannot be implemented if wastes can be trucked to another jurisdiction.

In some areas of public policy, where it may appear as if citizens have no choice in whether or not to conform and enjoy and consume. National defence is an example of a pure public good where citizens appear to have no choice in the realization of its benefits or costs. The same can be said of criminal-law enforcement by police forces. The voluntary or choice element may appear to be non-existent. Even in these cases, however, the exercise of choice is possible, although extremely costly to the individual. Exit to an alternative jurisdiction – local, provincial, or national – is one option, albeit a costly one, for citizens in relation to governmentally produced and regulated policies. The organization of an underground economy is another example. A third might be the organization of gambling and gaming clubs as leisure pursuits.

Two key questions may be asked about the interrelationships between government and the wider community over the commingling of social norms and government actions as institutional rules for public policy. The first question is, do governmentally inspired rules help or hinder the scope of voluntary collection action? The second question is, how can governmentally provided policies ever be successfully implemented in the face of the challenge (competition?) of voluntary collective action?

The answer to the first question is obviously a matter of empirical investigation. However, we should expect that some institutional rules can facilitate voluntary collective action, such as rules regarding corporate status, the limited liability of corporate officers, the periodic election of officers, and the payment of dues. Such is the case with voluntary collective action organized through churches and through condominium associations. Conversely, rules that expose voluntary collective action to the 'arbitrary and capricious' actions of public officials in the enforcement of governmental rules may drive out or drive underground such voluntary action. Such has been the fate of some child-care and children's aid associations in provinces where the scope of 'human resources' bureaucracies and rules has been extended.

The answer to the second question depends on the establishment of 'new' deconcentrated institutional rules for policy provision that incorporate citizens into the rule-making process. Such can be the case with the formulation of remedial action plans for the environmental improvement of rivers, estuaries, lakes, and harbours (Sproule-Jones 1990). In this way, the operational rules must withstand the scrutiny of those persons over whom they are to be monitored, enforced, and implemented. There is some evidence to suggest that deconcentrated institutional rule making is unstable in the face of the interests of public bureaucracies and elected officials (Sproule-Jones and Richards 1984). The basic logic of institutional rule provision may make these kinds of operational rules unsuccessful, in other words. If correct, this paradox has its roots in the design principles of the Canadian constitution.

Conclusion

The grand metagame of Canadian constitutional politics makes possible a wide range of institutional rules devised by executive governments within federal arrangements. The rules for policy provision, production, and regulation are set within the processes of executive federalism.

The institutional rules for policy provision are a product of the negotiations that take place within privy councils and government bureaucracies and between these bodies at different levels of government. The precise institutional-rule configurations in use are therefore difficult to predict at any one time, but they demonstrate the logic of joint and single provider and financier arrangements.

Similarly, the precise institutional-rule configurations for policy production reflect both this logic and the technical attributes of the policies in question. The rules for regulation reflect a critical third dimension, namely, the social norms developed by individuals as institutional rules and codified by courts as binding common laws.

The negotiations that take place over policy provision, production, and regulation are rarely those between parties with symmetrical, bargaining powers. Constitutional and institutional rules for negotiations create asymmetrical, interdependent relationships, whether in intergovernmental, intragovernmental, or public-private interfaces. The institutional rules-in-use for any public policy must be determined empirically for each public policy, using what we have called a 'bottom-up' methodological strategy of investigation. In this way, the operational rules – which synchronize the technical attributes of goods with the institutional rules-in-use – may also be empirically revealed. Part II of is book is explicitly designed with these goals in mind.

We should expect that our empirical analysis will reveal the influences of executive federalism and the logic of cartel behaviour set by the constitutional rules-in-use. We shall expect to find the dominating influences of producer values of both levels of government in the institutional rules-in-use. We should expect to find significant differences in the operational rules for each public policy, and in the precise configuration of institutional rules-in-use for any public policy in question. The rules for different public policies will, therefore, be 'stacked' according to the cumulative logic of operational, institutional, and constitutional arrangements, but the size and shape of the 'stack' will vary from one public policy to the next.

Finally, we must be alert to the possibility that our analysis will reveal the influence of non-Canadian rule-ordered relationships on our public policies. We might expect to see the influences of multiple constitutional, institutional, and operational rules on each of our public policies. Policies might then 'nest' within multiple 'stacks' of rules. The full meaning and evaluation of any rule 'nesting' will be addressed in chapter 11. At that time, 'the constitutive principles' or foundations of how governments work in Canada will be appraised.

Let the play proceed!

6

The Setting and the Site

Operational Rules-in-Use

Operational rules-in-use are the 'standard operating procedures' for the physical transformation of resources into goods. In a bureaucratic context, they may include service-delivery rules or, more rarely, comprise all of the service-delivery rules we have discussed previously. The operational rules-in-use are one element examined in policy and program evaluations; as we have seen, they may be assumed as constant exogenous variables in mainstream economic policy evaluations.

The 'standard operating procedures' will vary from one good to the next. The technical attributes of goods will require differing operational rules. The operational rules for education in the classroom will obviously differ from the operational rules for highway construction in the countryside. Less obviously, the configuration of operational rules-in-use may differ from one educational context to the next – such as from a classroom of young children to a classroom of high school students – and from one highway construction context to the next – such as from construction in the Rockies to construction on the Prairies.

Any examination of the operational rules-in-use will have intrinsic value for policy specialists. Different readers of this book will be interested in different public policies. We are all familiar with people who are erudite about, even occasionally fanatical about, health policies or environmental policies or peace and defence policies. Unfortunately not all readers will be interested in or erudite or fanatical about all public policies. Therefore the public policies selected for scrutiny here are those that provide insights into the rule configurations and rules-in-use in Canadian parliamentary federalism. This is what I have referred to previously as a 'bottom-up' methodology.

Part I of this book analysed the rule configurations and rules-in-use in Canadian parliamentary federalism so as to capture their basic logics. We examined the *consequences as a product of the incentives* of the actors involved in constitutional situations and in institutional situations of provision, production, and regulation. The incentive structures of these situations led to consequences that could be described in general terms. As we moved in our analysis from constitutional rules to institutional rules to operational rules, we noted how increasingly varied are the range of consequences of these rule configurations. Using such 'top-down' methodology, we could examine only the general patterns of institutional and operational rules, not the actual rules-in-use. In Part II, we begin to fill in more details about the rules-in-use as we shift to a 'bottom-up' methodology.

A 'bottom-up' methodology may be necessary for an understanding of Canadian parliamentary federalism, but it is not both necessary and sufficient. Additional methodological strategies must be adopted to make the analysis tractable. Two additional methodologies are adopted. Each will be discussed in turn.

We noted in chapters 2 and 3 that rules at all levels of analysis are designed to deal with the problems experienced by different communities of interest at different times and in different places. Sometimes rules-in-use will be made obsolete by the development of new knowledge about the goods in question or by the changing nature of individual preferences and communities of interest. Sometimes rules will be made inconsistent, as the interdependencies between goods may change. Sometimes new rules will be formulated at the institutional and constitutional levels, reflecting a misperception of their applicability to all operational circumstances. In other words, exigencies of time and place affect the synchronization of rules, individuals, and goods.

In order to take account of the constraints and opportunities of time and place, the analyst has two choices. He or she can examine public policies and their rules-in-use in the same site and in the same historical setting, or vary the site and the setting and examine one (or more) public policies over these differential circumstances.

In this book, I have selected the first option because our concern is less with the contingencies of time and place and more with the interface between rules and goods. Thus, the methodology is to examine three cases of public policy, all of which share a common historical and geographical 'heritage.' We thus examine the policy cases of commercial shipping, recreational boating, and water-quality management as they are exemplified in Hamilton Harbour, Ontario. A single site in one part of a country that constantly demonstrates its regional prides might seem a limited focus. However, we need to discover the micro operations of rules-in-use before we can safely generalize about the macro rule configurations for Canada. Thus Hamilton Harbour is simply an apt example in a theoretical sense.

The second methodological strategy is one designed to reinforce the distinctions between rules-in-use and rules-in-form revealed by the bottom-up methodology. The three policy cases presented are technically interdependent in so far as they all make use of the same body of water. These interdependencies can be compatible, as in the case of commercial shipping with virtually all water-quality conditions. They can also be in conflict, as in the case of recreational boating, including human contact with water (sailboarding) with some water-quality conditions. When technical interdependencies exist, rules may be designed to take account of the compatibilities and conflicts. These particular rules-in-use indicate the range of rules that may be designed for each policy situation. There is a danger that the range of rules-in-use may be understated by employing a bottom-up methodology in policy cases that are discrete rather than technically interdependent.

We are, therefore, engaged in this part of the book with a micro analysis of rules-in-use for three policy cases in one watershed in Canada. Before we can analyse these rule configurations, we must establish the historical and geographical contingencies for our policy cases. We begin with a brief overview of the policy cases, which are, of course, fully developed in later chapters. We then examine the history of the physical structure and aquatic ecologies of the harbour before examining the socio-economic history of the harbour's watershed. Finally we anticipate the thrust of the subsequent policy cases by noting the major consequence of the rules for the historical development of the site. This emphasis on the micro level will yield generalizations about the macro functioning of politics and public policy in Canada. We must engage ourselves in the workings of the rules in sites and times in order to build an accurate understanding of the logic of rule configuration in Canada.

Overview of the Three Policy Cases

Hamilton Harbour is the major naturally protected harbour on western Lake Ontario. Its waters measure some 40 square kilometres and are accessible to Lake Ontario by a man-made ship canal completed in 1830.

This site helps sustain our three policy cases. The harbour is a port that receives between 400 and 1,000 vessels during the ice-shortened season of the St Lawrence Seaway shipping transportation system.[1] Many of these vessels carry raw materials for two steel-making plants located on the foreshores of the harbour. Indeed, the foreshores are predominantly allocated to either port-related facilities (wharves, warehouses, and terminals) or industrial sites, present and planned. (See Map 1) In many respects, the harbour is the hub of the local and regional economies.

The harbour is, however, a natural resource that sustains additional policy activities. A major activity is for the free disposal of liquid wastes. Approximately 27 billion gallons of liquid wastes are discharged from industrial and municipal outfalls on an annual basis; this is equivalent to 40 per cent of the volume of the receiving waters. Some of the pollutants in these waste waters are treated, and some others are diluted before discharge. The harbour also receives run-off from a watershed larger than 500 square kilometres, and these untreated waters (apart from the area of the City of Hamilton's combined septic and storm drains) amount to 40 per cent of the volume of the receiving waters. It takes only three months for the harbour to flush itself into Lake Ontario, but the resident waters and sediments exceed conventional standards for many kinds of water pollutants.

Recreation – both pleasure boating and passive types on the foreshores of the harbour – is another major policy activity. It is estimated that sailing, canoeing, kayaking, and motorboating involve anywhere between 175,000 and 350,000 Hamilton residents in any one year. Walking, cycling, bird-watching, and ice-skating are other

1 The data in this section are documented in chapters 7, 8, and 9.

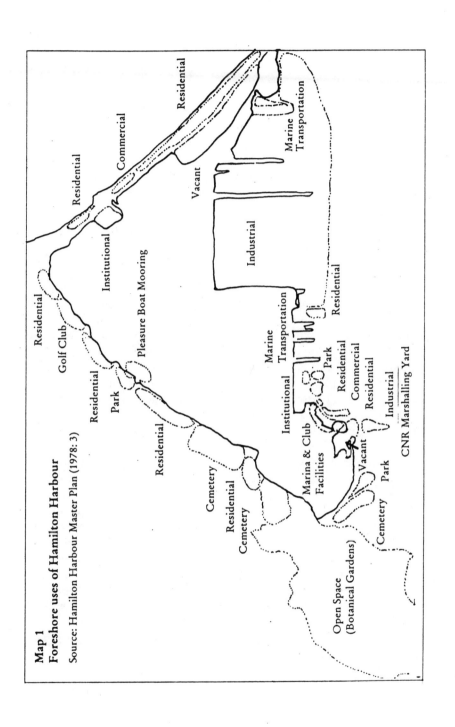

Map 1
Foreshore uses of Hamilton Harbour

Source: Hamilton Harbour Master Plan (1978: 3)

recreational activities on the harbour and its foreshores, although only 7 per cent of the shoreline is currently classified as open space, and one-half of this space is occupied by boating marinas.

The harbour also once supported a thriving commercial and recreational fishery. Because of infilling of spawning areas for expanded industrial sites on the southern and eastern shores of the bay, and because of sustained water degradation, these fisheries have disappeared. However, a variety of fish species, macrophytes, and benthic invertebrates still populate parts of the bay, and the prospect of improved dissolved-oxygen levels may presage a revival of these traditional activities in the harbour.

Finally, the harbour waters are used for industrial water supply. Some 2.3 million cubic metres are withdrawn daily, mostly for cooling water processes in the steel mills. Of this volume, 96 per cent is presently returned to the bay after use, but this proportion will drop to near to zero in the immediate future. Domestic water supply in the watershed is furnished largely from Lake Ontario. The City of Hamilton relied on wells and springs for domestic water supply prior to 1860, when water began to be pumped (for filtration) from Lake Ontario through a natural sand bar for storage and later distribution.

The present pattern of activities of Hamilton harbour has evolved for a number of reasons. First, the configurations of rules-in-use have regulated the compatibilities and conflicts between the policy activities to place emphases on certain priorities at particular times in the history of the site. Second, the rules-in-use have structured the situations facing policy actors in each policy activity. Third, the Harbour is a natural resource, available for use and exploitation in a variety of ways. Its physical characteristics create opportunities for and constraints on its use. In addition, the communities in the watershed and beyond place direct and indirect socio-economic demands on the harbour. Its location as a shipping port within an urban, industrialized watershed creates incentives and opportunities for different public policies that the harbour may not adequately be able to bear at the same time. Maps 2 and 3 show, respectively, the location of the harbour in relation to other Canadian ports and in relation to the watershed itself. These maps may help place the site for the reader in a context that includes international, national, watershed, and foreshore policy activities.

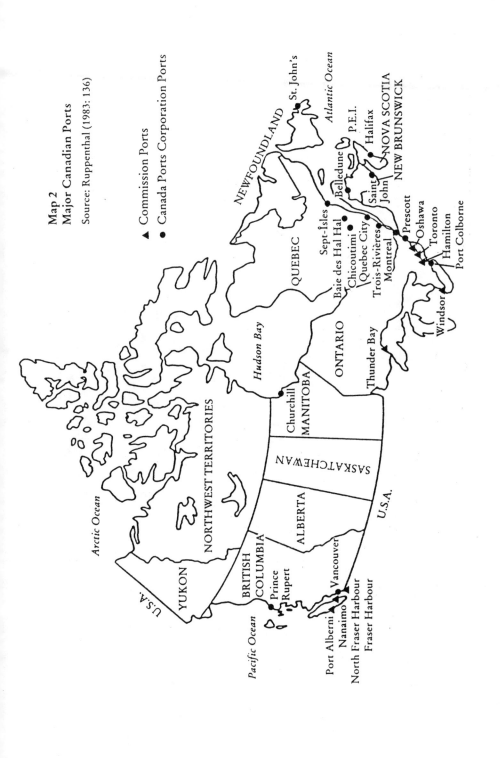

Map 2
Major Canadian Ports

Source: Ruppenthal (1983: 136)

▲ Commission Ports
● Canada Ports Corporation Ports

Map 3
Hamilton Harbour watershed
Source: Ontario Ministry of Environment (1985: 14)

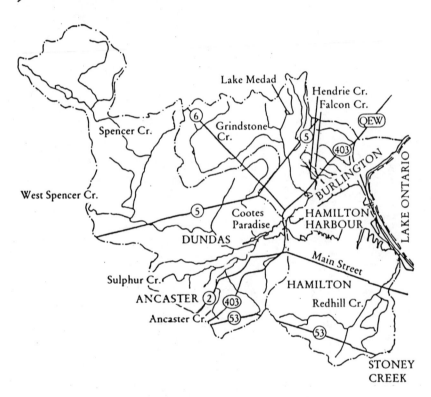

Changes in the Physical Structure and Aquatic Ecologies of the Harbour and Watershed

The last glaciation period established the basic physical structure of Hamilton Harbour. During this time, an ice lobe occupied the Lake Ontario basin and the adjacent lands. These lands included the Niagara Escarpment – an area of massive dolomite capping soft, easily eroded shales (Regional Municipality of Hamilton-Wentworth 1981; Putman and Putman 1979; McCann 1981).

The melting of the ice produced a series of lakes in North America, including Lake Iroquois. The surface of this lake at Hamilton was some 34 metres higher than the present Lake Ontario, and the action of waves at this time contributed to erosion from the escarpment face and deposition along the shore in a series of sand and gravel bars.

When the weight of the glaciers was finally removed, Lake Ontario emerged as a consequence of the uplift of the northeastern part of the continent. The lake flooded the area now known as the harbour, and penetrated and submerged the area known as Cootes Paradise, or the lower Dundas valley. At this time, a sand bar was formed that joined the northern and southern shores of the harbour, apart from a natural shallow outlet in the northeast of the harbour, now filled in (see map 4).

The physical structure of the harbour has undergone large-scale change in the last 150 years, and especially in the last 50 years (Hodson and Threader n.d.) The reasons will be examined in later sections of this chapter. The major man-made changes include:

1 / construction of the Desjardins Canal through Cootes Paradise to link the mill town of Dundas with the harbour and Lake Ontario between 1823 and 1830;
2 / construction of the Burlington Ship Canal, initially 27 metres wide, to provide secure shipping access between the harbour and Lake Ontario, in 1823. Between 1926 and 1969, the canal was more than doubled in size, to measure 88 metres wide by 10 metres deep;
3 / infilling of the bay for port activities and industrial land sites. This has resulted in a reduction in the size of the harbour waters by more than 20 per cent. The major reductions took place between 1926 and 1982, when the total area of open water was

Map 4
Site of Hamilton, c. 1800
Source: City of Hamilton (1984: 6)

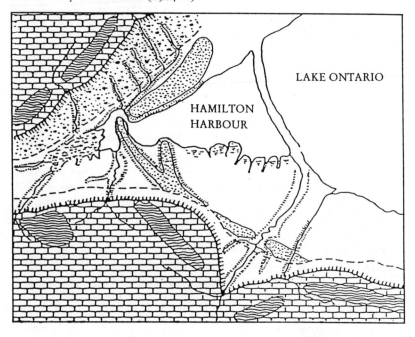

Iroquois sand and gravel bar		Shale	
Lake Iroquois shoreline		Moraine	
Niagara escarpment		Marsh	
Limestone plain			

reduced from 27.8 to 21.6 square kilometres. A comparison of maps 1 and 4 indicates the large-scale physical changes that have occurred, especially on the southern shore;

4 / non-point source run-off from the watershed, point-source discharges, and dredging, especially in the twentieth century, have resulted in bottom materials, consisting largely of mud, silt, and clay, replacing the extensive stretches of gravel and sand bottom in the harbour. Organic bottom materials that once covered Cootes Paradise, the north and easterly areas, and the southern inlets are now limited, because of infilling and burying, to the Cootes Paradise and northwestern corner of the bay.

The physical structure of the watershed has also undergone substantial change. Much of the forest in the watershed was cleared by pioneer farmers in the first half of the nineteenth century. The types of trees that prosper, and the types of agricultural crops that are predominant, vary significantly with the three types of soils that exist in the watershed. The escarpment and upland have a Silurian geological base on which the soils are mainly of two kinds – limestone and clay. The limestone areas to the north of Hamilton have topsoil depths of 10 centimetres or less and are covered with grasses, deciduous trees (such as maple, beech, and basswood), and the expanding edges of suburban and exurban settlements. The clay soils in the eastern part of the watershed have more than 35 centimetres of topsoil and became known in the twentieth century as part of the 'Niagara Fruitbelt.' Maple, ash, and hickory are standing forest species, although the lands are also subject to urban and suburban sprawl.

Lands below the escarpment consist of sandy dry plains, intermixed with moist sites of clay and marshland. Much of the marshland adjacent to the harbour has been filled, and other clay sites are spliced by tiling and drainage ditches.

Five creeks flow into the harbour from this watershed. Table 1 describes the current area and proportion of the watershed of each of the creek areas and the City of Hamilton.

Thus the physical structure of both the harbour and its watershed have undergone substantial natural and man-made changes. The man-made changes have mainly occurred and quickened in the last century.

TABLE 1
Watershed areas

Region	Area (sq. miles)	Percentage of watershed
Spencer Creek	76	40
Mineral Springs Creek	18	10
Rock Chapel Creek	8	4
Grindstone Creek	34	18
Red Hill Creek	24	12
City of Hamilton	30	16

Source: Forde (n.d.: 10)

The biology of Hamilton Harbour has changed dramatically in the last century (Holmes and Willams 1984). The ecological systems have not simply evolved, but have been substantially modified by changes in water chemistry (as a result of pollution) and changes in fishing effort (also as a result of pollution and of occasional overfishing). Generally, there has been a decline in both the multiplicity and the diversity of biological species, two accepted indicators of environmental degradation.

First, the abundance and distribution of benthic invertebrates that provide food for fish species have been reduced. Some species disappeared in the late nineteenth century, and others in more recent years. The southern shores contained no benthic invertebrates at all in 1981 because of complete anoxia or sediment chemistry, a situation that was reversed by 1989. Other areas, such as Cootes Paradise, are still home to abundant numbers of invertebrates such as snails, crustaceans, and oligochaete worms, and the last are now returning to the industrialized southern shores (Environment Canada 1987).

Second, the quantity and quality of the marsh area that provides habitat for fish and wildlife species have substantially declined. Some three-quarters of the marsh community in Hamilton Harbour has disappeared in the last 150 years (Willams, cited in Holmes and Willams 1984: 65). Even in postwar years the abundance and diversity of aquatic plants have been reduced. In the relatively unaltered Cootes Paradise, for example, the number of macrophyte families, genera, and species dropped by approximately one-half between 1949 and 1972. Substantial nutrient enrichment of the harbour has produced major changes in the dominant plankton taxa.

These changes have led to major changes in the abundance and distribution of fish species in the harbour. Cold-water species, such as trout, herring, and whitefish, were abundant in the harbour in the nineteenth century, and they sustained large commercial and sport catches. These species began to decrease in number and show signs of stress before the turn of the century, initially as a result of overexploitation. The loss of habitat and low dissolved-oxygen levels in the lower layers (thermocline and hypolimnion) of water in the summer months were major contributors in the total collapse of these fisheries in the 1930s and 1940s. Warmer-water species, such as catfish and especially carp, continue to provide angling opportunities on the northern and western shores, including Cootes Paradise. The ship canal to Lake Ontario provides further recreational opportunities to catch smelt, coho salmon, and trout. Recent studies have captured examples of fifty-nine fish species in Hamilton Harbour, with a greater abundance of smaller, short-lived species. Some larger resident species display indications of toxic water-quality conditions; white sucker fish, larger than 40 centimetres, appear highly susceptible to lip papillomas (tumours) (Great Lakes Water Quality Board 1984: Appendix).

Changes in the physical structure and aquatic ecologies of watersheds and bays are to be expected, even in wilderness areas. The changes that have occurred in Hamilton harbour and its watershed suggest much more than normal rates of evolution. Man has made substantial changes to the physical structure of the harbour and upland areas. The harbour itself is smaller, and its water chemistry and bottom materials much different from what one would expect from natural evolution. The upland areas, too, have undergone major changes as demands for agricultural, industrial, commercial, and domestic lands have replaced and restructured the physical geography of the region.

Finally, the ecological systems associated with the harbour and its tributaries have changed. Lower forms of biological life have been eliminated in some areas and changed in character in others. There is less abundance and diversity of biological life than one would anticipate from natural evolutionary change of aquatic ecologies.

Hamilton Harbour is thus as much a man-made artefact as it is a natural resource. It is a product, in part, of the socio-economic processes of the region.

The Socio-economic Structure and Its History

The Hamilton Harbour watershed is currently the home of more than 500,000 persons. Some 300,000 of these residents live within the municipal boundaries of the City of Hamilton, and the others within the municipalities of Burlington, Dundas, Ancaster, and Stoney Creek. The local governmental structure overlaps and divides the watershed of 900 square kilometres. Under a two-tiered local-government system established by the Province of Ontario in 1974, Hamilton, Dundas, Ancaster, and Stoney Creek are four of six 'lower tier' municipalities (the others being Flamborough and Glanford) within the 'upper tier' Regional Municipality of Hamilton-Wentworth. Burlington is a 'lower tier' municipality within the adjacent Regional Municipality of Halton. Hamilton Regional Conservation Authority, a special board dependent on both the regional and the provincial government for funding and statutory authority, is a major governmental body responsible for conservation and flood control in the basin. The rules of these local authorities and the rules of provincial, federal, and international governments are, as we shall see in later chapters, the major elements in the set of rule configurations for our three public policies.

Population growth in the area is significantly smaller than in the rest of Ontario and the rest of the country. In the last decade for which complete census data have been published (1971–81), population in the Hamilton Census Metropolitan Area (CMA) rose 7.6 per cent, compared with increases of 11.7 per cent for Ontario and 12.5 per cent for Canada as a whole.[2] In addition, the City of Hamilton itself, which once (1931) was home to 82 per cent of the population of the area, now has only 56 per cent of the area population, a trend reflecting the emergence of multiple growth centres and the population migrations characteristic of modern cities.

Employment opportunities in the area remain in the manufacturing and heavy-industrial sectors, despite regional population changes. Employment in the manufacturing sector is at 56 per cent, and 70 per cent of that is in the metal, machinery, electrical, chemical, and transportation-equipment industries. Employment in trade, services,

2 The Hamilton CMA includes the Town of Grimsby as well as parts of Burlington not in the watershed. Unless otherwise stated, the data in this section are from the 1981 Census.

and the public sectors is significantly less than in Ontario, or Canada as a whole. For example, public-sector employment in the area is at 11 per cent, compared with 22 per cent in Ontario and 26 per cent in Canada as a whole.

Personal disposable income per capita in the area reflects this predominantly blue-collar employment structure. It exceeds the provincial average purchasing power per person by more than 5 per cent. Average household rather than personal income parallels that of Ontario, however, reflecting, in part, the lower pay and lower labour-force participation rate of females in the area. At present then, Hamilton and its neighbouring communities within the watershed represent a relatively slow-growth area, primarily dependent for employment on the manufacturing and heavy-industrial sectors.

Population shifts within the area reflect the deconcentration of activities within the older central city, the locational competition of economic activities within the region, and also locational competition within the adjacent urban communities of Oakville, Mississauga, and Metropolitan Toronto. Economic competition is one of the enduring historical traits of Hamilton, and to this history we now turn.

The Early Years

The socio-economic history of Hamilton is, curiously, a history of politics in two different senses.[3] First, Hamilton's economy and society have developed because of political and military decision situations outside the region. Second, indigenous entrepreneurs – political as well as economic – have used the opportunities afforded by the rule configurations at the municipal, provincial, and national levels to develop, redirect, and restructure the economy. Hamilton is consequently as much an artefact of human design as is its harbour. These two political factors may also account for the persistent 'booster' culture of this 'artefactual' city and region, as well as of many other cities in Canada.

The early years of Hamilton's development – the years prior to Confederation – reflect these two political factors. The earliest set-

3 In this section, 'Hamilton' refers to both the city itself and other communities within the watershed of Hamilton Harbour.

tlers were Native Indians of the Neutral Nation, or Attiwandaronk tribe, who tried to maintain a neutral position in the tribal warfare of the seventeenth century (Johnston 1958: 8–10; Weaver 1982: 9; Woodhouse 1967: 4). Their numbers diminished by and having lost their tribal leaders to the plague, they were eventually eliminated by the Seneca Indians. Early European settlers preferred to locate away from the 'head of the lake' and closer to water-transportation routes such as the St Lawrence River and the portage between Lake Ontario and Lake Erie.

The American Revolution and its aftermath, including the War of 1812, laid the foundation for the early development in the region. Refugee Loyalists were attracted to the settlements of Dundas and Ancaster, seeking to exploit the milling potential of swift-flowing Spencer's Creek and Ancaster Creek. Governor Simcoe reinforced the development of the Dundas area by building a military road from the end of the marsh in Burlington Bay to the head of navigation on the Thames River (Craig 1963: 35). This military road, begun in 1793, was designed to maintain links with the interior of the continent should the Niagara frontier fall to the Americans. It had the effect of emphasizing Dundas as the outfitting and forwarding town for the interior.

The War of 1812 War launched the development of Hamilton itself, an area previously sparsely populated by squatter farmers. The British regular and militia forces were garrisoned on Burlington Heights (now in the Municipality of Flamborough) and provided both a measure of security for the inflowing population and a demand for local products and services (Watson 1964: 14; Campbell 1966: 42–43).

Two postwar political decisions of the Government of Upper Canada stimulated the development of the new community of Hamilton. First, the political influence of George Hamilton (after whom the city is named); his father, and former member of the Legislative Assembly, Robert Hamilton; local member of Legislative Assembly James Durand, and local wealthy merchant Nathaniel Hughson ensured that the site for a new district township would be on land owned by Hamilton, and formerly owned by Durand. From that time (1816) until 1841, appointed justices of the peace would organize and implement judicial, legislative, and administrative functions from the district townsite, and redirect local governmental business from Niagara-on-the-Lake to the south and York to the east (Crawford 1961: 22–5).

Second, the Government of Upper Canada financed the digging of a canal through the 'beach strip' sand bar in 1823 to enable merchant vessels to enter directly into Burlington Bay and to berth at the Hamilton waterfront. Almost immediately four wharves were built on the Hamilton waterfront and allied warehouses were constructed, and Hamilton superseded Dundas as the storage, outfitting, and distribution centre for western Lake Ontario. Attempts to restore Dundas's central role by building a man-made canal to the bay, with private and government funds, proved commercially unviable.[4] The advent of steam- rather than water-driven milling, the growth of banking and insurance companies, and the increasing imports and exports passing through the harbour all led to the absolute and relative growth of Hamilton in the region during the 1830s and 1840s.

Political and economic entrepreneurship created the next major developmental stage in Hamilton's growth. Sir Allan MacNab, the local member of the Legislative Assembly, was at the centre of successful organized attempts to construct a railway line linking Toronto with Buffalo through his lands adjacent to the harbour. The organization required capital from the Great West Railroad in London and, more important, the province's agreements (1849) to guarantee railway debt for lines that extended more than 75 miles once half the line was completed and (1851) to permit municipalities to undertake railway subscriptions on behalf of their taxpayers. The newly incorporated City of Hamilton pledged a stock subscription of £50,000 in 1851, when the total tax assessment of the city was only £94,000.[5] The railway was opened in 1853 and fully operational by 1854. It connected the harbour with the rail networks of New York and of Central Michigan, as well as connecting Hamilton to its hinterland and the City of Toronto. Once more, the opportunities

---

4 The Desjardins Canal was built between 1826 and 1837 with $31,000 of private funds and $68,000 of government funds from the colony. Neither the interest nor the principal was repaid (Kingsford 1865: 80–1).
5 Locally elected municipalities were made possible by the District Councils Act of 1841, passed by the United Parliament in the same year. Hamilton incorporated in 1846 (Johnston 1958: 135).

made possible by the rule configurations made viable the economic growth of Hamilton.

The remaining years before Confederation resulted in a short-run boom and growth, and a decade of recession and decline. The economic entrepreneurship of Hamilton's political élites proved disastrous to the city. The municipality had invested £104,600 sterling and $91,470 colony currency in four different railway schemes, and embarked on major public-works projects, including a waterworks scheme to pump water from Lake Ontario. The public works added £107,550 sterling and $46,789 colony currency to the debt load.[6] In 1861, Hamilton defaulted on its interest payments, and the province 'bailed out' the city. Two years later, the province refused a similar grant, and creditors eventually accepted restructured terms for the debt.

Hamilton's City Fathers had seriously misjudged the effects of economic competition from rival areas at home and abroad. Repeal of the Imperial Corn Laws resulted in freer trade between Britain and non-colonial countries of the world. The European revolutions of 1848 restricted alternative sources of demand for agricultural products. Americans built railways south of Lake Erie to divert traffic flowing to Michigan through the British colony. And the Grand Trunk Railroad, deliberately bypassing Hamilton, consolidated the dominance of Toronto and Montreal as the major import-export centres of the united colonies (now known as Ontario and Quebec) (Careless 1967: 113–25; Weaver 1982: 50–2). The Hamilton area would need major help to exploit the policy potentials of its harbour and watershed and to maintain employment for its lessening population. The exploitation of the decision situations made possible by rules, both in and outside the region, would provide such help in the next fifty years.

The Middle Years

The period from Confederation to the end of the First World War represented the major years of growth and consolidation of Hamilton as an industrial and commercial centre. During this period heavy industry became firmly established in Hamilton, and the harbour became significant as a site for industrial location and as an import-

6 One pound sterling equalled $3.85 colony currency (Miles 1979: xvii).

export docking centre. But these changes would not have occurred without major decision solutions outside the region, especially the national tariff policy and (of course) the First World War. As a result of such changes, the small-town service centre of 27,000 people became an industrial centre of quadrupled size.

Hamilton's industrial base at Confederation was established and linked to the iron industry, with the manufacture of stoves and farm implements as well as the rerolling of imported railway tracks the major elements. The continuing entrepreneurship of city politicians and business élites led to a five-year property-tax holiday for new industries and a five-year tax exemption for new machinery for existing business (Campbell 1966: 137). The policies of the Dominion government after 1878 were also significant in expanding the iron and steel industry. Not only was a large duty set on finished iron imports, but the doubling of the import duty on Scottish pig-iron meant that an expansion of Hamilton's own pig-iron production and rolling mills was feasible. The Dominion further offered a bounty to indigenous iron producers, and the municipality offered free land, cash bonuses, and long-term tax exemption (Roberts 1964). The removal of tariffs on the import of bituminous coal completed the set of favourable operational-rule changes for the development of the iron and steel industries in Hamilton. Iron ore from Lake Superior and coal from Appalachia could reach the harbourfront by relatively cheap water and rail transportation, and be made and finished into the products needed by an expanding agricultural economy, including the emerging Prairie market.

The success of these moves attracted the Hamilton Blast Furnace Company and led the city to grant ten-year tax concessions on any new industries and even greater bonuses for specially favoured companies, like the John Birge Company, the forerunner of the Steel Company of Canada.

More classical kinds of entrepreneurship brought hydro-electric power from DeCew Falls some 35 miles from the city and formed the basis of the electrical-appliance industry centred around Westinghouse. Similarly, the area became a major agricultural canning and meat-packing centre for both export and domestic consumption and a major centre for the manufacture of farm implements. And the availability of cheap electrical power; low-cost raw-material imports, especially cotton; and increasing waves of unskilled immigrants enabled the cotton and clothing industry to exceed the foundry and machine-products industries in terms of capital invested and total employment by the turn of the century (Census of Canada 1901: 184–5).

The early months of the First World War disrupted European demand for agricultural products and the derived demand for farm implements, and deepened the emerging economic recession of the times. By 1915, however, the production of munitions and farm products for war-torn Europe as well as the demand for troops, and military recruitment itself sharply reduced unemployment and contributed to the continuing restructuring of the economy from a small service centre to a large industrial centre that could capitalize on political events and arrangements beyond its boundaries.

Like many comparable Victorian developments, the industrial changes in Hamilton took place adjacent to water and rail transportation systems. Even the newer industries powered by electricity rather than steam concentrated in the same areas in Hamilton because of the availability of cheap uninhabited land. The swampy land and ravines that made residential settlement impractical but were important parts of the harbour's ecosystems were now infilled as sites for new and growing industries.

As pressure for industrial location adjacent to the harbour waters grew, the municipality successfully petitioned the Dominion to operate the navigation and shipping functions of the port. The rule configurations made possible, in other words, the substitution of one set of institutional rules for another. In 1912, the new Hamilton Harbour Commissioners (HHC) was established, with two Dominion and one municipal appointee to its board. The new board embarked on land reclamation as well as expanded wharfage, and these presaged a later period of conflict with the alternative goals of the municipal government. But later years brought fewer structural changes to the region's economy.

Modern Times

The First World War brought to Hamilton not only a booming economy but also rapid population growth as immigrants from abroad and at home sought the increasing numbers of unskilled jobs in the new manufacturing industries. Hamilton's population increased from 82,000 in 1911 to 114,000 in 1921, matching a proportional increase in the previous decade and a comparable increase in the subsequent decade. Outlying communities in the watershed gained little of this population increase. Ancaster, for example, was the same size in 1941 as it had been in 1871, and Dundas had increased only from 3,000 to 5,000 persons in the same seventy-year period (Census of Canada, various years). Table 2 indicates in gross terms how Hamilton dominated the watershed communities at the end of the First World War, continued to do so until 1951, and has played a lesser role since that time as population and employment opportunities have grown proportionately more without rather than within this Victorian city.

The 1920s were times of continued growth and prosperity for Hamilton, once the readjustment of the economy to peacetime conditions were made. Industrial production, especially in the heavy, capital-intensive industries, grew at wartime rates in response to demands from the transportation, agricultural, and construction industries. It would then be cut almost in half by the years of the Great Depression, as the 'new' economy of Hamilton was dependent on the state of the economy in the rest of Canada and abroad. Not until 1939 did the value of production rival that of 1925 at $152 million (Dominion Bureau of Statistics 1925–67). The worst year was 1933; one-quarter of Hamilton's families received relief payments during that spring, despite the fact that the textile mills had quickly recovered and reached 90 per cent of capacity (Weaver 1982: 135).

Once more the 'worst kind' of political decision, another world war, was to revive the regional economy and create growth and development in production and employment. Growth occurred in precisely those sectors that had profited from the First World War. The value of gross production reached $363 million in 1944, and employment levels increased by more than a third.

The economic entrepreneurship of Hamilton's political élites did not diminish during the booming 1920s or the depressed 1930s. The tradition of using rules and rule situations for economic gain and development manifested itself most notably in the activities of the Hamilton Harbour Commissioners. During these years the HHC began an aggressive policy for expansion and development that rested on two complementary strategies. First, the HHC wanted to see a large-scale expansion of the port activities, but at no cost to the shipping industry itself. Second, the HHC wished to use its lands and water lots as convenient sites for industrial development, fully cognizant

TABLE 2
Population in selected watershed communities, 1921–1981

Year	Hamilton	Burlington	Stoney Creek	Dundas	Ancaster
1921	114,151	2,709	n/a	4,978	5,586
1951	208,321	6,107	1,922	6,849	7,648
1981	306,434	114,853	36,762	19,586	14,428

Source: Census of Canada, 1941, 1971, 1981

of previous infilling and the demand for space north of the escarpment (Hamilton Harbour Commissioners n.d.; Cowan 1935; Ministry of Railways and Canals 1935). Both strategies were successful, as the following paragraphs indicate.

Shipping activities in the harbour increased spectacularly during the 1920s and continued to do so during the Depression and war years. One measure of shipping activities is tonnage imported and exported, and these were a trivial 80,000 tons in 1925.[7] By 1931, they exceeded 1.5 million tons, and were over 2 million tons in 1935, 2.5 million tons in 1938, and 3.25 million tons by 1945. The Dominion government contributed generously to this expansion. It completed the fourth Welland Canal, which would enable ships with cargoes of 25,000 tons to pass between Lake Ontario and Lake Erie. It also expanded the capacity of the Beach Canal between the lake and the harbour to accommodate the largest of the lake ships. The city government also subsidized the port activities. Between 1902 and 1927, it gave the HHC $4,000 per annum, but increased this grant to $10,000 per annum in 1927, and to $12,000 per annum in 1932. As a result, the HHC levied no user charges on ships until 1938.

The industrial location strategy was also successful and linked to increased cargo flows in the harbour. The HHC built two more public warehouses in 1924 and 1927, and enjoyed a useful rental income of almost $15,000 in 1938 from land reclaimed and infilled for development. More important, the HHC sold water lots to private interests to undertake the development of private docks. Lots were sold to Canada Steamship Lines (23 acres), Stelco (28 acres), Canadian National Railways (3 acres), Otis Elevators (29 acres), and

7 Tonnage statistics do not, of course, accurately reflect the value of cargo flows. Shipping and navigation within the harbour are the subject of chapter 7.

Hamilton By-Products (8 acres). Stelco would spend $8 million on its bulk-materials dock; Canada Steamship Lines some $2 million on expansion at its terminal; and Hamilton By-Products some $1.5 million on its new dock. The terms of the sales to these economic entrepreneurs were generous. Lots averaged only $50 per acre, except for Stelco, which paid $250 per acre. Once again, the rule configurations proved accessible, and the rule situations proved generous to the Hamilton's economic élites.

Postwar developments in the harbour extended the two pre-war strategies of the Harbour Commissioners. Shipping continued to increase, reaching a peak of 15 million tons in 1979, mainly in the form of iron ore and coal for the steel industry. As early as 1948, Hamilton exceeded Toronto as the major port on Lake Ontario, in terms of ship movements and tonnage imported and exported from the port.

The Dominion government continued to aid harbour developments. It agreed to fund 50 per cent of all harbour developments related to the establishment of the St Lawrence Seaway. Some $5.5 million in developments occurred, as a result, in the three years following the opening of the Seaway in 1956. This was approximately the same value as the capital developments in the harbour in the previous decade. The Dominion also further deepened the ship canal and reconstructed the bridge over the canal. During the 1950s, some $60 million was spent on harbour improvements.

The HHC continued a vigorous 'privatization' of water lots until the mid 1970s. The majority of water lots were sold to Stelco and Dofasco, culminating in a politically contentious 'land swap' of 106 acres of lots fronting the steel companies for 313 acres on the eastern shores that the commissioners wished to develop independently. Some 40 acres of water lots in the northwestern harbour that were alienated in 1959 were ultimately purchased by the city government, who, along with the Hamilton Conservation Authority, became increasingly opposed to the developmental strategies of the HHC.[8]

The wider economy of Hamilton and adjacent communities has changed, if not developed, in postwar years. Now some half of all

8 The conflict over the developmental strategies of the commissioners were only exacerbated by the 'kickback' dredging scheme established by the city appointee to the board of commissioners. The appointee was convicted and jailed in 1975.

manufacturing employment is in the steel and iron industries, and the once-booming textile industry has dwindled to a mere 3 per cent of total manufacturing employment. Hamilton itself has stabilized both its population growth and its level of employment, excepting the recession years of the early 1980s. Events outside the region, including economic change and development, continue to determine the structure and size of the activities within Hamilton harbour's watershed. These events have and continue to have been made possible by the rule configurations within and without Canada. The local political élites have a continuing tradition of attempting to exploit the rule situations for economic gain.

Parallel Artefacts

We have seen that Hamilton harbour is as much an artefact of human decision making as it is a product of physical, biological, and natural change. As a purely natural resource, the harbour and the watershed have been altered by construction, infilling, and wastes disposal, and by use as a source of food, water, and energy. As a centre of population and commerce, the watershed as well as the waters have provided economic opportunities, opportunities for settlement and immigration, and locations for industry and transportation. Neither the harbour nor the watershed bears much resemblance to the lands sparsely occupied by refugee farmers of two hundred years ago, nor indeed much resemblance to the small commercial town with the abundant trout and herring fisheries of 1867. Both the resource and the socio-economic structure have been fashioned and designed by human invention. In this sense, Hamilton Harbour is an artefact of human design.

Artefacts will be designed only if the designers can capture most, if not all, of the benefits of the design. Hamilton has provided ample opportunities for individuals and groups to capture such benefits. They have seized the opportunities of war to build munitions, clothe and feed troops, and supply agricultural machinery to Western farmers who have fed beleaguered populations. To do so they have used the rule configurations of Canadian parliamentary federalism to attract railways, protect and subsidize industries, privatize public water lots, and finance public improvements. It is true that Hamilton possessed locational advantages to which the flows of technological innovations could be directed and enhanced (Weaver 1983: 197–217).

But these, too, have been made possible by the exploitation of the rule situations at some time in Hamilton's history. In other words, the incentives provided by multiple rule configurations have been seized with alacrity by Hamilton's political and economic entrepreneurs.

Hamilton and its surrounding communities are thus 'artefactual' communities designed by man and subject to error and exploitation by human design. The errors to date are manifest mostly in the biological communities of the harbour itself. Plant, fish, and other biological life in the harbour have been severely reduced in numbers and in kind. Natural habitats have been replaced with landfill and concrete. Bottom sediments are covered with mud, silt, and clay that contain alarming proportions of heavy metals and toxic chemicals. Larger resident fish species may have a one-in-four chance of contracting lip cancers.

Errors in design may extend to the socio-economic structure of the community. In designing and responding to wartime economies and protected markets for capital goods, the local economy has increasingly concentrated on the capital-intensive manufacturing sectors of the economy. The opportunities and benefits have not always been weighed and balanced by the longer-run costs and limitations of this practice. The future of a socio-economic structure based on heavy industry remains uncertain, as does the future of the policies physically linked to the harbour waters.

Conclusion: Time, Place, and Events

Hamilton Harbour is the site of our micro-level policy studies. It is a site that is shared by the policy cases of commercial shipping, recreational boating, and water quality/wastes disposal. The kinds of 'sharing' that currently takes place on this body of water does so within the rule configurations currently in use.

However, the opportunities and constraints are also affected by the history of past decision situations. These decision situations have, in turn, taken place within the rule configurations in use during many previous years. There is a cumulative accretion of opportunities, constraints, and burdens for the present generation. These are reflected directly in the nature of the goods or policies we shall examine, and in the nature of the operational, institutional, and constitutional rules-in-use.

All of the above is implied in the findings that the physical and biological properties of the harbour and its watershed are as much an artefact of human design as they are a given of the natural world. We now move into an examination of the three policy cases, aware of these contingencies of time and place and previous events. These situational contexts are important for estimating the precise effects of rules-in-use on policy outcomes and impacts. We begin with our policy case of commercial shipping.

7

Commercial Shipping

Canada's settlement patterns have been and remain intimately linked to transportation. Most early settlements were based on or near accessible and navigable waters (Bellan 1972). Later these settlements were to be linked by rail, and today the urban form is dominated by road transportation networks.

The transshipment of goods by water remains the core of economic activities in many Canadian cities, such as Vancouver, Montreal, Saint John, and Halifax. We saw how Hamilton's growth was based around its harbour and the opportunities it provides for cargo flows and industrial location. Yet few, if any, social scientists bother to explore the public policy of commercial shipping and navigation and its role in understanding how government works in Canada. We explore this public policy at the 'micro-site' of Hamilton for reasons previously explained.

Our policy case explores the relationships between rules-in-use and the nature of the good. We evaluate the rule configurations and their consequences for the operation of the port. More specifically, we discover that:

1 / the constitutional rules-in-use do not fit with a more orthodox 'top-down' view of shipping and navigation as an exclusive function of the Canadian federal government. We discover, instead, that the constitutional rules-in-use include non-domestic constitutional rules and domestic constitutional rules that predate the confederation settlement for parliamentary federalism. The policy case thus 'nests' within multiple constitutional (and other) rules.

2 / The institutional rules are also multiple and configurative in form. They include rules for policy provision, production, and regulation based on the delegated legislative powers of the federal government and the Ontario provincial government, although the balance is predictably asymmetrical – in this case in favour of federal arrangements. The institutional rules also include, however, those formulated in an organization called the Hamilton Harbour Commissioners, which possesses property rights that stem from its own constitutional status that is, legally independent of the Constitution Act. Not only does the policy case 'nest,' it also is 'stacked' within these multiple constitutional- and institutional-rule configurations.

3 / The institutional rules-in-use create an incentive for the implementation of operational rules that make the Port of Hamilton a commercial competitor with other ports and transportation systems in eastern Canada and the eastern United States. These operational rules create incentives for the creation of a 'market niche' for the transshipment of particular kinds of cargoes and for port facilities. The nature of the good thus interacts with and is synchronized with the institutional rules-in-use through the creation of particular operational rules of port management. The 'public economy' or 'provision system' for commercial shipping and navigation is thus wide in geographic scale, and the particular place of the Port of Hamilton within the public economy for shipping is evaluated by using economic and non-economic indicators of performance.

4 / The rule configurations at the constitutional and institutional levels also create an incentive for the port to compete with other organizations over the uses of the foreshores of the harbour. Operational rules have again been created to synchronize port management with the nature of the good, in this case the water-land docking and road and rail transfer facilities. The policy case of shipping and navigation is interdependent in this instance with other public policies, and the rules for regulating the competitive interactions between policies are continually subject to dispute. The consequences are more fully evaluated in our later policy cases (chapters 8 and 9). They include both economic and non-economic impacts on the harbour watershed.

Our analysis proceeds as follows: We first examine the constitutional and institutional rules-in-use for the port. We then note the basic logic of these rule configurations, namely, the incentives for competitive behaviour on the part of the Port of Hamilton with other ports and with other foreshore uses. Third, we examine the nature of the good as exemplified in the operating rules of the port and, in a fourth section, in terms of the cargo flows transshipped through the harbour. We evaluate the operational rules of the policy in a fifth section, and, in the concluding part of the chapter, we return to an analysis of the findings of our policy case for understanding how government in Canada works.

Constitutional and Institutional Rules-in-Use

Commercial shipping for the Port of Hamilton is based on a configuration of constitutional and institutional rules. The basic logic of these rules-in-use is to make operational rules for the port subject to the monopoly jurisdiction of the Hamilton Harbour Commissioners (HHC). Other governmental bodies, property owners on the bay (riparians) and private organizations and citizens who may have an interest in the policy in question have limited legal authority to influence port management. Rules pertaining to other ports do, however, make a difference, as we shall see. We shall examine the structure of domestic constitutional and institutional rules that establish the jurisdiction of the HHC; however, first I offer some comments about the common law of shipping.

Common Law

A primary legal foundation for port management in Canada is the common-law doctrine that the right of free navigation is a public right paramount and superior to all others on navigable waters. Owners of adjacent land have no ownership rights to the water or the water bed, and cannot construct or do anything that would interfere with the primacy of navigation.[1] So-called riparian rights – of landowners adjacent to the banks of a watercourse – are thus strictly

1 *Arsenault* v. *R.* (1917), 16 Ex CR, 271 at 277; *Moore* v. *R.* (1915), 16 Ex CR, 264 at 267. The most frequently cited case is *Wood* v. *Essen* (1884), 9 SCR 239.

limited, whether or not the riparians are private persons or public bodies: 'the right of the Crown to sail in ... public navigable waters is subject to the right of passage, and any grantee of the Crown must take subject to such right ... this public right includes all such rights, as ... are necessary for the convenient passage of vessels along the channel.'[2]

In other words, the starting-point for understanding the legal framework for shipping and navigation is the common-law doctrine of free navigation. This doctrine remains important even when other constitutional laws and statute laws have limited this paramount use of navigable waters; the courts have subjected constitutional sections and statutes to greater judicial scrutiny. The doctrine, sometimes known as the doctrine of navigable servitude, is important in resolving conflicts between shipping and other policies in the harbour. It may even be considered a basic constitutional rule, as it is used to determine some of the paramountcy issues among various heads of legislative powers granted to the two levels of governments in Canadian parliamentary federalism. We shall return to this rule in later chapters.

Constitutional Rules

By virtue of the Third Schedule (operated through section 108) of the Constitution Act, 1867, the Crown in the right of the government of Canada was granted authority to control shipping and navigation in 'public harbours.'

Case law has established that the public harbours designated under section 108 – those watercourses that were operating as 'public harbours'– belong, in both a proprietary (ownership) and a legislative sense, to the federal Crown (government), and that federal ownership extends to the bed and foreshores of the harbour.[3] While there is no clear definition of what actually constitutes a 'public harbour,' there must be at least some physical characteristic distinguishing from a place merely used for purposes of navigation. Since Dominion ownership does not extend beyond that part of the water-

---

2 *Wood* v. *Essen*, 246–7.
3 *Holman* v. *Green*, 1881, 6 SCR 707; *Fader* v. *Smith*, 1885, 18 NSR 433; *A.G. Canada* v. *A.s G. Ontario, Quebec, and Nova Scotia (Reference re Provincial Fisheries)* (1898), AC 700 (PC)

body or watercourse that is actually used for harbouring purposes (anchoring ships and landing goods), the federal government cannot claim proprietary jurisdiction over a waterway adjacent to a harbour that is too narrow or shallow for navigability, or claim to own a section of river bank to bank if only a sheltered cove of the river is used to anchor ships.[4]

In harbours where the federal government can *clearly* claim proprietary jurisdiction, its authority over all aspects of harbour development is absolute. The federal government has the power to control all activity on the watercourse as well as the port that services it (the 'port' in a federal harbour refers to all lands and buildings involved with the operation of shipping, and courts have generally defined these boundaries to include shoreline adjacent to the harbour, although not land uses indirectly connected with a harbour beyond the shoreline, for example, road access).

Under these constitutional rules, the federal government has formulated a number of institutional rules governing port management and commercial shipping for use of harbours in Canada. Some of these, especially the ones directly affecting Hamilton Harbour, are discussed below. However, the constitutional authority of the federal government over Hamilton Harbour is much more limited than that over many rival ports.

Hamilton Harbour's Exceptional Constitutional Status

The authority of the federal Crown over 'public harbours' is limited in the case of Hamilton Harbour because Hamilton Harbour was not, in 1867, a public harbour within the meaning of section 108 and the Third Schedule of the Constitution Act, 1867. In 1846, the statute incorporating the City of Hamilton defined the boundaries of the city to include 'the harbour of said town.'[5] Section 5 of the same act provided that 'all of the Bay to the opposite shore thereof laying in front of the said City shall vest in the City council of the said City.' In other words, the harbour was vested in the Municipality

4 *City of Montreal* v. *Montreal Harbour Commission* (1926), 1 DLR, 840 AC 299
5 Canada, Legislative Assembly of Upper Canada, *Provincial Statutes of Canada, 1846*, c. 73, s. 3, An Act to Alter and Amend the Act Incorporating the Town of Hamilton, and to Erect the Same into a City. Unfortunately, the act has no short title.

of Hamilton at the date of Confederation, rather than in the Province of Ontario. The provisions of section 108 and the Third Schedule vested in Canada 'the public works and property of each province enumerated,' not the property of municipalities. Municipal property is legally the property of the municipal corporation, although municipal corporations are merely political entities created by provincial legislation.[6]

Currently proprietary ownership of the bed of the harbour, of water lots, and of harbour lands (not expressly alienated) is held by the Hamilton Harbour Commissioners, a public corporation established by the federal government in 1912. Ownership is no longer vested in the municipality, nor is it vested with the provincial or the federal government. The HHC acquired proprietary authority in 1948 as a result of an agreement among the City of Hamilton, the Province of Ontario, and the Dominion of Canada, which was designed to end some fifty years of disputes over ownership issues.[7]

The federal Crown can, however, claim legislative, not proprietary, jurisdiction over the use of the waters of Hamilton Harbour through the constitutional authority over shipping and navigation assigned it under the Constitution Act, 1867. This jurisdiction includes legislative control over beacons, buoys, and lighthouses; a specification that shipping lanes connecting a province with any other country are excluded from the jurisdiction of the provinces; and a main authority-creating provision that explicitly assigns legislative power over 'shipping and navigation' to the federal government.[8] Because this power is strictly legislative, the HHC remains owner of navigable waters as well as their water beds.

Theoretically, the Province of Ontario can challenge the use of the waters of Hamilton Harbour, for example, for industrial or do-

---

6 The precedent-setting case for all such harbours in Canada was *R.* v. *Saint John Gas Light Co.* (1895), 4 Ex CR 326, in which it was ruled that the harbour of Saint John, New Brunswick, did not vest in the Dominion by virtue of the British North America Act, 1867 (now the Constitution Act, 1867), c. 3, s. 108.

7 The deed from the city was no. 148343NS, registered 8 November 1948; Provincial Order-in-Council 266/47 was passed 13 February 1947; and the Dominion Order-in-Council PC5427 was passed 26 November 1948.

8 Constitution Act, 1867, sections 91 (9), 92 (10), 91 (12). Case law establishes that no proprietary right accretes to the federal government under these sections. *A.G. Canada* v. *A.G. Ontario,* 1898, AC 700; *Re Water and Water Powers,* 1929, SCR 200; *R.* v. *Moss,* 1896, 26 SCR 322

mestic consumption. In practice, this form of control is highly cir-
cumscribed, because the courts, using the doctrine of navigable
servitude, have declared the paramountcy of navigation over other
harbour uses.[9]

The federal government thus retains considerable authority over
Hamilton Harbour because of its constitutional powers over navigation rather than its constitutional powers over public harbours.
Unlike the case in most public harbours, it cannot claim exclusive
jurisdiction over waterfront lands not expressly used for shipping
and navigation; it shares concurrent jurisdiction with the province
over such lands. The Province of Ontario has granted authority to
the City of Hamilton to exercise these concurrent proprietary rights,[10]
although these rights do not extend in the matter of business assessment of the Harbour Commissioners for taxation purposes.[11]

Institutional Rules for Provision and Regulation

The federal government, through powers that flow from the appropriate sections of the Constitution Act, 1867, is thus able to legislate
for the provision and regulation of shipping and navigation throughout the country. Under these powers, the federal government has
recognized or established four kinds of ports authority to manage
some seven hundred harbours.

First, in small harbours that serve mainly pleasure craft and smaller
fishing fleets, the federal government recognizes 'public harbours'
in which wharves, ramps, jetties, and breakwaters are administered
by a federally appointed harbour-master, who may or may not collect
berthage duties for operating and maintenance costs.

Second, the federal government permits the operation of so-called
'private' ports, in which the commercial shipper operates the port
normally as an adjunct economic activity of the extraction of a natural resource (such as copper from a mine). There are twenty-two
such private ports within Ontario alone. Management over these

9 *Ireson* v. *Holt Timber Co.* (1913), 30 OLR 209; *Elec. Development Co. of Ontario* v. *A.G. Ontario* (1917), 38 OLR 383 [reversed (1919) AC 687 (PC)]
10 *Hamilton Harbour Commissioners* v. *City of Hamilton et al* (1978), 91 DLR
   (3d), 353 at 376, 1 MPLR 133; 21 OR (2d), 459 (CA), 6 MPLR 183
11 *City of Hamilton* v. *Hamilton Harbour Commissioners and the Regional Assessment Commissioner for the Regional Municipality of Hamilton-Wentworth* (1984), not reported

first two kinds of ports is largely accomplished through regulations of the Department of Transport under the Canada Shipping Act, 1970; the Government Wharves and Piers Act, 1964; the Fishing and Recreational Harbours Act, 1964; and the Canada Ports Act, 1982.

More important in terms of the movement of goods are the third and fourth types of ports in Canada. Some fifteen ports are managed by local port corporations under the authority of the Canada Ports Corporation, which was established as a 'super' Crown corporation in 1982. These ports were known as the National Harbour Board ports prior to the 1982 passage of the Canada Ports Act. The changes were introduced in 1982 with the ostensible purpose of allowing ports to develop some independence in financial and other management operations; the National Habour Board ports operated under a centralized structure established in 1936 after the bankruptcy of a number of ports. More than 50 per cent of Canada's water-borne tonnage is handled through these fifteen ports, and more than 90 per cent of container traffic flows through the four ports of Montreal, Halifax, Saint John, and Vancouver.[12]

The final type of port in Canada is the so-called harbour-commission port. Some nine ports have their own enabling statutes that grant broad discretionary authority in management to these local public corporations. The Canada Ports Act, 1982, and the Harbour Commissions Act, 1964, impose some of the financial, borrowing, and reporting practices on the harbour commissions, although Hamilton and Toronto harbours were expressly excluded from the provisions of the 1982 act. Hamilton is thus one of the more decentralized ports in Canada that operates under its own act and is subject to relatively little federal government regulatory authority, made possible by the legislative (as opposed to ownership) rights of the federal government.

The key statute for understanding port operations in Hamilton is the Hamilton Harbour Commissioners Act, 1912. The Hamilton Harbour Commissioners is a public corporation with powers to 'hold,

12 The Canada Ports Corporation, the Minister of Transport, and the Treasury Board still retain considerable legal authority over local port-corporation operations, and it remains moot whether local ports can become fully responsive to customers under such a structure. For example, capital expenditures in excess of $10 million still require Treasury Board approval, but prior to 1983 National Harbour Board ports required approvals for expenditures over $50,000 (see Goss 1983: 3–87; Ruppenthal 1983: 122–69).

take, develop and administer on behalf of the City of Hamilton in the harbour as defined by this Act ... all property which may be placed under the jurisdiction of the Corporation.'[13] The limits of the harbour as defined by the act include all the waters of Burlington Bay, together with all the inlets (except for the Burlington Ship Channel, which was to remain the express dominion of the federal Department of Transport) and all waterfront property, water-lots, piers, docks, shores, and beaches in and along the bay. The only exception is the body of water known as Cootes Paradise, which is legally owned by the Royal Botanical Gardens, a provincial Crown corporation.[14]

Like most public corporations, the Hamilton Harbour Commissioners enjoys considerable autonomy from the federal government. The federal Crown appoints two commissioners; the City of Hamilton appoints a third. Beyond this, the HHC has authority to appoint and fix remuneration of its own personnel; borrow and spend; and acquire, own, sell and lease land. The HHC is, within the limits of its act, 'master of its own house.'[15] It is an archetypal example of bureaucratic discretionary rules made possible by delegated provision rules of the federal government.

The power conferred by the act on the HHC includes absolute jurisdiction on lands owned by the HHC to be developed for shipping and navigation or harbour purposes.[16] With respect to privately owned lands, and properties controlled by the City of Hamilton, or by other municipalities, or by the Province of Ontario, the act confers authority on the HHC to enact by-laws controlling the use of such lands to the extent that the use of those lands might interfere with the navigation and shipping activities of the harbour,[17] but the HHC may not exercise its authority in such a way as to affect the

13 Hamilton Harbour Commissioners Act, SC 1912, c.98 [amend. SC 1951, c. 17, SC 1957–8, c. 16] s. 14(1); the act was consolidated in the *Revised Statutes of Canada,* 1970.
14 The Royal Botanical Gardens received proprietary rights (full property rights) to Cootes Paradise, delegated by the Province of Ontario through its 1941 act.
15 Mr.Justice Griffiths, in decision of *Hamilton Harbour Commissioners* v. *City of Hamilton et al,* at 360
16 Hamilton Harbour Commissioners Act, s. 14. The corporation also has ownership of the bed of the harbour, as previously noted.
17 Ibid., ss. 15(1) and (2); the regulatory instruments for this authority are Hamilton Harbour Commissioners by-laws 81 and 88.

proprietary rights of public or private landowners.[18] The practice observed generally where any harbour construction, dredging, or other operation is to be carried out on either a private or a public basis is for the party or government involved to apply to the HHC for a permit authorizing the necessary operation.

In terms of the regulation of shipping in the bay, the HHC is permitted to pass its own by-laws, provided they do not conflict with two major pieces of federal legislation: the Canada Shipping Act and the Navigable Waters Protection Act.

Under the Canada Shipping Act, Transport Canada, or its commissions, oversee the registration of all ships (except certain classes of small or open boats); certification of all maritime personnel; the appointment, powers, and duties of shipping-masters; the frequency and extent of shipping inspections; the administration of pilotage authorities; and the pollution of water by commercial ships.[19] Thus, all ships entering Hamilton Harbour are, from the time they enter the Burlington Ship Canal through to when they exit the harbour, under the exclusive regulatory control of HHC authorities, who supervise every aspect of the ships' stay in the harbour. Conversely, shipping vessels are not required to respect any legal prohibitions or restrictions outside those existing as regulations under the Commissioners Act or the Canada Shipping Act. As a result, municipal by-laws and provincial statutes are of no effect with ships that fall under the guidelines of the act, since such ships are *ultra vires* the jurisdiction of any level of government other than the Federal level.[20]

A more important statute in the context of Hamilton Harbour is the Navigable Waters Protection Act, a federal statute that was passed in 1886 with the intent of preventing interference with navigation. Under the act, a person cannot construct a work in navigable waters without the approval of Transport Canada (in practice, the agency is the Coast Guard) or a representative commission, such as the Harbour Commissioners.[21] 'Work' is defined as including any bridge, boom, dam, wharf, dock, pier, tunnel, landfill, or excavation of materials from the bed of navigable waters that may interfere with navigation.[22] This approval must be obtained even if the work is

18 Ibid., s. 12
19 Canada Shipping Act, RSC 1970, c. S-9
20 *R.* v. *Canada Steamship Lines* (1960), 127 CCC (Ont.), 2:05
21 Navigable Waters Protection Act, RC 1970, c. N-19, s. 5(1)
22 Ibid, s. 3

constructed by a riparian or the owner of a private water lot, and even if it is far away from existing or potential shipping lanes. If any work is built without such approval, or not maintained as required, the work may be declared by the minister to be a public nuisance, and he or she may order it to be removed or destroyed, even if it has very great public benefit and is an obstruction in the slightest degree.[23] While any interference with the public right of navigation can also be declared a nuisance by a court of law (which can then order it abated), it can do so notwithstanding any approval of the Minister of Transport under section 5 of the act.[24] Thus, if a party that obstructs navigation does so under the statutory authority of the minister, he or she is immune from any and all court actions that might be launched by other affected parties.

Thus the institutional rules for shipping and navigation in Hamilton Harbour grant the Harbour Commissioners a virtual monopoly in devising, monitoring, and enforcing the operational rules for port management. The HHC does not simply possess the relative independence of all public corporations; it possesses independent property rights over the bed of the harbour, water lots, and all lands that are related to shipping and navigation. The Canada Shipping Act and the Navigable Waters Protection Act are the only major legal constraints on the port-management function of the HHC. And the port-management function – the field of shipping and navigation – is granted legal paramountcy over all other uses of the harbour under the common-law principle of 'navigable servitude.'[25]

The Basic Logic of the Constitutional- and Institutional-Rule Configurations

While the law grants the Hamilton Harbour Commissioners a virtual monopoly of powers with regard to shipping and navigation in the harbour, the HHC is paradoxically subject to intense rivalry and com-

---

23 Ibid., s. 6(1); *Stephens and Mathias* v. *Macmillan* (1954), OR 133. High wires strung over navigable water that did not directly impede navigation were nevertheless held to be a public nuisance under the terms of the act.
24 *A.G. Canada* v. *A.s G. Ontario, Quebec, and Nova Scotia*. The Judicial Committee of the Privy Council also held that the act gives the governor-in-council the statutory authority to permit erection of what would otherwise be a common-law nuisance in navigable waters.
25 *Hamilton Harbour Commissioners* v. *City of Hamilton et al*, 378; *R.* v. *Hamilton Harbour Commissioners* 1977, 7 CELN, Ont., 130

petition in two respects. First, the port is a rival to all other ports in the Great Lakes (and to those ports with access to marine traffic) for water-borne traffic and commerce. Second, the port is a rival to some other uses of Hamilton Harbour itself, in so far as these other uses require foreshore land that may or may not be related to shipping and navigation in the foreseeable future. Each of these rivalries is discussed in turn.

The Competition between Ports

Hamilton Harbour competes with other ports on the Great Lakes and on the eastern seaboards of Canada and the United States for the transshipment of goods. Indeed, it competes with other transportation modes (railways, road trucking, and air freight) and relies on them for transferring cargoes from their origins to their destinations. In this environment, ports seek out a 'market niche' that may give them a comparative advantage over potential competitors. Hamilton, as we shall see, is no different from other ports in this regard.

The market area that Hamilton Harbour serves is bounded, in part, by the drainage area of the Great Lakes (see map 5). This area is served by four larger transportation systems other than provided by lakes ports (Peat Marwick and Partners et al., 1894, 3:1), namely: the Mississippi river system; the U.S. Midwest–Atlantic rail system with important intermodal transfers at the ports of Baltimore and New York; the Canadian rail system with key intermodal transfers at Thunder Bay, Montreal, Saint John, and Halifax; and the Trans-Canada and U.S. Interstate highway systems.

Only 19 per cent of the inland water traffic in this area involves a Canadian port on the Great Lakes–St Lawrence Seaway system.[26]

Hamilton Harbour has benefited from man-made improvements on the Great Lakes. The U.S. federal government built and maintains four locks and a ship canal on the St Mary's River. The Canadian federal government built and maintains the Welland Canal with eight locks, the last major improvements occurring in 1932 and 1959. Both governments built and maintain the St Lawrence Seaway between Montreal and Lake Ontario, a system consisting of seven locks and a dredged depth of 35 feet. These developments made possible the

26 The percentage is for tonnes for 1982.

Map 5
Great Lakes–St Lawrence waterway and ports

Source: Ruppenthal (1983: 136)

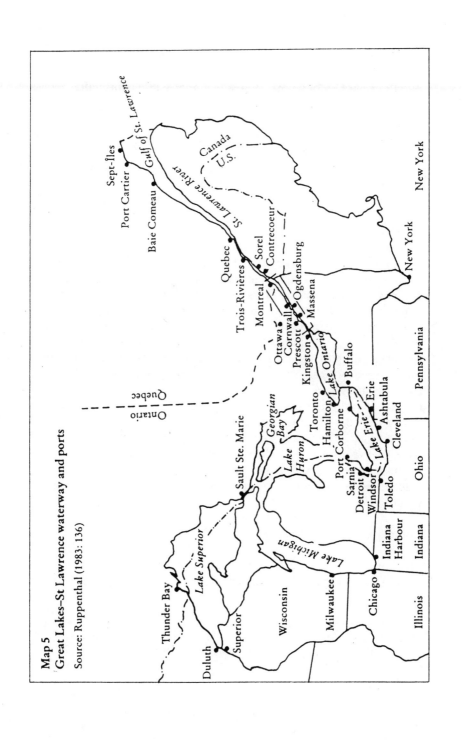

movement of bulk materials such as iron ore and coal throughout the Great Lakes without offloading at ports in the upper lakes, at Buffalo, or at Quebec ports. It also made possible continental access for smaller seagoing vessels (those with a draught of 35 feet or less) carrying general cargo (break bulk and containers). Hamilton benefited more than most Ontario ports from these developments, as almost all of its cargoes use either the Welland or the St Lawrence itself. It can also accommodate the larger vessels of up to 730 feet in length, and the more efficient ships, such as the self-unloading bulk carriers, that have largely replaced the smaller and older 'lakers' (Peat Marwick and Partners et al., 1884, 4:4; Ruppenthal 1983: 170–9).

However, the advantages Hamilton Harbour has gained from improvements in the Great Lakes have magnified its existing specializations in the market rather than made possible newer forms of competition with other ports. The improvements were of importance in emphasizing Hamilton's comparative advantage in the import of bulk commodities for the steel companies located on the foreshores of the harbour. The locational advantages of Thunder Bay for the loading of Western grain, and federal government subsidies for rail transportation of grain from southern Ontario to Montreal, have meant that the largest bulk-commodity flows on the Great Lakes by-pass Hamilton. Similarly, the locational advantages of Montreal have allowed it to capture much of the regular container-ship movements to eastern Canada and for it to challenge rival ports such as New York–New Jersey.[27] Hamilton Harbour thus tends to specialize in those types of cargo flows in which it has a comparative advantage, albeit within a network of rival ports and rival transportation modes.

Competition over Foreshores

The courts, as previously indicated, have given the Harbour Commissioners priority in the management of shipping and navigation

---

27 The container feeder system is dominated by the rail and road transportation modes rather than by water transportation. Toronto Harbour has suffered from road-rail competition and transshipment through Montreal, Halifax, Saint John, New York, and Baltimore, and has been more unsuccessful than Hamilton in establishing a market 'niche.' See Peat Marwick and Partners 1984, vol. 4.

over alternative uses of the bay. In terms of the impact of shipping and navigation on other uses on the waters themselves, the consequences are few. Larger ships create some extra turbidity in the waters, but the regulation of spills of fuel and bulk goods can be easily monitored and enforced (see chapter 9). Similarly, shipping and navigation have few consequences for recreation on the waters, subject to clearly defined and policed shipping lanes, which again are easily monitored and enforced.

Shipping and navigation are, however, rivals to other uses when it comes to foreshore lands. Shipping and navigation require dredged channels and berths, storage space, intermodal transfer space, and access to such space by road and rail. The extent of lands required for such purposes will be subject to different interpretations and, ultimately, to negotiations by other user interests that have proprietary and legislative controls over some foreshore aspects.

Currently, more than one-third of the shoreline is allocated to commercial shipping and allied activities – wharves, warehouses, terminals. More than one-half of the waterfront is committed to industrial sites; as we saw in chapter 6, the Harbour Commissioners pursued, between 1926 and 1982 especially, a systematic policy of infilling water lots in the harbour and retailing these lots as industrial sites. Furthermore, the harbour waters have diminished by more than 20 per cent since 1850.

The major rival to the Hamilton Harbour Commissioners over the allocation of the foreshore land to use for shipping and navigation is the City of Hamilton. The powers of the City to regulate foreshores stem from the Provincial Planning Act (so, 1983, c. 1) and the Provincial Municipal Act (rso, 1983, c. 302). Under section 34 of the Planning Act, the City is authorized to prohibit or regulate the use of all lands and improvements in the municipality, subject to the approval of the Ontario Municipal Board (a provincial tribunal). This act does not require the City to establish recreational foreshore uses, although, according to a general common-law principle, municipalities have a duty to advance the common interests of its residents (and these common interests could be recreational).[28] The

28 *Re Howard and Toronto* (1928), 61 OLR 563; *Leitch* v. *Strathroy* (1923), 53 OLR 655 at 669; *Re Foxcroft and London* (1928), 61 OLR 553 at 556; *Eastview* v. *Episcopal Corp. of Ottawa* (1918), 44 OLR, 284 at 297; *Re Labute and Tilbury North* (1918), 44 OLR, 522 at 528 (CA); *Upper Canada College* v. *Toronto*

Municipal Act also provides that the City and Regional Municipality of Hamilton-Wentworth can, at their discretion, acquire land for and establish public parks.[29]

The City of Hamilton has used the powers vested in it by the Planning Act to create By-law 6593, which was passed on 25 July 1950 and revised on several occasions since. This general zoning by-law, according to its preamble, is intended to 'Prohibit Certain Uses of Land, Building and Structures and to Regulate the Height, Bulk, Location, Spacing, Character and Use of Buildings and Structures in the City of Hamilton.' The territorial application of By-law 6593 is defined in section 3(1) as follows: 'Saves as in this section otherwise provided, the provisions of this By-law shall apply throughout the various districts of the City of Hamilton as shown in the various maps appended to and forming part of this by-law, and to the adjoining shores of Hamilton Harbour, Cootes Paradise and Lake Ontario, including land covered by water wherever there is or may be erected any jetty, boathouse, pier or other building or structure.' Thus the by-law is intended to include all parts of Hamilton Harbour, including those areas under the jurisdiction of the Hamilton Harbour Commissioners, although it does specifically exempt public parkland managed and controlled by another government body from the operation of the by-law. This exemption is intended to exclude the lands of the Hamilton Regional Conservation Authority from the terms of the by-law.

The City of Hamilton thus asserts its rivalry to the Harbour Commissioners in its own by-laws. The courts have found such by-laws legal, provided they do not conflict with the by-laws of the Harbour Commissioners, in which case the latter has paramountcy since shipping and navigation are the paramount uses of the harbour.[30]

The judicial decisions are of little practical import in determining solutions when the rule configurations for different policies conflict. Because the HHC operates on a not-for-profit basis, an incentive is created to pre-empt larger blocs of foreshore land for port pur-

---

(1910), 22 OLR 178 at 179 (CA); *Re Hassard and Hamilton* (1907), 9 OWR, 731 at 733

29 *Municipal Act* (RSO 1982), s. 208, paras. 51–3, and *Regional Act* (RSO, 1980), c. 437, s. 155

30 *Hamilton Harbour Commissioners* v. *City of Hamilton et al*, 378

poses. Put another way, the courts have sanctioned an overuse of the foreshores for shipping and navigation because any surplus revenues (over expenditures) by the HHC do not accrue to non-shipping activities: 'In this context, "profits" does not mean excess of revenue on expenditure sumplicate ... What are excess profits in any particular year I leave for determination in those proceedings or preferably to the common sense of the parties themselves. My decision is confined to the principle that the commissioners do not have their preponderant purpose the making of a profit on their undertaking.'[31]

In sum, while it may appear that the Hamilton Harbour Commissioners is operating from a monopoly perspective in its ports management, it is, in fact, subject to rivalry from other ports and transportation modes as well as to rivalry in its occupation and use of foreshore lands. Some further implications of these rivalries will become apparent when we look at the operating characteristics of the Port of Hamilton.

Operating Rules

Operating Rules in General

The Hamilton Harbour Commissioners operates as both a landlord and a management organization. On the foreshores that it owns in Hamilton Harbour, it both leases parts of this property and directly manages other parts. In other portions of the bay, it regulates traffic and charges levies for traffic destined for privately owned wharfage. Key designations in this latter respect are the docks owned by the two steel companies, Stelco Inc. and Dofasco Inc., and what used to be the private dock owned by J.I. Case Inc., the agricultural implement company previously known as International Harvester. This last dock was purchased by the HHC in 1988.

The port may thus be described as a 'mixture' of differing organizational forms, all of which are made possible under the broad terms of reference of the Enabling Act. Section 14(2) of the Hamilton Harbour Commissioners Act, 1912, states that the HHC: 'may acquire, expropriate, hold, lease and otherwise dispose of such real estate, building or other property as it deems necessary or desirable for

31 Ibid, 48

the development, improvement, maintenance and protection of the Harbour.' Critical to an understanding of port operations in Hamilton are the revenue and budgetary policies of the HHC. Under the terms of the federal Harbour Commissions Act, 1964, commission ports (but not Hamilton) are required to be self-financing, to be autonomous in setting rates and charges, to adopt a common accounting system (based on historical accrued values), and to operate on a not-for-profit basis. The HHC is also self-financing and autonomous in setting rates and charges, adopts the same accounting systems as commission ports, and operates on a not-for-profit basis. The accounting systems are adopted by the HHC because the federal government requests such systems for general reporting purposes; they are 'guidelines' rather than rules. Surplus revenues received by the Hamilton Harbour Commissioners, defined as revenues in excess of costs, are to be paid to the City of Hamilton rather than to the Receiver General of Canada. The Toronto and North Fraser harbour commissions share this last requirement of the payment of any surplus revenues to their adjacent municipalities.[32]

The financial policies of the Harbour Commissioners create an economic incentive to 'overexpand' port operations in the harbour. They create an incentive to balance the *total* costs of operations with the *total* benefits of those operations, rather than to balance the *marginal* costs of operations with the *marginal* benefits of revenues derived from operations. Given that the marginal revenues from larger-scale operations will be less than the marginal costs of these operations, the HHC would be more efficient by restricting the scope of port operations to more limited levels.[33] However, the surplus revenues (profits) generated under such a system would only be lost to the Port of Hamilton.

In addition, port operations typically display large economies of scale that could supplement or replace the previous incentive for expansionary activities.[34] Viable ports require large-scale investments in docks, terminals, and, especially, allied road and rail infrastructive developments. These are largely of a fixed-costs nature

32 Harbour Commissioners Act (RSC 1970), c. H-1. See also Ministry of State for Urban Affairs (1978: 45–6).
33 The port provides an illuminating example of the so-called Niskanen hypothesis about government service levels (Niskanen 1971).
34 Marginal cost pricing will normally result in financial deficits where there are economies of scale.

and thus less sensitive to the volumes of port imports and exports. The greater the volume of traffic, the more that these fixed costs can be spread out over more port users. In short, the larger the port, the lower the costs. This economic incentive has the same expansionary impetus as does the not-for-profit incentive.

These incentives for port expansion require opportunities for capital investment and financing. In historical terms, rather than in terms of current port policy, the HHC has pursued the lowest-cost options of responding to the incentives. It has filled in the water lots that it owns on the edge of the harbour's waters and has either resold these lots or entered into long-term lease arrangements with shippers and other industrial users.

Today, with more than two-thirds of the shoreline committed to land uses that depend on shipping and navigation and auxiliary rail transportation, and with some water lots and piers without tenants, the HHC relies on leasing arrangements as its major strategy for maintaining the scale of port operations.[35] This strategy is consistent with the economic advice of the World Bank's study *Port Pricing and Investment* (Bennathan and Walters 1979: 179–83).

Two conclusions may be reached from these broad economic considerations. First, the Hamilton Harbour Commissioners operates within a structure of institutional incentives that lead to an overexpansion of shipping and navigation uses for Burlington Bay.[36] Second, the negative impacts of this overexpansion are evident in the water quality and recreational uses of the foreshores and waters of the harbour, as larger blocks of wharfage areas have been constructed from marshlands, creeks, and points of access on the bay (see chapter 9).

Within the broad institutional-rule configurations, including those resulting in the market conditions for vessel-traffic flows on the Great Lakes, the HHC adopts revenue and pricing policies that maintain the financial viability of the port. Unlike the Toronto Harbour Commission, the Hamilton Harbour Commissioners has not required

35 Principally, the water lots known as piers 1, 2, and 3, and the so-called East Port Development, piers 25, 26, and 27. Approximately thirty tenants occupy the leased property of the HHC.

36 The federal government has historically provided grants for capital expansion of the harbour; they are provided on a 'case by case' basis for harbours throughout the country.

a municipal subsidy of its operations since 1938 (when user charges on vessels were first adopted).

Revenue and Pricing Policies

The financial processes for the Hamilton Harbour Commissioners consist of, first, estimating the total costs of port operations; then, setting charges to cover these costs; and, finally, adding extra charges to generate revenues 'for future harbour improvements.'

Table 3 summarizes the effects of these processes in generating revenues that exceed operating expenditures. Over a twenty-year period, the HHC has been able to set aside excess revenues in all but four years, and has enjoyed excess revenues as high as 34 per cent (1980 and 1982) when the steel industry was working at major-capacity levels. It is noteworthy that the budget process has, since 1979, generated revenues well in excess of operating expenditures. The only exception is 1983, when the HHC would have sustained a loss of almost 12 per cent without the sale of land to the Government of Ontario for the Skyway Bridge Expansion, the twinning of a four-lane bridge over the sand bar that divides the harbour from Lake Ontario.

Table 3 also indicates the large fixed costs of harbour operations. Operating expenditures have also altered significantly since 1977. What has changed in this period of time is the revenue, particularly that revenue derived from cargoes and shipping fees. Table 4 shows the excess revenues as a proportion of total revenues for the HHC. As the table indicates, revenue during the period varied from a high of more than $8.5 million (1982) to a low of $3.75 million (1977, after the sale of land to Halton Region is deducted).

Income for the Harbour Commissioners from two sources appear highly elastic. First, the 'terminal income,' or charges assessed against cargoes, is sensitive to the demands of shippers and tenants, and, second, charges assessed against ships for the use of the harbour (which also vary by type and weight of cargo) are similarly sensitive.[37] For instance, in the recession year 1983, terminal income fell to $900,199 from $4,485,495 the previous year and harbour user fees

37 Terminal income and harbour-use income are based on either the weight or the volume of different classes of cargo shifted through the port. While the rates are published annually, negotiations on asking prices frequently occur.

TABLE 3

Hamilton Harbour Commissioners: Excess of revenues over expenditures as a
percentage of operating expenditures

Year	Excess of revenue over expenditures	Operating expenditures	Percentage
1965	54,061	1,697,347	3.19
1966	69,762	2,014,717	3.46
1967	90,948	1,992,736	4.56
1968	188,866	2,340,371	8.07
1969	100,517	2,356,750	4.27
1970	253,259	2,325,593	10.90
1971	245,283	2,528,786	9.70
1972	-193,559	3,370,001	-5.74
1973	-176,129	3,151,090	-5.59
1974	-79,703	3,244,405	-2.46
1975	9,404	3,487,484	0.27
1976	N/A	N/A	N/A
1977	-46,061[a]	3,956,425	-1.16
1978	126,086	4,093,026	3.10
1979	783,578	5,050,437	15.52
1980	1,866,430	5,499,553	33.94
1981	982,281	5,497,794	17.87
1982	1,737,009	5,162,066	33.65
1983	4,501,274[b]	3,834,521	117.39
1984	729,972	3,772,216	19.35
1985	999,372	4,234,694	23.59
1986	1,885,019	2,641,154	71.37
1987	2,023,636	2,905,562	69.65
1988	4,092,720	3,836,208	106.69
1989	4,121,727	3,653,471	112.82
1990	2,587,075	3,914,934	66.08

Notes:
[a] Indicates sale of land to Halton Region for the Burlington Sewage Treatment
Plant
[b] Indicates $4.9 million sale of land to Ontario for the Skyway Bridge 'twinning'
Sources: Hamilton Harbour Commissioners, annual reports, 1965–90

to $845,995 from $1,041,296. In contrast, rental income from tenants
on HHC land grew from $1,430,392 in 1982 to $1,655,250 in 1983.
Rental income has been increasingly important since 1977. The fourth
major source of income – dockyard income, primarily for marina-
slip and facility rentals, may also provide an expanding source of
revenue for the port (see chapter 8).

Capital financing of port operations comes from several sources.

TABLE 4
Hamilton Harbour Commissioners: Excess revenue as a percentage of total revenues

Year	Total revenues	Excess revenues	Percentage
1977	3,910,364	−46,061	1.18
1978	4,219,112	126,086	2.99
1979	5,050,437	783,578	14.62
1980	7,365,983	1,866,430	25.34
1981	5,497,794	982,281	17.87
1982	8,604,542	1,737,609	20.19
1983	5,000,195	4,501,274	90.02
1984	6,264,078	729,972	11.65
1985	6,925,370	999,372	14.43
1986	7,412,281	1,885,019	25.43
1987	7,949,433	2,023,636	25.46
1988	11,250,553	4,092,720	36.38
1989	11,432,326	4,121,727	36.05
1990	10,002,730	2,587,075	25.86

Source: Hamilton Harbour Commissioners, annual reports 1977–90

'Excess revenues' (as defined above) are earmarked for capital development and are supplemented, where possible, by grants from governments. The East Port Development project of the Hamilton Harbour Commissioners is a current attempt to develop industrial sites on water lots reclaimed by the deposition of dredge spoils made necessary by annual dredging of shipping lanes. These industrial sites require, in turn, intermodal transfers by water, rail, and road, and hence long-term capital financing. In sum, capital developments are largely self-financed, except in so far as land sales and/or grants from government may supplement the available funds. The HHC does not possess any independent taxing authority on tenants; it simply transfers realty taxes imposed by the City of Hamilton from tenants to the city.

The capital value of the assets held by the HHC may give an additional picture of the finances of the port. The HHC assesses its fixed assets at acquisition cost, and depreciates these assets on a straight-line basis at the following rates: docks and improvements at 2, 5, 10 and 20 per cent; buildings at 2, 5, 10, and 20 per cent; and vessels and equipment at 10, 15, and 20 per cent.

The depreciation formulas are consistent with federal government

TABLE 5

Hamilton Harbour Commissioners: Capital growth (selected years)

Capital as of 31 Dec.	Capital as of 31 Dec.	Percentage annual growth
1964: $16,225,479	1965: $16,504,421	1.72
1969: 17,823,641	1970: 18,078,321	0.43
1974: 17,017,745	1975: 17,027,149	0.06
1979: 17,129,146	1980: 17,495,576	2.14
1980: 17,495,576	1981: 19,559,267	11.80
1981: 19,559,267	1982: 21,181,463	8.29
1982: 21,181,463	1983: 23,372,305	10.34
1983: 23,372,305	1984: 26,157,868	11.92
1984: 26,157,868	1985: 27,130,663	3.72
1985: 27,130,663	1986: 30,200,915	11.32
1986: 30,200,915	1987: 34,999,351	15.89
1987: 34,999,351	1988: 36,110,307	3.17
1988: 36,110,307	1989: 38,538,998	6.73
1989: 38,538,998	1990: 49,626,073	28.77

Source: Hamilton Harbour Commissioners, annual reports, 1965–90

accounting practices, and the commissioners' adopting of these practices is discretionary.[38]

Table 5 indicates that the port has enjoyed modest increases in the value of its capital assets over the last twenty years. The only years in which the growth in the value of assets has exceeded 10 per cent have been 1981, 1985, 1986, and 1989; in 1983 and 1984 were years of extraordinary land sales and government grants, respectively. In general, the modest accumulation of capital assets reflects the operational-policy rules of the HHC to follow federal government accounting procedures that, in turn, are designed to impose a not-for-profit regime on port operations in the country.[39]

Operating Rules for Cargo Flows

Hamilton Harbour receives ships some six hundred times per annum (see table 6). Vessel arrivals give an indication of port activity, but

38 Changes were imposed in each year from 1964 through 1968, with the general impact of adding extra charges to capital accounts.
39 Since 1966, dredging conducted by Public Works Canada is considered as both an expenditure and an income, irrespective of impact on capital assets of the ports.

TABLE 6
Hamilton Harbour: Vessel arrivals, 1976–90

Year	Arrivals	Year	Arrivals
1976	876	1984	682
1977	800	1985	564
1978	847	1986	626
1979	959	1987	820
1980	895	1988	878
1981	741	1989	772
1982	564	1990	776
1983	565		

Note: The same vessel may arrive a number of times in any one shipping season.
Source: Hamilton Harbour Commissioners, annual reports, 1976–90

as Great Lake ports are experiencing a secular rise in the size (gross registered tonnage) of ships (Ruppenthal 1983: 170–9), the number of arrivals in any year is not a good indicator of the tonnage, volume, or value of imports and exports.

Cargoes handled by ports are typically classified into dry bulk goods, liquid bulk goods, and general cargoes (or break bulk goods). An example of dry bulk goods is potassium chloride (muriate of potash), which, as a fertilizer, began to be exported through the Port of Hamilton in 1979. The major liquid bulk good 'handled' by the port is fuel oil. 'General cargoes' is a general category of goods imported and exported that do not fall into the bulk-goods categories. They are often transported by containers that may or may not be broken up on harbour waterfronts into smaller units for transshipment by road or rail. Typical general cargoes handled by the Port of Hamilton are machinery and other capital goods, which are exported rather than imported through the HHC's own facilities.

Cargo flows for the Port of Hamilton are dominated by two major factors. First, the port is primarily for the import rather than the export of goods. Second, the tonnage moved to (rather than from) the port is dominated by the demands of two private docks owned by the steel companies, Dofasco Ltd and Stelco Inc. Table 7 summarizes both of these dominant characteristics over a twenty-seven year cycle. Rarely do port exports exceed 7 per cent of total port tonnage. Imports of steel inputs are rarely less than 80 per cent of total port tonnage. Figures 6 and 7 present these characteristics graphically.

TABLE 7
Total port tonnage: Exports and imports of natural resources for the steel
companies 1963–90[a]

Year	Total tonnage	Total port exports	% of total	Steel inputs tonnage	% of total steel inputs
1963	8,935,303	528,718	5.9	7,390,377	82.7
1964	9,392,558	699,470	7.4	7,365,865	78.4
1965	10,293,615	712,715	6.9	8,167,725	79.3
1966	10,718,678	695,209	6.5	8,692,714	1.1
1967	10,593,080	604,732	5.7	8,794,156	83.0
1968	11,998,424	746,903	6.2	10,133,702	84.4
1969	11,119,409	789,722	7.1	9,129,428	82.1
1970	12,881,123	798,33	6.2	10,624,935	82.5
1971	11,985,793	617,434	5.1	9,942,510	83.0
1972	12,680,908	569,811	4.5	10,754,217	84.8
1973	13,097,147	458,997	3.5	11,385,919	86.4
1974	11,869,371	437,533	3.7	10,184,199	85.8
1975	14,270,367	561,215	3.9	12,677,692	88.8
1976	13,325,524	667,236	5.0	11,784,180	88.4
1977	13,233,665	490,625	3.7	11,740,685	88.1
1978	13,854,276[b]	unavailable[c]		11,600,346[b]	88.9
1979	13,127,192[b]	unavailable[c]		unavailable[c]	unavailable[c]
1980	14,197,741	1,138,142	8.0	12,292,835	86.5
1981	10,333,876	454,820	4.4	9,023,748	86.4
1982	7,277,773	1,000,478	12.6	6,461,743	81.5
1983	9,613,224	294,496	3.1	8,786,831	91.4
1984	12,373,190	unavailable[c]		11,218,980	90.7
1985	10,305,896	unavailable[c]		8,987,753	87.2
1986	10,412,793	306,996	2.9	9,082,297	87.2
1987	10,934,762	279,771	2.6	8,889,072	81.3
1988	12,933,195	358,227	2.8	10,321,574	79.8
1989	12,508,359	250,763	2.0	10,059,048	80.4
1990	11,860,194	323,875	2.7	9,772,904	82.0

Notes:
[a] Iron ore, ore concentrates, scrap, coal, coal products are inputs; total iron ore
loaded are exports.
[b] These figures vary more than 5 per cent from tonnage statistics reported by the
Hamilton Harbour Commission. Statistics Canada warns that domestic tonnage
statistics may have a 10 per cent error margin, and international statistics a 10
to 20 per cent error margin. In general, Statistics Canada reports lower tonnage
statistics than the Harbour Commission because of voluntary compliance.
[c] Statistics Canada discontinued data gathering in these years.
Sources: Dominion Bureau of Statistics, *Shipping Report, Part II: 1960–1969*, and
Shipping Report, Part III: 1970–1977 (Ottawa: Ministry of Industry, Trade, and
Commerce, annual from 1961 to 1969); Statistics Canada, *Coastwise Shipping
Statistics, 1978–1982* (Ottawa: Ministry of Supply and Services, annual); Statistics

There has been a significant change in the source of the iron ore, scrap, and iron-ore concentrate landed in the port. Most is now a product of 'coastwise shipping' rather than 'international shipping,' indicating that the dry bulk is now shipped in a vessel of Canadian registry plying between two Canadian ports. This change may reflect Quebec-Labrador sourcing of iron ores (Ruppenthal 1983: 177).

It is doubtful whether cargo flows through the port will significantly change in volume or type in the next fifteen years. Demand-forecast studies conducted in the early 1980s suggested that the port might be able to develop major thrusts in terms of the export of corn and potash and the export of break bulk goods (Peat Marwick and Partners et al. 1984, IV: 18–19). However, the decline in agricultural prices and the downturn in break bulk goods handled by the port suggest that these forecasts were optimistic. Much depends on the types of industrial tenants attracted to the new East Port Development piers adjacent to the major highway known as the Queen Elizabeth Way, as well as (of course) the stability of the steel industry. Hamilton's major rival on Lake Ontario, the Port of Toronto, may not even enjoy stable cargo flows as shippers intensify their preference for the road-rail-water connections through the Port of Montreal.

One final feature of the cargo flows through the port deserves mention. The Harbour Commissioners has one small container crane, which is actually a modified fork-lift. This gives the port a modest ability to expand its break-bulk tonnage shipped in containers. Highly specialized container traffic that does not depend on regular scheduled routes may still prefer Hamilton to rival ports. An indicator of the potential capacity to handle container traffic may be found in statistics for 1980, when general cargoes were at their recent most peak: some 227 containers were handled that year.[40]

In sum, the Port of Hamilton is, in terms of cargo tonnage imported and exported, the major port on Lake Ontario and the fifth-

Canada, *Shipping Report, Part II and Part III, 1970–1979* (Ottawa: Ministry of Industry, Trade, and Commerce, annual); Statistics Canada, *International Seaborne Shipping Port Statistics, 1980–1983* (Ottawa: Ministry of Supply and Services, annual to 1985); Statistics Canada, *Shipping in Canada* (Ottawa: Supply and Services, annual from 1986–1990).

40 Containers are measured in twenty-foot-equivalent units (TEUs) as most containers measure 20 feet by 8 feet by 8 feet.

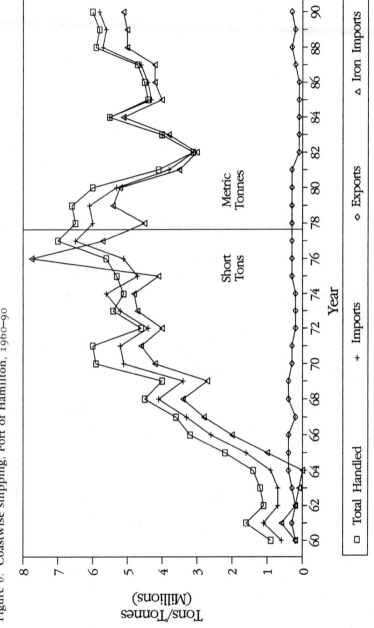

Figure 6. Coastwise shipping, Port of Hamilton, 1960–90

Figure 7. International shipping, Port of Hamilton, 1963–90

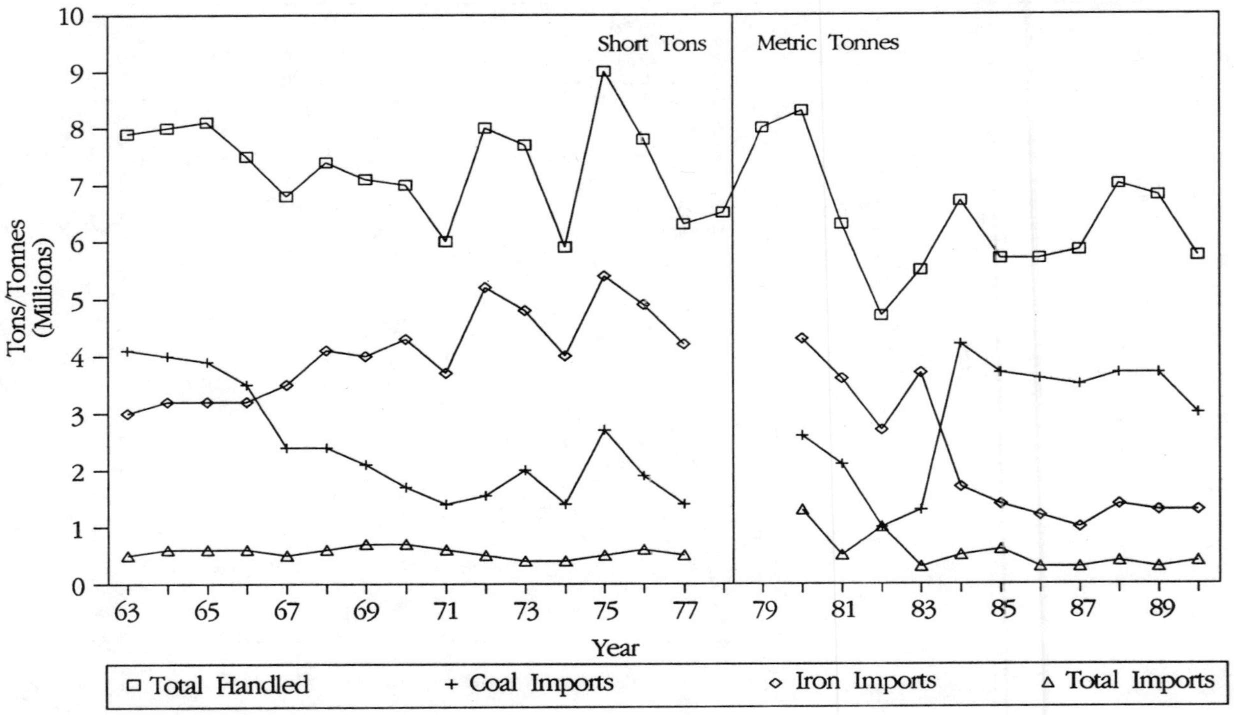

largest port in Canada. However, tonnage statistics, like vessel arrivals, can be a misleading indicator of the importance of a port. The economic value of cargo flows may give a different picture. Until 1990 the Harbour Commissioners possessed no information on the economic value of its cargo flows, a point discussed further below.

An Evaluation of the Operational Rules

Performance Indicators in General

The commercial-shipping activities within any port can be assessed in two broad ways – first, in terms of physical indicators of performance, and, second, in terms of financial and economic indicators. Each of these categories will be discussed in turn.

Physical indicators are measures of port performance that are non-monetary in form. Examples include vessel waiting-times for berths or vessel turn-around times at berths. Other examples are labour (and other input) obstacles that restrict cargo flows and theft and product deterioration on wharves. These factors may not be easily measured in dollar terms, but they could act to influence both the demand for and the supply of wharfage space and allied port activities. Vessel waiting-time and turn-around times are often critical for the viability of a port. Congestion and delays in ports may induce charterers of vessels (normally not the shipowners) to seek alternative ports. As one commentator expresses it: 'Considering a ship on an ordinary voyage charter, it is likely that the faster turnaround time will be reflected in less demurrage, more dispatch money (neglecting the customary difference between these) or in a lower charter rate and that the lower stevedoring costs, payable directly by the ship, will (since they must be predictably lower) be reflected in a lower rate for the charter since the charter will have been arranged in a competitive market' (Goss 1983: 57).

Financial and economic indicators directly address the economic performance of ports. Indicators include operating ratios (ratios of operating expenses to operating revenues) and increases in the value of capital assets over time.

What these multiple indicators of port performance draw attention to are those aspects of commercial shipping that can be made subject to the operational rules of a port commission, and those aspects that are subject to the rules of other governments that may require a port to act inefficiently. We have already noted, for example, how the federal government imposes requirements for inefficiency in its financial regimes for all commission ports (other than Hamilton and Toronto). Within these broader institutional and operational rules-in-use, port management may still operate effectively. We will now apply the physical and economic indicators to the operations of the Port of Hamilton.

Performance Indicators for Hamilton Harbour: Physical Indicators

1 / Ship waiting time: Hamilton Harbour experiences no congestion in its port facilities. It holds berthing capacities for approximately thirty ships, yet reports no waiting time for berths within the past ten years.
2 / Ship turn-around time: Turn-around time varies as a function of cargoes and weather. As the port is primarily a bulk-import port for iron ore and coking coal, and these commodities are off-loaded mechanically at private docks, the turn-around time is largely a matter beyond the control of the HIIC management.
3 / Theft and product deterioration: The nature of the cargoes handled at the port restricts the opportunities for theft and product deterioration. Bulk imports have little resale value (in small quantities) and the break-bulk imports (especially when containerized) offer little scope for theft. The volumes of fruit and vegetables shipped through the port are small; they consist primarily of soya beans, malts, and sugar products. Approximately 75,000 tonnes (mostly imports) are shipped annually, which is three to four times less tonnage than was shipped in the mid 1960s. In sum, theft and product deterioration are likely to be small. Until 1986, the Harbour Commissioners had its own police force of seventeen officers and three gate guards. They reported clearance rates of 5 per cent of crimes against property, and 75 per cent of crimes against persons.[41] The private docks maintain their own independent security forces.

41 In 1986, the Hamilton-Wentworth regional municipality began to police the harbour. Their clearance rates are approximately 19 per cent of property crimes and 76 per cent of person crimes, but because of the unique characteristics of port thefts it is impossible to state whether harbour policy will change clearance rates. These data, which represent five-year averages, were supplied by Dr James C. McDavid from his unpublished comparative analysis of police forces in larger cities in Canada.

4 / Physical indicators of input constraints (labour, capital, and land) on cargo flows: The port has had no strikes, work slow-downs, walk-outs, or lock-outs since 1961 in terms of the labour relations with the International Longshoremen's Association (locals 1879 and 1654). Adverse labour relations on the private docks can, of course, directly affect the HHC's income from cargo flows (terminal income and harbour operations), but these relations are beyond the control of the HHC management. The HHC has, under its 1912 act, no constraints on capital financing or on the sale and disposition of land and water lots that its owns. Its lacks sufficient back-up lands for road-rail-water terminals in the West Harbour (proposals for remedy have long been a source of conflict with recreational users of the bay), but the East Port Development may alter this constraint. More important, market demand for the use of Hamilton Port does not indicate changes in the type and character of cargoes; Hamilton and other Great Lakes ports will not become major container and general-cargo ports because of the physical constraints of the St Lawrence Seaway and the commercial competition from such rival ports as Montreal, Halifax, and New York.

Four sets of physical indicators of performance suggest that the management of the Port of Hamilton is effective but within the rules-in-use that lead to market competition and within the rules that are beyond the influence of the HHC itself.

Performance Indicators: Market

As mentioned previously, the Hamilton Harbour Commissioners generates excess 'income' annually in terms of the operating ratios between revenues and expenditures, but since the port covers total operating costs, this is not a good measure of performance either for ports generally or for Hamilton Harbour. Again, the value of the capital assets of the HHC has grown only modestly largely because of the financial rules followed by the HHC in accordance with federal 'guidelines' governing asset depreciation and accumulations. The HHC has nevertheless, enjoyed some success in risk-averse capital expansions, in view of secular declines in bulk-goods movements on the Great Lakes and the high cost of relocation of industries on the Hamilton waterfront that depend on water-borne movement of natural-resource imports (Norcliffe 1982: 53–72).

While these market indicators suggest that the Port of Hamilton is largely constrained and influenced by financial and economic rules and by the physical attributes of Seaway shipping, it is important to note that until 1990 the Port of Hamilton lacked information over port impacts that might induce alternative management strategies within these rules. Partly because of the findings in this study, the HHC moved to acquire such information.

The Hamilton Harbour Commissioners possessed, until very recently, no information about the economic impacts of different cargo flows, which, in turn, might form a viable strategy for risk investment. For example, the 1972 Economic Impact Study of the Port of Montreal indicated that the total economic impact of general cargo was almost nine times that of bulk cargo, and containerized cargo almost four times that of bulk cargo (Port of Montreal 1973). This kind of study suggests that the future of ports lies in determining the precise economic value of different cargo flows into their hinterlands, assessing their multiple effects, and reorienting management strategies to cater to and seek revenues from the higher-valued cargo flows. The Hamilton Harbour Commissioners has only just begun to reach a stage of knowing the parameters within which a strategic cargo-management program could be established. This picture should be balanced against the highly effective management of the port in terms of physical indicators of performance.

There may well be further impacts of port operations in the harbour on alternative uses or public policies. These are suggested in chapters 8 and 9. These would be a consequence of the configurations of rules-in-use on multiple policies that share the same site. In the narrow sense of the impacts of commercial-shipping rules, alternatives are not systematically appraised.

Conclusions

The Port of Hamilton has developed an unusual mix of commercial-shipping operations and operational rules in response to the incentives of the institutional rules-in-use. Major port operations are dominated by the private docks owned by the two steel companies located on the waterfront, Dofasco and Stelco. Most of the vessel traffic and most of the goods passing through the port are generated by the demands of the steel companies for coking coal and iron ore. This vessel traffic is managed by the Hamilton Harbour Commissioners, a federal government agency incorporated in 1912.

The HHC is also a landlord (it leases foreshores and docks) and manager of most general cargo flows through the port. In these respects, the HHC is the manager of vessel traffic within the physical boundaries of Hamilton Harbour.

The size and types of cargoes imported and exported through the Port of Hamilton reflect, in part, the rivalry and competition for movement of goods from other ports and from road and rail linkages within the Great Lakes and Mississippi Valley areas of North America. Hamilton retains a comparative advantage in the import of bulk commodities for the steel companies, and in small break-bulk general cargoes. It has avoided direct competition in larger-scale and regular container movements that give other ports, especially Montreal and New York–New Jersey, comparative advantages on the east coast. The St Lawrence Seaway development and the development of larger, direct off-loading bulk carriers have reinforced the specializations of Hamilton's port. The port remains the largest in Lake Ontario and the fifth-largest in Canada in terms of cargo tonnage imported and exported. In these respects, the institutional rules-in-use provide the incentives for competitive economic behaviour on the part of the Harbour Commissioners, even though the rules would apparently suggest monopoly economic behaviour.

The Hamilton Harbour Commissioners is a highly effective manager of port operations by conventional physical indicators of performance. Ship waiting-time for berths has been zero for the past ten years. Ship turn-around time varies only as a function of cargoes and weather and not of organizational practices. Theft and product deterioration are small. Finally, input constraints on cargo flows, especially those of labour relations, are minimal. Land constraints for road-rail-water terminals are eased with the East Port Development.

The HHC is also a highly effective manager in financial terms of performance. Through a variety of charges and fees, the HHC has operated since the Second World War without municipal or federal subsidies, and in most years can set revenues to generate working capital for the port. The exception to these management practices was the absence of information until 1990 on the economic impact of alternative cargo flows to the port and its hinterland; such information could now prove useful, enabling the HHC to adapt its management practices to place an emphasis on alternative kinds of facilities for alternative kinds of cargoes that would benefit the community and the agency. Evidence from other ports suggests that the specializations of the Port of Hamilton yield fewer multiplier benefits in the community than do other types of cargo flows.

While the HHC is effective as a port manager, it also adopts financial rules that suggest that commercial-shipping operations are larger and more inefficient for managing the *multiple* uses of Hamilton Harbour. The HHC equates its total costs of operations with its total revenues rather than balancing its marginal costs with marginal revenues. Moreover, were this policy to be changed, and marginal-cost pricing strategies pursued by the HHC, any surplus revenues would simply accrue to the City of Hamilton rather than to the port because of the rules within the Hamilton Harbour Commissioners Act of 1912. In other words, the 1912 act may create an incentive for certain elements of inefficiency. In practical terms, it means that some commercial-shipping operations on the waters and foreshores are cross-subsidized by more profitable operations in the port. It also means that more of the foreshores and waters of the harbour are dedicated to commercial-shipping uses than can be justified on commercial grounds alone.

Nevertheless, rule configurations grant the Hamilton Harbour Commissioners a monopoly over commercial-shipping operations on the waters of the harbour itself. The HHC can use its monopoly powers to sustain, legally, any inefficiencies it wishes to pursue as a matter of institutional discretion. It does mean, however, that the rivalries over the uses of the foreshores of Hamilton Harbour, in particular with the City of Hamilton, retain an intense political and legal flavour.

More generally, the policy case does illustrate the 'nesting' features that can occur within any multiple rule configurations. The operational rules for the port are devised within constitutional- and institutional-rule configurations that are both domestic and international in source and span both shipping and alternative bulk-goods transportation modes as public policies, on the one hand, and shipping and alternative forshore uses, on the other. Within these complex and multiple rule configurations, the HHC, as one set of decision makers, act largely in response, to the incentives of rivalry.

It illustrates also how constitutional and institutional rules that might, from a 'top-down' perspective, mislead the reader into interpreting the behaviour of the HHC in terms of the delegated legislative powers of the Canadian federal government, rather than the behaviour of an institution operating within rule incentives for the transshipment of goods in the eastern parts of North America. Although the HHC was established by federal statute, it responds to a quite different set of incentives. While it is true that some rules are 'stacked' in one domestic hierarchy, other rules not so stacked provide alternative incentives.

The case further suggests that the operating rules must deal with the attributes of a good at particular times and places, and that the consequences show up in terms of performance indicators. They also show up in terms of the interdependencies between policies at particular times and places. The character of the good, in a technical sense, dictates some of the characteristics of the operating rules. These manifestations are also revealed in subsequent chapters. Governments 'work' in often surprising ways.

8

Pleasure Boating

Recreation policy is one that takes place largely outside the bounds of governmental rules. It is true, of course, that governments produce some elements of recreation in the way of libraries, swimming pools, or hockey arenas, and if they do not produce them themselves they subsidize their costs, as they do with the National Ballet or B.C. Place stadium. It is also true that governments seem to like regulating recreational pursuits, whether these be the content of television programs or the use of trail bikes in national and provincial parks. But recreation and other leisure pursuits are largely inspired and produced by individuals, by clubs of private citizens, or by educational and health-related organizations. This makes it extremely difficult to synchronize the institutional rules of production and regulation to the nature of the good.

For example, think about the most popular recreational activities, such as walking and watching television. The frequency and scale with which people indulge in these activities is virtually impossible to monitor and predict. Conditions of time and place, like climate for walking or location for watching American soap operas without cable, have far more impact on when and how people will walk or watch television than governmental rules about sidewalk snow shovelling or Canadian content in 'The Beachcombers.' Similarly, anyone who has sunbathed on the coast or a lakefront and had to endure the high volume from the ghetto-blaster of a strutting teenager will realize the difficulties of devising, monitoring, and enforcing rules to take account of the obvious technical interdependencies between different recreational pursuits. Any operational rules devised to regulate leisure pursuits are likely to be either obsolete or unenforceable. It is far more likely that social norms (when these are treated as operational rules) will better predict, constrain, and make available opportunities for leisure pursuits than any governmental regulations.

These considerations make it difficult to analyse recreation as a public policy. Recreational activities are multiple, varied, and often even easily substitutable. While determined in part by time-and-place circumstances, recreational activities are subject to rapidly changing technologies and individual-preference orderings. Further, any social norms as operational rules of conduct are highly variable and difficult to enforce in larger urbanized settlements. Finally, the operational rules for governmental regulation and production are, as we have implied, frequently obsolete and/or unenforceable; they take on the characteristics of rules-in-form rather than rules-in-use. Recreational policies are, as it were, like prohibition policies writ large!

An analysis of pleasure boating as one form of recreation is a little more tractable. Many kinds of pleasure boating involve substantial capital expenditures on the part of an individual or group of individuals, and these sunk costs tend to have a stabilizing effect on preference orderings and the substitutability between leisure pursuits.[1] Further, the use of sailboats and powerboats requires facilities such as moorages, ramps, and road-access points, that are largely fixed and hence more easily measured than those facilities needed for other leisure pursuits, including sailboating, canoeing, and kayaking. Finally, pleasure boating often takes place on waters that may not have the carrying capacity to easily accommodate the number of craft that wish to use those waters. Rules, such as 'rules of the road,' may have to be devised, monitored, and enforced. This last consideration is amplified when the waters in question are subject to multiple activities – when this recreational policy is technically interdependent with other water-related policies – as when a harbour is used for both pleasure craft and commercial shipping.

Because of these considerations, we are likely to find operational rules-in-use in the context of Hamilton Harbour. Further, the operational rules-in-use are likely to be both configurative (multiple rules for interdependent goods) and subject to multiple and varied

---

1 Given the relatively high transaction costs of market exchanges in sailboats and powerboats

institutional rules for provision, production, and regulation. Constitutional rules-in-use for the institutional rules also exist.

As we shall see, the policy on site is subject to rule 'stacking' by operational, institutional, and constitutional levels. It also 'nests' within multiple rules, including those at a constitutional level. In these regards it is similar to the policy already examined in chapter 7, that of commercial shipping. The policy and its rules-in-use differ, however, from the rule-ordered policy of commercial shipping:

1 / the rules-in-use constrain and limit any competition between pleasure boating and alternative activities for harbour waters and foreshores. The opportunities forgone are measurable by economic indicators (in part), and they reflect the operational and institutional rules (including property rights) for the uses of the harbour waters themselves; and

2 / the rules-in-use permit competition between pleasure-boating facilities (such as marinas) both within the harbour and at accessible sites on adjacent shores of Lake Ontario. However, these rules include direct governmental production of some facilities in the harbour and governmental subsidization of the capital costs of private marina operators within and outside the harbour. In this rule-ordered environment, there are few indicators of an insufficiency of boating facilities within the harbour itself.

We thus see how the basic logic of the rule configurations for pleasure boating differs from that for commercial shipping. Some of the difference obviously stems from the nature of the good itself. Commercial shipping, for example, involves a magnitude of capital expenditures on docking facilities that is barely comparable with those on pleasure-boating facilities.

But, as important as the nature of the good is the institutional rules-in-use. Pleasure boaters have highly attenuated property rights to access and use harbour waters. They have what are essentially 'squatter's rights,' with no legal remedies available to permit them to enjoy the harbour waters except at the discretion of the landlords in question. The 'landlord' of the waters is the Hamilton Harbour Commissioners. The landlord of the foreshores are private riparians, the HHC, and the municipalities of Hamilton and Burlington. Herein lies the paradox of pleasure boating in Canadian harbours. Most recreational activities take place beyond the bounds of rules; pleasure boating on harbour waters takes place only when sanctioned by rules.

The discussion in the chapter proceeds as follows: We first briefly review the constitutional and institutional rules-in-use for pleasure boating on Hamilton Harbour. Many of these rules parallel those in use for commercial shipping, so the discussion will be limited. We then describe the moorage and related facilities, and the economic value and magnitude of pleasure boating on the bay. Third, we assess the performance of the rules-in-use for pleasure boating. Finally, we return to the thrust of the entire book, namely, an analysis of how government works in terms of rules and policies.

Constitutional and Institutional Rules

The constitutional rules-in-use for pleasure boating in Hamilton Harbour include the rules of navigable servitude, the rules for the legislative authority of the federal and Ontario governments, and the rules granting proprietary rights to the Hamilton Harbour Commissioners outside the Constitution Act, 1867. The rule of navigable servitude is a common law that allocates priority to vessels in navigable waters, subject to multiple uses. The rules for the legislative authority of the federal government are largely those in section 91 of the Constitution Act, which assigns legislative power over shipping and navigation to the Dominion rather than to the provincial government. The rules for the legislative authority of the Government of Ontario are largely those in section 92 of the Constitution Act, including the jurisdiction over municipalities and the general power to legislate for 'property and civil rights.' Finally, the rules for the proprietary authority of the Hamilton Harbour Commissioners stem from the pre-Confederation era, when the City of Hamilton possessed these rights; they were not transferred to the federal Crown in 1867, but were transferred, by agreement of the municipality, the province, and the Dominion, to the HHC in 1948. All of these constitutional rules were examined at length in chapter 7.

The institutional rules-in-use for pleasure boating are also similar to those for commercial shipping. The federal government legislated the establishment of the Harbour Commissioners in 1912. This act delegates authority to the HHC to make all decisions affecting the use of harbour waters by commercial and pleasure craft, provided they do not conflict with the Canada Shipping Act, 1970, and the

Navigable Waters Protection Act, 1886. As a result, the HHC has established its own by-laws as regulations for the conduct of pleasure-craft and moorage operators. Three sets of regulations are important for the pleasure craft themselves:

1 / Boating Protection Regulations: These establish requirements for signs, lights, foghorns, and lifebuoys. They set restrictions on speeds and requirements for permits for regattas and races. Fines of up to $50 and imprisonment of up to 30 days are potential sanctions for non-compliance.
2 / Pleasure Yachts Marking Order: This sets standards as to how registration numbers are to be displayed.
3 / Small Vessels Regulations: These provide for registration of vessels and set detailed standards regarding required safety and navigation equipment. The 'rules of the road' and collision regulations are also described. Licensing of vessels that use the harbour is no longer compulsory; the requirement was deleted when the Regional Municipality of Hamilton-Wentworth assumed responsibility for harbour policing on the abolition of the Hamilton Harbour Commissioners' force in 1986.

The regulations for marina and moorage operators are partly developed from the purposes of the Navigable Waters Protection Act, namely, to prevent the physical obstruction of vessels as the paramount users of such waters. In practice, this means that the commercial marinas and riparians on the harbour must seek written approvals from the HHC in order to build moorages and ramps. In addition, because the HHC possesses independent proprietary rights, it may sell or lease water lots adjacent to the foreshores for specified purposes, including the operation of boating clubs, marinas, moorages, and ramps.

It is also important to note that the HHC possesses full statutory and proprietary authority to own and operate its own moorage and related facilities. As a consequence, it operates the largest facilities on the bay.

Moorage and access to moorage facilities are jurisdictionally more complex than the above rules imply. They also involve the discretionary authority of the municipalities of Hamilton and Burlington made possible by the provincial Planning Act, 1983, and the Municipal Act, 1983. (The Regional Municipalities of Hamilton-Wentworth and Halton also possess some discretionary authority for the acquisition of land for the establishment of public parks.) We have already discussed, in chapter 7, how the City of Hamilton exercises its discretionary authority under the Planning Act. In brief, it has passed by-laws as regulations for the uses of land, buildings, and structures for all parts of Hamilton Harbour and its foreshores, except those public parklands managed and controlled by another governmental body. The exception is intended to exclude those lands of the Hamilton Conservation Authority, a provincial Crown corporation with a local board of directors, funded by provincial and local governments. The Conservation Authority regulates and manages lands within the harbour watershed, but not adjacent to the harbour waters themselves.

The jurisdiction of the municipalities, especially Hamilton, for the uses of foreshore lands and improvements directly conflicts with the jurisdiction of the Harbour Commissioners for shipping and navigation, as they pertain to foreshore lands and infilled water lots. Case law has established, as we saw previously, some general principles to resolve conflicts between Hamilton and the HHC over foreshore land uses. Let us briefly review those principles.

The City of Hamilton, pursuant to section 34 of the Planning Act, can validly pass zoning by-laws affecting land use within the harbour so long as it does not explicitly attempt to prohibit or regulate the use of land for purposes related to shipping and navigation. Similarly, the Harbour Commissioners can validly pass by-laws to regulate and control the use and development of land within the harbour for purposes related to navigation and shipping. Only if conflict arises with respect to the use of a parcel of land within the limits of the harbour would the paramountcy of HHC, authority cause the operation of the by-law of the city to be suspended, because the federal government and the HHC occupy the paramount field of shipping and navigation.[2] These same general principles were used by the courts to limit the authority of conservation authorities to regulate infilling of the harbour.[3]

Unfortunately, pleasure boating is treated by the courts and the HHC exclusively as a form of shipping, rather than as both a form

2 *Hamilton Harbour Commissioners* v. *City of Hamilton et al*, 1978, 91 DLR (3d), 378
3 *R.* v. *Hamilton Harbour Commissioners*, 1977, 7 CELN, Ont., 130

of shipping and a type of recreation. Consequently, the institutional rules-in-use may be appropriate for devising operational rules for small vessels, but they are not always appropriate for devising operational rules for those aspects of recreational boating that take place on harbour foreshores. In other words, the operational rules-in-use are not fully tailored to the nature of the good. The consequences show up, as we shall see, in the economic opportunities forgone because of the operational limits placed on pleasure boating by the institutional rules-in-use.

These limits, imposed in practice by the HHC and its discretionary authority to give priority to commercial shipping over pleasure boating, are reinforced by historical circumstances. Most of the foreshores of the harbour are held in fee simple by riparians. Only 7 per cent of the total shoreline of 45 kilometers is legally classified as 'open space,' namely marinas, parks, and a golf course. The remainder is owned by private industries; a (nationalized) railway company; the HHC, all three levels of government, in the form of public buildings and roads; and by private residents.[4] Each of these riparians has the legal right to prevent trespass on his or her property and to block access to the waterfront for pleasure boaters and other recreationists. In other words, the institutional rules embodied in the property rights over foreshore lands grant no rights to pleasure boaters over most of the harbour waterfront, given the way the foreshores have been occupied during the history of the harbour.

We mentioned previously that, when on the waters of the harbour, pleasure boaters possess no legal property rights to use and enjoy the resource. They are legal squatters, allowed to use the waters at the discretion of the Harbour Commissioners. In addition, on the foreshores of the harbour, they possess only the legal rights of access and withdrawal on those parcels of land and water lots expressly sold, leased, or dedicated as open space. On other parcels of the foreshore, they could be legal squatters were they to use these properties for recreational purposes.

With these constitutional and institutional rule configurations-in-use, we can turn to describe briefly the moorages in the harbour before we assess the value and magnitude of pleasure boating. Given the rules-in-use already described, we can anticipate that these values and magnitudes will be limited.

4 Unpublished 1984 data from the Hamilton Conservation Authority

Moorage Description and Facilities

Hamilton Harbour is home to six marinas, the total number of slips amounting to 681 in 1989, which represents an increase of 75 per cent since 1974–6 when 390 boat slips existed in the bay (Public Works Canada 1976). Table 8 documents the number of slips, wet moorings, dry moorings, and boat ramps available for pleasure boating at the two publicly owned and four private marinas.

The number of slips and berths available for boaters in the harbour is not an accurate indicator of the number of vessels that use the harbour during the open season. It excludes those craft that are put in and taken out of the water on a daily basis, especially canoes and sailboards. The publicly owned facility of the Hamilton Harbour Commissioners is expanding its moorings and ships (in part because of the influence of this chapter's findings).

The number of pleasure-boating facilities on the harbour is constrained by land access. Map 6 shows existing marina locations on the bay. All but one are located in the same region of the harbour and are accessible only through a road system designed for neighbourhood residential trips. New commercial marinas on the Harbour are unlikely to develop, therefore, without public investment in improved access and public subsidies for capital construction. Two sets of indicators reinforce this conclusion. First, as table 9 indicates, most marinas do not have waiting lists for berthage, and the largest marina (the publicly owned marina of the Harbour Commissioners) reported a surplus of slips for larger vessels until 1986. Second, the estimated net earnings, before taxes and financial charges, for commercial marinas on the Great Lakes is only 9 per cent.[5] This suggests that commercial marinas rely on public subsidies for capital construction, such as was available under the federal Fishing and Recreational Harbours Act, 1977–8.

A final feature of moorage facilities available in the harbour must be emphasized. Commercial marinas do not appear to be able to capture a large proportion of the expenditures of boaters on pleasure boating without public subsidies of capital costs and access. Revenue per slip per annum averages only $622 in terms of rental

5 Public Works Canada (1976). The estimate is based on a survey conducted by the National Association of Engine and Boat Manufacturers and is probably downwardly biased.

TABLE 8
Moorage facilities, 1985

Marinas	Slips	Wet moorings	Dry moorings	Boat ramps
Hamilton Harbour Commissioners[a]	231	210	0	1
La Salle Marina	219	Included in the 210 belonging to HHC[b]	0	2[f]
Leander Boat Club	0	0	Sculling facilities[d]	0
Macassa Bay Yacht Club	100	0	0	0
Scott MacDonald Marine Services	50	2	0	0
Hamilton Yacht Club, 1888	81	Unlimited[c]	155[e]	1[g]
TOTAL	681	212+	155+	4

Notes:
[a] Public marina operated by the Harbour Commissioners, later expansion from 1989 to 1991
[b] 160, excluding the 50 included in the HHC total
[c] No present constraints due to congestion
[d] Rental facilities available
[e] Includes 120 storage facilities and 35 laser facilities
[f] One public ramp plus one run by boat club
[g] Boat winch

and maintenance costs, or some $4 per day for a typical season of 160 days. This is less than 10 per cent of the annual direct expenditures on boating by owners who use the bay.[6] However, boatowners themselves appear prepared to own rather than to rent slips. Table 9 indicates that a substantial market in this commercial asset exists at La Salle Park. In this case, some of the bundle of legal property rights of foreshore 'lands' for pleasure boating are expanded from that of mere access and withdrawal from the waters. Pleasure-boat owners have the legal rights of access, withdrawal, management, exclusion, and partial transfer of their property rights in their own slips.[7]

6 From calculations reported below.
7 The resale of slips must be made only to the Burlington Boat Club at an admin-

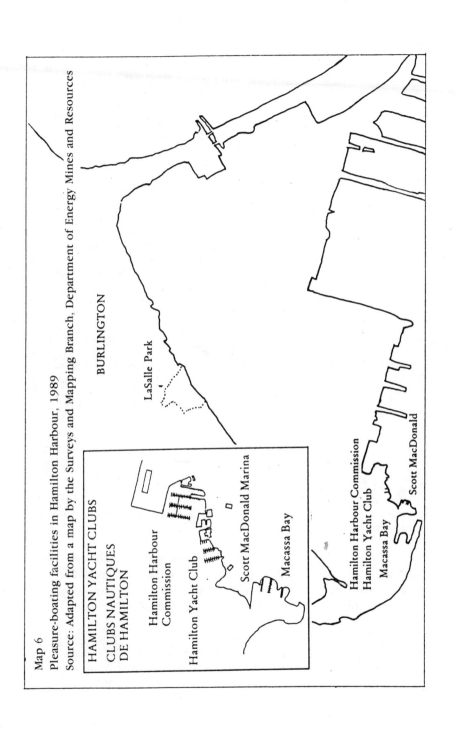

Map 6
Pleasure-boating facilities in Hamilton Harbour, 1989
Source: Adapted from a map by the Surveys and Mapping Branch, Department of Energy Mines and Resources

BURLINGTON

LaSalle Park

HAMILTON YACHT CLUBS

CLUBS NAUTIQUES
DE HAMILTON

Hamilton Harbour
Commission

Hamilton Yacht Club

Scott MacDonald Marina

Macassa Bay

Hamilton Harbour Commission
Hamilton Yacht Club

Macassa Bay

Scott MacDonald

TABLE 9
Sufficiency and availability of moorage, 1985

Marinas[a]	Waiting lists	Memberships/Access
Hamilton Harbour Commissioners	None; slips for large craft available in 1985; 210 wet moorings available for purchase at $470, but these include 160 at La Salle Park	No membership necessary
La Salle Park	Waiting list[b]; 219 slips available for purchase at average price of $4,800[c]	No memberships; operated by Burlington Sailing and Boat Club
Macassa Bay Yacht Club	5-year waiting list for active membership	Social membership of 150 at $20 required before active membership of 100 at $50 per annum
Scott MacDonald Marine Services	None	No memberships necessary
Hamilton Yacht Club, 1888	None	Variety of memberships available for purchase; a resident membership includes $1,000 initiation fee, $690 annual fee, $600 club fee

Notes:
[a] Excludes Leander Boat Club
[b] Size is unavailable
[c] Price increases 10 per cent per annum under current policy; hence, occasional vacancies occur.

Thus we see that different types of moorages and moorage facilities are available for pleasure boaters on Hamilton Harbour. We also see that there is little unavailability and insufficiency of moorages, as indicated by marina waiting lists. Further, most of the mar-

---

istered price of 10 per cent per annum above the sale price. The owner of the slip thus does not capture the full economic benefits of the property rights of ownership.

inas are organized as clubs or produced by a government agency directly (the HHC) and have benefited from public subsidies and cross-subsidization, respectively, of their capital costs. The operational rules-in-use for access to the harbour waters may thus compensate for the limited physical access across riparian lands on the bay. However, it should be noted that these operational rules-in-use are devised only as part of the discretionary authority of governmental agencies, including the Harbour Commissioners, the former federal Small Craft Harbours Branch, and the road transportation agencies of the municipalities and the province.

The Value and Magnitude of Pleasure Boating

General Considerations

Pleasure boating is not, by definition, a commercial activity. Once a boat is purchased, rented, or leased and access to the water is secured at either private or public expense, the benefits of boating are non-market in nature. The value of pleasure boating to the participants is not signalled or indicated by dollar signs. Use of the waters of Hamilton Harbour or Lake Ontario is not sold on the market, and the recreational, aesthetic, and sports-fishing benefits of pleasure boating are not easily calculable. This is not, of course, to deny that pleasure boating generates economic consequences for marina operators, manufacturers of boats and equipment, and the owners of such facilities as restaurants and tackle shops that derive 'secondary' benefits from boaters.

A number of economic techniques exist for estimating the value and magnitude of pleasure boating in the absence of market indicators (Eby and Partners 1979; Goodwin 1982; Hough and Partners 1979 and 1985). While few economists would claim that such techniques yield perfectly accurate calculations, they do none the less give an approximation of the extent of the benefits associated with this form of recreation. Unfortunately, no data exist on the value and magnitude of pleasure boating in the harbour. I report, as a consequence, our own estimates, based on indirect indicators. I was unable to survey boaters to calculate directly the actual number of users on the waters on any one day and then to elicit from them their own estimates of the benefits they derive from this type of recreation. Doing so would have enabled me to estimate certain attributes of pleasure boating, like the 'quality' of the boating experience or the boaters' willingness to pay for using harbour waters. Instead, I had to derive many of my estimates from census data and data obtained from marina operators, using the economic methodology of the Ontario Recreational Boating Studies (hereafter cited as RBS) of 1979 and 1985, both of which excluded Hamilton Harbour (Hough and Partners 1979 and 1985). This methodology has the key advantage of allowing us to compare the actual economic value of pleasure boating in Hamilton Harbour with the expected value derived from provincial data. In such a fashion we can make some inferences about the performance of the governance system for this use of Hamilton Harbour compared with Ontario-wide norms.

The Magnitude of Boating

The boating season for the harbour runs from April to mid-November, in terms of the 'first-in' and 'last-out' boat. This season is approximately 240 days, twice as long as the Ontario average season of 120 days. Most of the boating occurs between the Victoria Day and Thanksgiving Day holidays, and in many of our calculations we use a season length of 160 days. (We exclude ice boating from our analysis.)

Table 10 shows a variety of estimates of the number of boats of various kinds that use the harbour or are resident within the Census Metropolitan Area. The range of over 300 per cent indicates that some of these estimates are unreliable.

A more reliable estimate of the extent of boating on Hamilton Harbour is derived from the number of boating opportunities made possible by existing moorage and ramp facilities on the bay. The RBS calculates that moorage and ramp facilities make possible a specified number of opportunities for boating in any one day, and that an annual calculation is subject to the length of the season and socioeconomic constraints on boating (as recreational uses cannot be spread evenly over the number of days of the week). Calculating the number of boating opportunities made possible by existing facilities in the harbour, using a season length of 160 days and a socioeconomic constraint factor of 0.5,[8] we discover that 264,480 boating

8 The ratio of facilities to opportunities is an Ontario-wide average, namely, 3.5 opportunities per day per slip or wet berth and 62.5 opportunities per day per

TABLE 10
Estimates of boating numbers, 1985

Source of data	Boat estimation	Comments
Canada Customs Licensing Division	52,000	Hamilton Metropolitan Area estimate
Hamilton Harbour Commissioners' Police Force	32,000	Some 1,701 vessels complied with registration requirements of HHC by-laws; estimated at 75% of total
Statistics Canada data on family expenditure by household income	22,930	Adjusted to fit income earners of 15 years and older in Hamilton CMA
Statistics Canada data on family expenditure by homeowners or rental status	15,243	Adjusted to fit tenure status in Hamilton CMA

opportunities exist each year on Hamilton Harbour, or 1,653 opportunities on an averaged daily basis.

Not all of the craft are associated with these businesses use the harbour itself, so we confine our analysis of the size of the boating industry to the marina operators resident on the habour shores. In table 11, we indicate the size of marina operations by calculating the moorage revenues of the five major marinas on the harbour (we exclude the Leander Boat Club).

The Boating Industry

The Hamilton Harbour watershed is home to a variety of boating businesses. As table 12 shows, we estimate that a total of 33 private and public enterprises are engaged in marina operations, boat building and repairs, boat sales, boat transportation, boat excursions, boating instruction, and boat rentals and charters.

These revenues represent the primary as opposed to the secondary expenditures associated with moorage on the harbour. Secondary expenditures include club memberships, restaurant expenditures,

---

ramp. Season length is 160 days rather than the 120 days for Ontario as a whole, and the constraint factor of 0.5 corresponds to province-wide estimates.

TABLE 11
Moorage revenues, 1985

Marinas	Rental and capital sales	Maintenance	Total
Hamilton Harbour Commissioners	250,199	98,700	348,899
La Salle Park	43,800	1,051,200	1,095,000
Macassa Bay Yacht	20,000	Nil	20,000
Scott S. MacDonald Marine Services	37,500	Nil	37,500
Hamilton Yacht Club, 1888	71,425[a]	Nil	71,425
TOTALS	422,924	1,149,900	1,572,824

Note: [a] Includes storage

and expenditures on tackle and so on, generated from primary expenditures on boats and moorage. It is worth noting that expenditures on the rent and maintenance of moorings amount to only 27 per cent of total expenditures on moorings, once capital sales of moorings are included. Again, the importance of the acquisition of property-ownership rights in moorages to the boatowner is apparent.

Economic Impact

The previous findings would suggest that recreational boating in the harbour is a very small economic activity. However, expenditures on moorage represent a small proportion of the expenditures made by boaters. It is possible to estimate the full economic impact of pleasure boating made possible in the harbour by using standard economic techniques. Our estimates are, in fact, downwardly biased because they are limited to sailing and motor boating and do not include canoeing, kayaking, and windsurfing. (Canoeing, kayaking, and windsurfing are excluded because no data on the magnitude of their use in the harbour exist and no estimate of magnitude can be made from the number of slips and ramps existing in the harbour.)

The basis for the calculations is our previous estimate of annual boating opportunities made possible by the existing facilities in the harbour (264,480). As table 13 indicates, the facilities in the harbour contribute almost $9 million into the economy and lead to the employment of almost 800 persons.

TABLE 12
Number of boating business, 1985

Marinas	6
Boat builders and repairs	9
Boat dealers	9
Boat transporters	1
Boat excursions	1
Boat instructors	5
Boats – rental and charter	2
TOTAL	33

Source: Bell Canada, *Regional Municipality of Hamilton-Wentworth, Burlington and Surrounding Area*, directory; comments from the Hamilton Harbour Commissioners.

We thus find that recreational boating in Hamilton Harbour has important benefits both to the recreationist and to the local economy. Although these benefits can be calculated in economic terms, previous work at other sites and times indicates that the pleasure boater derives as much if not more non-economic benefit from these kinds of recreational activities. (The calculated benefits pertain only to the local economy. A fuller accounting might be necessary for different purposes than ours.)

In sum, despite the institutional constraints, including those of property owners, on access to and use of the harbour, foreshores, and waters, pleasure boating is a highly valued use of the resource. But what are the net effects of the existing institutional and operational rules-in-use for pleasure boating and other activities of the harbour on the value of pleasure boating itself? How well does the system perform? Partial answers to these questions will now be suggested.

Performance

In some ways, each harbour waterfront site in Canada is unique. In each case, the activities and uses of the waters, foreshores, and watershed generally have grown partly in response to the geographic characteristics of the site and partly in response to historical circumstances of rules and their operational effects. In this way, it is invalid to compare Hamilton Harbour with, say, Toronto Harbour

TABLE 13
Economic impact of sailing and motor-boating, 1985

Economic indicator	Total
Direct expenditure[a]	$3,033,585.6
Total economic output[b]	7,098,590.3
Income generated[c]	8,873,237.9
Direct employment[d]	285.7
Indirect employment[e]	505.7
Total employment	791.4

Notes:
[a] Estimated at $11.47 per occasion. 'Occasion' is defined in the next section. All multipliers are those used in RBS (1985: 16–18) and are chosen for comparability purposes.
[b] Economic output is the total regional output necessary to produce the direct expenditures; multiplier of 2.34
[c] Value of regional wages, salaries and profits; multiplier of 1.25
[d] 32.2 person years per $1 million of expenditures
[e] Multiplier of 1.77

with respect to recreational boating: Toronto Harbour generates approximately $37 million of annual income and 2,700 person years of employment.[9] It would be just as invalid to compare the positive economic performance of commercial shipping in Hamilton with the continuous deficit positions of that harbour use in Toronto.

It may be possible to assess the scope of pleasure boating in Hamilton Harbour, however, by comparing *current* impacts and facilities with what the economic inputs and facilities would be were residents in the watershed to use the harbour in proportion with how Ontario residents use their adjacent waterways.

Some methodological procedures should be detailed in order to clarify the comparative assessment.

1 / The Ontario Recreational Survey, which remains the only comprehensive study of the characteristics and behaviours of recreationists, estimates that 4.1 is the annual per-capita participation rate in boating of all kinds for mid-sized popu-

9 Calculated on the basis of facilities, using the same season length, opportunities per type of facility, constraints on opportunities, and multipliers as used in our previous calculations for Hamilton Harbour (see Johnson et al 1985: 15, 26, 53).

lation centres (100,000 to 499,999 persons). We applied this rate to the population, age twelve and older, of the Hamilton Census Metropolitan Area.[10]

2 / These calculations yielded a figure of 1,855,557.5 occasions, which we define as Hamilton's participation in pleasure boating at least once during a year. We deflated this figure by one-third, by using the province-wide standard that one-third of all boating occasions are satisfied out of the area in question (RBS, 1979: 37).

3 / We then further deflated this figure of 1,237,038 occasions by 56.2 per cent, which is the province-wide proportion of boating occasions satisfied by motor-boating and sailing rather than by canoeing, kayaking, and rowing.

4 / We finally applied the same parameters and multipliers as were used in table 13 to yield a performance standard from which to assess the sailing and motor-boating uses of the harbour.

Our calculations reveal some significant findings about the performance of the governance system in relation to pleasure boating in the bay (see table 14). The opportunity costs associated with current motor-boating and sailing facilities, access, and usage in the harbour vary from almost $5 million of direct expenditures to $14 million of lost watershed income. More than 450 person-years of direct employment is forgone, and almost 1,300 persons-years could be generated in the watershed from enhanced motor-boating and sailing. In fact, we estimate that a potential recreational industry worth $14 million alone in direct expenditure is available for capture by appropriate harbour facilities, access, and pleasurable conditions for boating. This figure includes canoeing, rowing, and kayaking, as well as sailing and motor-boating. This figure would merely bring the harbour into equivalence with Ontario-wide norms (see table 15). Such a standard would require, *inter alia*, the construction and maintenance of 1,529 slips or 86 ramps, or some combination of both. Because of probable congestion with commercial shipping and navigation, it is doubtful that all of these facilities could be feasibly constructed and maintained.

It is important to emphasize that the deficiencies we have iden-

10 Data sources are *Ontario Recreation Survey 1975–1979*, vol. 2, 107, and Census of Canada, Population ... selected characteristics.

TABLE 14
Comparative performance indicators

Indicators	Expected performance	Actual performance[a]	Deficit[b]
Direct expenditure	$ 7,945,742.7	3,033,585.6	4,912,157.1
Total economic output	18,593,307	7,098,590.3	11,494,717.7
Income generated	23,241,633	8,873,237.9	14,368,395.1
Direct employment	748.4	285.1	462.7
Indirect employment	1,324.7	505.7	819.0
Total employment	2,073.1	791.4	1,281.7

Notes:
[a] From table 13
[b] Expected performance minus actual performance

tified in the performance of the governance system of rules-in-use are only crude indicators of performance. First, they are exclusively economic in nature. Second, they include the interdependent effects of rules-in-use for other harbour activities on pleasure boating; these would show up as net benefits rather than net losses for such activities as commercial shipping and waste disposal. We now return to our analysis of the rules-in-use for pleasure boating with these crude performance indicators in mind.

Conclusions

Pleasure boating is a major activity on the waters of Hamilton Harbour. It generates economic benefits for the community and has a value for the pleasure boater that is only approximated by economic indicators. Unfortunately these benefits appear to be less than one would predict for individuals who engage in recreational boating in similar-sized communities. Why is this the case?

Our analysis suggests that three sets of reasons are major contributable factors to the deficiencies. First, historical decisions and geographical circumstances limit the value and magnitude of recreational boating in the harbour. In chapter 6, we saw how the harbour is as much a man-made artefact as a natural resource. Over time, and particularly in the last one hundred years, the rules-in-use have

TABLE 15
Indicators of potential boating performance: All vessels

Direct expenditure	$14,188,826
Economic output	33,201,853
Income generated	41,502,316
Direct employment	1,336
Indirect employment	2365.4
Total employment	3701.4

placed a low priority upon recreation, in general, and pleasure boating, in particular. This situation is evidenced most visibly in the limited acreage set aside on the foreshores of the harbour for recreational access. Property-rights arrangements have been built up without consideration of the demands of future generations.

Second, we have noted at length how the rules-in-use for pleasure boating grant discretionary authority to the Harbour Commissioners to allow as much boating, where and how, on harbour waters as it sees fit. Further, the rules-in-use for harbour foreshores and water lots, which are expressed in legally enforceable property rights, preclude access to and enjoyment of the land-water interface. Pleasure boaters enjoy squatters' rights, as legal rules, on the waters and on more than 90 per cent of the foreshores of the bay. On the remaining foreshores, they have attenuated property rights that are limited to access and withdrawal.

Third, the rules-in-use for multiple activities or legal uses of the harbour place a low priority on recreational activities relative to that accorded commercial shipping and waste disposal. Recreational boating is treated as the same public policy or good as is commercial shipping rather than as a form of recreation as well as boating. Consequently, the rules-in-use for the alternative uses of the harbour and its foreshores bias, if that is the correct word, the rules-in-use for recreational boating. This is best exemplified in the written policy of the Harbour Commissioners which states: 'First and foremost, increased trade and development at the port through commercial shipping shall be promoted' (Hamilton Harbour Master Plan 1978: 8). The legal doctrine of navigable servitude makes this priority a feasible operational rule-in-use.

In broader terms, we can conclude with these more general observations about how governments work. First, the public policy is stacked (in a hierarchy of multiple rules) among operational, institutional, and constitutional rules. In terms of the basic logic of Canadian parliamentary federalism, the rule stacking is asymmetrically weighted towards federal authorities, including their Crown corporations, i.e., the Hamilton Harbour Commissioners. It must not be forgotten, however, that the conflicts over foreshore uses are between provincial instrumentalities, such as the City of Hamilton, and federal instrumentalities, such as the Harbour Commissioners.

Second, it must also not be forgotten that the HHC enjoys some independent constitutional status over proprietary rights to the harbour waters. Further, the operational rules-in-use are legally interdependent, as well as technically interdependent with the rules-in-use for other goods, such as commercial shipping and waste disposal. Recreational boating thus 'nests' within configurations of rules (that are non-hierarchical in source) both for itself as a public policy and for other public policies manifested in the bay.

Third, the basic logic of the rule configurations of rules-in-use for pleasure boating is to limit competition between boaters for harbour waters and foreshores, and to constrain the competition between pleasure boating and alternative uses. Again the property rights accorded to public and private riparians and to the public waters exemplify this configuration and its consequences.

Finally, it should be noted how the rules-in-use sanction the discretionary expenditure of public funds on boating marinas and facilities. It appears as if the rule configurations make it easier for governmental agencies to spend money to enhance recreational boating in the harbour than it is for them, in concert with others, to promote the change of the configurations of rules-in-use. This is what is to be expected when government works through the delegated discretionary authority of public agencies.

9

Water-Quality Management

This chapter could be titled 'Pollution Control' or 'Waste Management' or 'Environmental Policies' as those activities occur in our micro-laboratory setting of Hamilton Harbour. Unfortunately, each of these terms is ambiguous and subject to rival interpretations. Indeed, the same could be said of the title 'Water-Quality Management.' Let me explain.

The term 'pollution control' can connote that the thrust of this chapter is the monitoring and enforcement of institutional rules, including the criminal law, on known polluters of harbour waters. This chapter has a much broader focus. It attempts to deal, *inter alia*, with the nature of the complex good of water in its quality dimensions, and the problems associated with synchronizing these dimensions to rules.

Similarly, the term 'waste management' might imply, to some readers, that we are concerned solely with the operational rules for the treatment, modification, or total banning of waste materials discharged into harbour waters. Rather, we are concerned with a number of water-quality parameters, their sources and effects, and the ways in which multiple configurations of rules-in-use are effective in modifying these parameters.

Third, the chapter differs from 'environmental policy' studies, as this term is often used. We are not concerned, as such, with the formulation and implementation of rules about the aquatic environment of Hamilton Harbour, and how these may or may not be balanced or integrated with economic policies or health policies. We are concerned with rules-in-use and their consequences on the water-quality dimensions of the harbour. Our various theoretical chapters would imply that environmental policies cannot be considered as tradable, or balanced, or integrated with other public policies in a direct sense. Each policy is a product of a configuration of rules-in-use, and it is through the design of rules that different public policies may be manipulated and coordinated. A prior step is to understand the rules-in-use for each policy.

Finally, the term 'water-quality management' may disappoint some readers. It is true that we deal with issues associated with water and not with other resources and their interrelationships with human and other biological ecosystems. However, we will deal with water-quality management for the harbour as if the system of rules and the aquatic environment were 'open systems.' We acknowledge the multiple linkages between, on the one hand, water-quality parameters in harbour waters and sediments and, on the other hand, their probable causes and effects, which may extend into ecosystems within and beyond harbour boundaries.

Our analysis of water-quality management is, in fact, predicated upon two major scientific principles: the 'materials balance' principle and the 'ecosystemic' principle. (Other scientific principles and findings are dealt with in the body of the chapter.) The 'materials balance' principle states that the weight of resources processed, manufactured, and consumed in society equals the weight of resources returned to the environment, albeit in a transformed physical state (Kneese Ayres, D'Arge 1970). In the light of this principle, all waste materials are simply 'residuals,' some of which may have a 'polluting' effect, especially if they are concentrated in a site that cannot easily store or assimilate them. A simplified illustration of the 'materials balance' principle is presented in figure 8. We would simply expect any urbanized and industrialized watershed to be a site where residual wastes will be a potential problem. In this respect, Hamilton Harbour is no exception. Its exceptionality is solely a matter of geographic conditions on site, historical conditions of residuals disposal on site, and the accumulated legacies and current operations of rules-in-use for water-quality management on site.

The second principle, the 'ecosystemic' principle, states that biological and physical processes are interconnected in terms of their functional relevance for the stability of ecosystems (de Groot 1986, as adapted). In terms of human ecosystems, the other ecosystems found in nature provide four basic functions:

Figure 8. The 'materials balance' principle

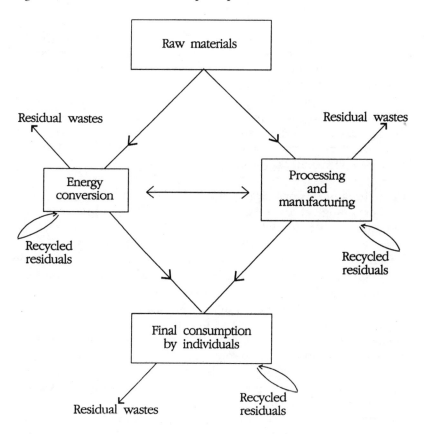

1 / The regulation function: the capacity of natural ecosystems to regulate and maintain ecological processes and life-support systems, such as the continuous recycling of nutrients that takes place in wetlands
2 / The carrier function: the capacity of the natural environment to provide space and a suitable substrate for human activities (i.e., an ecological niche), such as the capacity of a watershed to be used for human settlements, industry, waste disposal, recreation, and other uses
3 / The production function: the capacity of the natural environment to provide raw materials and energy, such as the ways in which water can be drunk, be used in industry, or provide a medium for waste disposal
4 / The inspirational function: the capacity of the natural environment to provide opportunities for cognitive development and recreative experiences over and above normal experiential recurrences, such as many of the experiences sought by pleasure boaters, swimmers, or birdwatchers

In the light of this principle, pollution represents a chemical, physical, or biological 'disturbance' of one or more of these ecosystem functions with potential consequences for human ecosystems. We may indicate these 'disturbances' by examining water-quality parameters in a specified site, like Hamilton Harbour. The causes and consequences of the 'disturbances' are bound up with the limits of scientific knowledge. The rules-in-use for water-quality management represent a strategic intervention into ecosystem functions within the uncertain boundaries of scientific knowledge.

Our examination of the rules-in-use for water-quality management for Hamilton Harbour reveal some superficial similarities with those for commercial shipping and pleasure boating. First, rules are 'stacked,' but what is especially noticeable is that they are stacked asymmetrically in favour of the provincial rather than the federal government at the institutional level. This situation is the converse of our previous cases. Our theory of the basic logic within Canadian parliamentary federalism predicted that asymmetries would be associated with different public policies.

Second, the rules are also 'nested' in configuration, but again in a different way than found previously. This time it is not the independent constitutional status of the Hamilton Harbour Commissioners that is of prime relevance. Rather, the institutional rules articulated in the Great Lakes Water Quality Agreements with the United States are of greater import, implying that the set of constitutional rules for water quality in the harbour embrace those of both the United States and Canada.

Third, the number of institutional and operational rules is wider than those in the previous cases. The configurations of rules-in-use are larger. This feature reflects the technical attributes of the good in question. Given the ecosystem principle (where ecosystemic principles have functions of varying scales), we should expect to find rules governing or at least taking into account events occurring beyond the harbour and its watershed, and events having different implications for the ecosystem functions.

Finally, we find that the rules-in-use do not fully 'mesh' or are not fully synchronized with the nature of the good. This finding reflects in part the scientific uncertainties as to water-quality conditions in the bay and their exact causes and effects. It also reflects in part the limitations of any system of rules as regulations on the conduct of a multitude of socio-economic decisions made daily within an urbanized watershed. But it also reflects something in the basic logic of Canadian parliamentary federalism: the dominance of public agencies within the public economy of water-quality management, and the discretionary exercise of this dominance through delegated authority. To these limited degrees, the configurations of rules-in-use may be evaluated as to their effectiveness and value.

The format of the chapter follows the model of the previous two. We examine the constitutional and institutional rules-in-use for the case. We then examine the current water-quality conditions in the harbour, with reference to their geographical and historical origins. The scope and effectiveness of the operational rules-in-use are then analysed and evaluated. Finally, the conclusion reflects on the importance of the findings for our understanding of rules, rules-in-use, and how government works in Canada.

Constitutional and Institutional Rules-in-Use

The basic logic of the rules-in-use for water-quality management in Hamilton Harbour gives pre-eminence to the institutional and operational rules of the Province of Ontario. While certain rules of the Dominion cannot be ignored, especially those made through its constitutional treaty power with the United States, the constitutional rules-in-use grant asymmetric authority to the provinces in matters related to water-quality management. Before we examine the constitutional rules-in-use, we shall first summarize the common law regarding pollution. Common law formed the basis of rules-in-use prior to the 1960s.

Common Law

Common law provides that riparians, those holding land adjacent to or under a stream, lake, or harbour, have legally enforceable rights to the quality of waters that they use.[1] The basic principle is that 'every riparian proprietor is ... entitled to the water of his stream, in its natural flow, without sensible diminution or increase and without sensible alteration in its character or quality. Any invasion of this right causing actual damage or calculated to fund a claim which may ripen into an adverse right entitles the party injured' (*John Young and Co.* v. *Bankier Distillery Co.* [1893], AC 691 at 698). A riparian may sue for damages or injunctions or both to restrain an offender from polluting the water that passes by his or her land, even if the offender is also a riparian. Although a riparian has the common-law right to drain into a stream, this affords him or her no defence in a civil action – pollution is unlawful no matter who does the polluting, and in itself constitutes a nuisance. As well, the plaintiff need not prove material damage to maintain his or her action: the fact that a riparian right has been violated is sufficient to constitute damages in law.

This is not the case for parties whose lands are not bounded by a polluted watercourse, but who none the less depend on it for some purpose and suffer damage through its continued pollution. The common-law remedies available to such persons are much more limited and much more difficult to invoke. The only common-law action that a non-proprietary user of a waterbody can undertake is a 'public nuisance' action (as compared with a 'private nuisance' action available to a riparian). 'Public nuisance' concerns wrongs against the public at large. Unfortunately, the 'public' that is injured by a polluter currently cannot, in Ontario, as in all other provinces

---

1 There are no common-law property rights vested in water flowing in a defined channel until rendered for use. *Embrey* v. *Owen*, 1951, 6 Ex 353

except Quebec, collectively launch a 'class action' suit; only individuals (or organizations, such as public and private corporations, that have standing as legal persons to sue other parties) are allowed to pursue nuisance actions. In the case of public nuisance, the common law denies any individual the standing to sue unless he or she can show that the damage he or she has suffered is 'special' and 'unique,' that is, different from that which could be expected to be suffered by other members of the public. Otherwise, the action may only be brought under the authority of the provincial attorney general. As mentioned, in Quebec, the provincial government has granted the availability of class actions by statute to overrule these 'judge-made' rules. As of time of writing, the Ontario government plans to introduce a comparable provision as part of an environmental bill of rights.

Partly because of these limitations of the common law of nuisance, and partly because of the evidentiary problem facing individuals wishing to pursue 'private nuisance' actions, the common law has been largely extinguished by statutes at the provincial level. The result is to strengthen the discretionary authority of the provincial Crown.

Constitutional Rules

The authority of the province is established through a variety of heads of legislative power in section 92 of the Constitution Act, 1861. Under section 92, the province has legislative authority over the management and sale of public lands (92[5]), municipal institutions (92[8]), local works and undertakings (92[10]), matters of a merely local nature (92[16]), and especially property and civil rights (92[13]). Proprietary jurisdiction over water resources is allocated to the province under section 109, but in 1947 the province (as well as the federal government and the City of Hamilton) transferred its proprietary jurisdiction by order-in-council to the Hamilton Harbour Commissioners, as was discussed in chapter 7.

Federal jurisdiction for water-quality management in Hamilton Harbour is also legislative in character. Under section 91, the federal government is granted the power to legislate for the 'peace, order and good government of Canada' and in relation to navigation and shipping (91[10]), seacoast and inland fisheries (91[12]), and criminal offences (91[27]). Other relevant constitutional rules include the treaty power (section 132) and the spending power (91.[1A]). Even this partial listing of constitutional rules may overestimate the number of rules-in-use. Neither the navigation nor the fisheries powers may be used to mount broad-scale public controls over the water quality of the harbour, and in any case the federal government delegated to the province its power to legislate over inland fisheries in the 1850s. Criminal offences against environmental degradation are limited to prohibitions of criminal negligence, nuisance, and mischief, and in any case are rarely used because of the necessity to prove *mens rea* for successful convictions (Law Reform Commission of Canada 1988). The 'peace, order and good government' clause may become relevant in water-quality matters since the *Crown Zellerbach* case of 1988 (1 SCR 401), discussed in chapter 4. It remains to be challenged in the case of inland *fresh* waters, although it is used as legal justification for the new Environmental Protection Act, 1988, discussed below. It is safer to conclude, at present, that the federal powers are less than those of the province and rest largely on the navigation power, the spending power (and resulting requirements for environmental-impact assessments – see below), and the treaty power.

Neither the provincial nor the federal legislative powers rest explicitly on a constitutional rule about water quality or pollution. Water quality was not a constitutional decision problem for the Fathers of Confederation. These powers have been inferred from other institutional rules.

Institutional Rules-in-Use

A plethora of institutional rules as statutes characterizes the rule configurations for Hamilton Harbour. A casual reading of all of these provincial and federal rules could imply a 'tightly coupled' regulatory regime, in the sense that the operational rules would take account of all of the uncertainties in establishing, monitoring and enforcing rules about water quality in the bay. A closer reading would suggest, however, that they represent, in part, an attempt to accumulate discretionary power into the hands of provincial and federal agencies. This power is limited in two key respects, however. The nature of the good imposes constraints in terms of scientific knowledge about water-quality conditions, their causes and effects, and how to appropriately construct effective operational rules. Second, regulations established by agencies as third parties to the socio-economic interactions within an urbanized settlement can never be as successfully monitored and enforced as those established by mutual agreement of the parties to an interaction. Some legal persons will probably be indifferent or hostile to the operational rules.

We review the many institutional rules of the provincial and federal governments with the above caveats in mind. Although provincial and federal rules are treated separately below, they do work, in tandem as a rule configuration for public policy. Both levels of government have passed a plethora of statutes affecting water quality, not all of them relevant for Hamilton Harbour (such as the federal Arctic Waters Pollution Prevention Act); the statutory bases for water-quality management in the harbour and its watershed are outlined below.

Provincial Rules

Four major provincial statutes and a number of minor ones have relevance for Hamilton Harbour. First, the Ontario Water Resources Act, 1961 (OWRA) essentially vests all riparian rights to the uses of water in the provincial Crown (Campbell, Scott, and Pearse, 1974). The provincial Crown allows riparians to maintain their legal rights to water uses at the discretion of the relevant minister responsible for the act (currently, the minister of the environment). Newer (since 1961) larger-scale withdrawals of water for other than domestic or farm use require a permit from the minister, and the minister may prosecute and impose penalties for the impairment (pollution) of water. What is important to note about this legislation is the discretion afforded to a minister of the provincial government. Thus approved sewage-treatment plants operated by municipalities are exempted from prosecution for pollution under this act. Only if such municipalities contravened the terms of a licence (issued under a different act – the Environmental Protection Act [EPA], 1971) would then be exposed to legal action, and only then if the contravention occurred because of negligence on their part. Thus, the regional municipalities of Hamilton-Wentworth and Halton, which operate sewage-treatment plants that discharge into Hamilton Harbour and two of its tributaries, are not liable for damages caused to riparians on the bay, as these plants operate under licence from the ministry of environment.[2] Conversely, riparians cannot seek legal redress for pollution of Hamilton Harbour by licensed dischargers, even when the riparians include the Hamilton Harbour Commissioners, which owns the harbour bed.

The Environmental Protection Act, 1971, that is a more important provincial statute for regulating polluting in Hamilton Harbour because it has primacy when in conflict with other provincial acts. Section 14 of the act suggests its broad scope for pollution control:

No person shall deposit, add, emit or discharge or cause or permit the deposit, addition, emission or discharge, into the natural environment of a contaminant that:
  a) has an offensive odor
  b) may endanger the health or safety of any person
  c) may injure or damage or cause injury or damage to
    i) real or personal property
    ii) plant or animal life.

The Ontario Ministry of Environment is empowered under the act to regulate the discharge of wastes into Hamilton Harbour. The ministry implements the act by requiring all point-source waste dischargers that discharge directly into the harbour to seek and receive a certificate of approval or permit. The certificate sets dilution criteria for each type of known residual waste in the effluent of the discharger. The dilution criteria are, in turn, established on the basis of provincial 'Water Quality Objectives,' which are, in fact, standards established by the findings of various scientific tests (includ-

2 *R.* v. *Sault Ste Marie* (1976), 30 CCC (2d) 257, 13 OR (2d) 113, 70 DLR (3d) 430, affirmed (1978) 2 SCR 1299, 3 CR (3d) 30, 4 CCC (2d) 353, 21 NR 295, 7 CELR 53. In this case, the City of Sault Ste Marie was being held liable for the actions of a company it had hired to dispose of garbage, and which had already been convicted of polluting under the provisions of the Ontario Water Resources Act. The Supreme Court held that the City could not be held absolutely responsible because the procedure involved in trying such an offence afforded the City no opportunity to defend itself by proving that it took all reasonable care to avoid the offensive result. The Ontario Water Resources Act extinguished the successful injunction brought against the pollution associated with a new municipal sewage-treatment plant in the Village of Richmond Hill: *Stephens* v. *Richmond Hill* (1956), 4 DLR 572, DR 88 (CA).

ing bioassays) to protect 'aquatic life and recreation in and on the waters' of the province (Ontario Ministry of Environment 1984: 10 – the so-called Blue Book). The 'objectives' are compilations of scientific studies conducted in sites across North America. These rules are further disaggregated by three key institutional 'subrules.' First, the standards are termed 'objectives' because the ministry officially recognizes that they may not be met by all dischargers of different residuals for technological reasons and reasons of scientific uncertainties about 'safe standards.' Second, direct dischargers are granted certificates on a case-by-case basis because the ministry officially recognizes that the assimilative characteristics of the receiving water body may make province-wide standards redundant. Third, the ministry officially recognizes that compliance with the 'objectives' cannot take place instantaneously, so it empowers its officials to grant interim legal approvals as operational rules; these are variously termed 'control orders,' 'requirements and directions,'[3] and 'approvals to proceed.' The third institutional rule meets the procedural requirements of administrative law and absolves the discharger from potential damage suits under common law.

The net effect of these rules established under the statutory authority of the EPA is to transform the regulatory process into a bargaining process between ministry officials and the waste discharger's officials. Thus bargaining can take place over 1 / the residuals to be subject to permit; 2 / the dilution criteria; 3 / the technologies for residual modifications; 4 / the schedules for compliance; and 5 / methods for assessment of compliance with the effluent-dilution criteria. Bargaining is endemic in all pollution-control regulatory regimes (Holden 1966; Sproule-Jones 1981; Dorcey 1985). The institutional rules in the EPA establish the bargaining powers for the ministry of environment. They are extensive and discretionary in application.

Since 1986, the ministry is supplementing these point-source effluent-permit processes with new institutional rules aimed at limiting the discharge of toxic wastes into provincial waters – the so-called Municipal-Industrial Strategy for Abatement (MISA). The object is to minimize the *total* loadings of designated toxic wastes in

3 These particular terms are part of the Ontario Water Resources Act rather than the EPA.

direct discharges, thus replacing dilution standards with effluent limits.[4] The institutional rules envisage the setting of the standards by industrial sectors (with municipal sewage-treatment plants as a sector) rather than on a case-by-case basis. Limits have recently been set (1989) for the iron and steel sector, the sector (other than the municipal sector) of relevance for Hamilton Harbour. The limits are specified in relation to which of two institutional rules is the more stringent in each site, namely, the best available technology that is economically achievable and the estimated impacts of designated 'toxics' on the immediate receiving waters ('mixing zone'). Again, the net impact of these newer institutional rules is to increase the bargaining powers of the ministry in relation to the designated residuals and designated methods of abatement for (identifiable) point-source dischargers.

A third major provincial act is the Public Health Act, 1956. As in many parts of Canada and other countries, concern about pathogenic pollution and associated human diseases preceded the modern environmental movement by many decades (Sproule-Jones 1981: 103–5). It was under the authority of this act that the chief medical officer of the City of Hamilton banned swimming in the harbour in 1930 (Forde n.d.: 3). Many of the pollution provisions of the Public Health Act are now encompassed by the EPA, but it is still under the authority of the Public Health Act that the chief medical officer (now of the Regional Municipality of Hamilton-Wentworth) samples harbour waters in the summer for evidence of pathogenic pollution and 'recommends' that the waters are unfit for swimming. The Hamilton Harbour Commission, under its by-laws, reinforces this 'recommendation' by banning swimming.

The fourth major piece of provincial legislation affecting water-quality management in Hamilton Harbour is the Environmental Assessment Act (EAA). This act requires all public-sector 'undertakings' and major private-sector projects to seek pre-project approval from the minister of the environment. Proponents of such undertakings must file an assessment document explaining the rationale for the

---

4 The limits are set in terms of units of concentration and either mass loadings per day or load per day per unit of production. The last two criteria are, in turn, established statistically in terms of a long-term average performance and maximum variations normally expected to determine a maximum permissible daily value.

project; alternatives to the project and its implementation, estimates of the effects of the project on the environment (defined to include physical, ecological, social, economic, and cultural conditions); actions to prevent, change, mitigate, or remedy the effects; and, finally, an evaluation of the specific alternatives to the project. The act also contains extensive opportunities for public participation – before a ministerial review of the documents; later, in requesting a hearing before an environmental assessment board or tribunal; and, finally, in appeals to the cabinet. At a number of stages in the process, the minister has the legal authority to intervene. He or she can exempt projects from the process, treat smaller projects as a 'class assessment' in which the format is simplified for frequently occurring undertakings such as road widenings, waive the rights to a board hearing, and importantly change the reported content and scope of the documents through the environmental assessment branch of his or her ministry. Thus the act adds pre-project approval mechanisms to the post-project emission controls in the EPA and OWRA (Gibson and Savan 1986; Roman 1983; Lucas 1981). Again what is important to note about these rules is the discretionary authority lodged within the Ontario Ministry of the Environment as to projects subject to the process and enforcement of the process. Only federally sponsored projects are officially excluded from this authority.

In terms of Hamilton Harbour, the EAA has had limited application, reflecting more the stable character of waterfront and water-body uses of the harbour than the discretionary application of the regulations. The application of the act has been limited to a forty-acre site on the western foreshores that the City of Hamilton envisaged as a recreational/park site; at the time of writing, the application is suspended until the City revives a plan for physical restructuring of the site.

There are other provincial statutes of relevance to water-quality management in Hamilton Harbour. Under the terms of the enabling statutes for the regional municipalities of Hamilton-Wentworth and Halton, these local governments own and operate sewers and four sewage-treatment plants. The two largest plants (in Hamilton and Burlington) discharge effluent directly into the bay, and the two smallest (in Dundas and Waterdown) discharge into tributaries in the watershed. The Hamilton-Wentworth region also owns twenty-six storm drains that discharge into the harbour. (These drains are not subject to provincial permit, and their largely unknown effluents are supplemented by sewage overflows in high-rainfall periods; most of the City of Hamilton has combined sewage and storm-water drains.) These two regional governments, the upper tiers of two-tier local government systems in southern Ontario, also are granted by their respective enabling legislation the power to pass by-laws regulating the wastes discharged into their sewer systems. Both governments have established effluent (dilution) standards as the basis of these by-laws. As in the case of direct provincial regulations on direct dischargers, the by-laws establish the bargaining powers of the regional engineering departments over 'hook-ups' to municipal sewers. Enforcement of the by-laws is discretionary. Only when the treatment plants do not operate according to predictable standards is there an attempt to locate the source of possible non-compliance. The by-laws follow a 'model' by-law suggested by the ministry of environment. The new MISA program will require changes in the by-laws and in these enforcement rules. Both regions also own eight landfill sites in the watershed, one of which (Burlington) is still used for solid-waste disposal, and four of which have their leachate collected and treated at sewage-disposal plants.

The Conservation Authorities Act, 1970, is of some relevance for water quality in the harbour, especially in terms of its potential for controlling water quantity (and hence the assimilative characteristics of the bay) as well as some of the soil erosion in the watershed. Under this act, the Hamilton and Region Conservation Authority (with membership appointed from municipalities in the watershed) has the authority to conserve, restore, develop, and manage the harbour watershed. The courts have declared, however, that its powers under section 27(1)(ii) to regulate or prohibit the dumping of fill in any water-body in its jurisdiction does not extend to the activities of the Hamilton Harbour Commissioners or to the activities of the Canadian National Railway (a riparian on the bay). In these cases, it was held that the (federal) Navigable Waters Protection Act and the (federal) Railway Act were, respectively, paramount over the Conservation Authorities Act.[5]

Finally, a number of provincial statutes can affect the nature and type of non–point source pollution in the bay. The one that is of most direct relevance is the previously mentioned Environmental Protection Act (Part IX, ss. 79–112), which imposed unlimited and

5 R. v. *Hamilton Harbour Commissioners*; R. v. *CNR* (1975), 4 CELN 78 (Ont.)

retroactive absolute liability (i.e., where *mens rea* and due diligence are not defences) on pollutant spills of a sudden and accidental nature (the so-called Spills Bill amendment of 1985).[6] Other land-use controls are generally the responsibility of municipalities under the Municipal Act and the Planning Act. (Flood plains are the responsibility of the conservation authorities). All lower-tier municipalities in the watershed have zoning and other land-use regulations in their by-laws, and are required by the province to see that changes in these regulations conform with official plans. These by-laws have not been framed to take account of non–point source pollution, however. Indeed, by-laws passed by the City of Hamilton to regulate foreshore uses have been deemed by the courts to be *ultra vires* provincial authority when they conflict with the use of the foreshores for shipping and navigation (see chapter 7). Thus the use and development of the foreshores of Hamilton Harbour are subject to the by-laws of the Hamilton Harbour Commissioners for purposes related to navigation and shipping, and only when they are not do the planning by-laws of Hamilton and Burlington apply to waterfront property. These same general principles were applied by the courts to limit the authority of the Hamilton and Region Conservation Authority to regulate infilling of the harbour (see chapter 8). In sum, land-use regulations in the watershed are not designed for environmental purposes in general or for harbour water quality in particular. They may have inadvertent relationships with the Harbour and thus may be classified as rules-in-use. But the regulatory regime essentially ignores most non–point source pollution.

Federal Rules

The federal government has passed a number of statutes that deal with environmental pollution, but many of these are of limited relevance for Hamilton Harbour. The key federal statute for water-pollution control in Canada is the Fisheries Act, 1868, amended most recently in 1970 and 1977. Section 33(2) is, the key clause for pol-

---

6 In 1981 the Ontario government established the Ontario Waste Management Corporation to dispose of toxic and other containable wastes. The formulation of rules is still to be established, monitored, and enforced, because of an inability to find an acceptable site on the lands in Ontario. Currently, toxic wastes are trucked to New York State or stored or illegally dumped.

lution abatement as it prohibits the deposit of any deleterious substance into water frequented by fish or in any place where the substance could enter such waters.[7] Under a century-old interdelegation of powers (confirmed in 1984), the Ontario government (the ministry of natural resources) manages fisheries in the Great Lakes. Thus the major rule for federal water-quality management reinforces the extensive provincial authority, and federal water-quality guidelines, which are effluent standards established by industrial sector, are rules-in-form rather than rules-in-use. The province has never seen fit to use the Fisheries Act in Hamilton Harbour, as is witnessed by the destruction of the commercial fisheries and their habitats in the bay.

In 1988, the federal government passed a new Environmental Protection Act. This act consolidates a number of previous federal statutes, including the Environmental Contaminants Act, the Clean Air Act, the Ocean Dumping Control Act, and parts of the Canada Water Act and Department of Environment Act. The main impact of the new act is likely to centre on rules for the release, sale, import, and export of 'toxic substances' and rules that new chemicals must be proved 'safe' before being introduced to the market-place. Experience under the Environmental Contaminants Act suggests that this new act will be used to prevent the release of specified chemicals (such as PCBS). The act also contains provisions granting members of the public the right to sue for the sake of environmental matters in conjunction with personal health. This may change the definition of legal standing depending on whether the courts grant paramountcy to federal regulations under the *Crown Zellerbach* doctrine.

Other relevant federal statutes affecting the institutional rules-in-use for Hamilton Harbour are limited. The Canada Water Act, 1970, is designed to permit the federal government to enter into agreements with the provinces to conduct research or to establish 'water-quality management' areas. To date, no such agreements have been signed with the Government of Ontario. However, it should be noted that under this act, rather than the Fisheries Act, regulations limiting the flow of nutrients (especially phosphorous) into fresh waters have been passed.

---

7 *R.* v. *Northwest Falling Contractors Ltd.*, 1980, 32 NR, 541, 53 CCC (2d) 353, 113 DLR (3d) 1

Three federal statutes affecting shipping and navigation in Hamilton Harbour have relevance for its water quality. First, commercial shipping in the harbour is regulated by the Hamilton Harbour Commissioners. Under the terms of its enabling act, the HHC has passed by-laws to implement provisions of the Canada Shipping Act and the Navigable Waters Protection Act. The former act permits the HHC to regulate all vessel pollution in the bay, and the latter requires the HHC to approve any 'work' (such as landfills, excavations, or physical structures) that may be planned for the harbour. The major pollution concern of the Canada Shipping Act is with oil pollution from commercial ships. The main concern of the Navigable Waters Protection Act is gravel, cinders, ashes, soils, and so on, rather than chemical substances, and the infilling of some 20 per cent of the waters of the bay between the First World War and 1972 suggests that water-quality management has not historically been of concern to the HHC. As we have already noted, the powers of the HHC in these regards supersede the powers of the Hamilton and Region Conservation Authority. The powers of the HHC also supersede the powers of the cities of Hamilton and Burlington to regulate foreshore lands and their uses and, hence, certain forms of non–point source pollution. However, it should be noted that pollution, primarily from the sewage-treatment plants of Hamilton and Burlington have altered the chemical composition of the dredgeate owned and sold by the HHC for landfill. No rules exist to maintain the commercial value of this dredgeate because of concerns about any leachate on watercourses.

The federal government Environmental Assessment Review Process (EARP) for evaluating the likely impacts of projects prior to their initiation does not rest at present on any statutory grounds. It stems directly from the constitutional spending powers of the federal government on any object of public policy concern. It also has fewer procedural requirements than the Ontario process, and proprietary Crown corporations (such as Canadian National Railways, which has exclusive waterfront property on the harbour) and federal regulatory agencies, as opposed to federal departments of government, are invited rather than required to participate. Essentially, the proponent or sponsoring federal department determines whether any potential adverse effects of a project are 'significant,' and if it so decides, a formal review process is triggered (Fenge and Smith 1986). The formal process, in turn, consists of public servants delegated from federal departments within each region of the country (Ontario is a region for these purposes) who will sponsor studies and solicit public comment in a variety of ways, following guidelines issued by the federal Environment Assessment Review office. This last body is a division of Environmental Canada. The guidelines themselves are procedural requirements that cannot, since court cases in 1988 and 1989, be waived on pain of legal injunction. At present, the federal government plans to make the guidelines a statutory requirement. Final decisions on substance and as to proceeding with a project are left to the minister of the environment and the minister of the proponent department. It is under this EARP that the so-called clean-up of Windermere Basin at the eastern end of the harbour is proceeding. In this case, the Harbour Commissioners voluntarily submitted its plans for dredging and dyking a highly silted and contaminated portion of the harbour to the EARP. It is the only project affecting harbour waters to be submitted to the federal process.

Perhaps the most important federal authority for water-quality management in Hamilton Harbour is the Boundary Waters Treaty, 1909. This treaty provided for the establishment of the International Joint Commission (IJC) with the United States. The IJC is charged under a series of Water Quality Agreements (1972, 1978, 1987) with the overseeing and review of water-quality objectives for the Great Lakes. The IJC can only make recommendations to the two national governments. However, its recommendations provide an institutional opportunity for the federal government to negotiate 'appropriate' regulatory rules for water-quality management on the Great Lakes with the Ontario government.

The IJC acts on recommendations provided by a Great Lakes Water Quality Board and the Great Lakes Science Advisory Board. These bodies have established 'objectives' or hypothesized standards for the presence of a number of water-quality parameters for the Great Lakes. The thrust of the earlier recommendations was to publicize the need for phosphorous load reductions in the light of eutrophication in Lake Erie, especially (Dworsky 1986). Later recommendations have expanded the scope of the 'objectives' to include a larger number of hazardous pollutants and the range of abatement procedures consistent with an 'ecosystem' approach.

In terms of Hamilton Harbour, the major impact of the IJC has come in the form of its identification as one of forty-three 'areas of concern' on the Great Lakes (seventeen are located in Ontario). These 'areas of concern' are bays, harbours, and rivers where major pollutants consistently exceed the IJC objectives. In 1986, the federal and Ontario governments signed a Canada-Ontario agreement (COA) to develop a Remedial Action Plan (RAP) for these areas, including Hamilton. The planning process is a microcosm of the discretionary exercise of delegated authority by, in this case, both levels of government acting in concert. A COA review board made up of provincial and federal public servants makes recommendations to the IJC Water Quality Board on the basis of plans submitted by the Hamilton Harbour Remedial Action Plan 'writing team' and coordinated by a RAP steering committee for the seventeen Ontario areas. Both of the latter two committees are composed exclusively of federal and provincial public servants. After the IJC Water Quality Board reviews the plans, the COA Review Board submits the plans to the Ontario and federal ministers of the environment, to the relevant U.S. department, and then to the IJC itself. As of the time of writing, Stage One of the plans for the harbour – 'Goals, Problems and Prospects' – has passed the approval process. Stage Two has entered the approval process.

The RAP planning process for Hamilton Harbour is an oddity compared with the process for other 'areas of concern.' The writing team allowed forty-nine representatives from interest groups, the general public, organizations using the harbour, and local governments (called 'stakeholders') to set the 'use goals' for the harbour rather than to act as advisers to government on such goals (Sproule-Jones 1990).[8] For three years, attempts by the stakeholders to have a continuous open monitoring of the implementation of the plans, by both stakeholders and the general public, were consistently vetoed or delayed by one or more Ontario officials. An auditing body of stakeholders, the Bay Area Restoration Council, is now incorporated because of private-sector lobbying. However, the province managed to delay for three years the function of a Bay Area implementation team of agency heads responsible for carrying out the fifty recommendations listed in the Stage Two report. The reasons appeared to be associated with central department–field branch conflicts over the allocation of funds, rather than the global budget

---

8 The stakeholders did act as advisers in terms of the specification of necessary scientific data to be collected and analysed, and in terms of priorities among the remediation measures.

approved for RAP. This kind of capricious behaviour can be expected by the large discretionary delegated statutory authority of the Ontario government. The initial strategy or 'error' of sharing decision-making powers with 'stakeholders' may be attributed to a lack of experience with the RAP processes.[9] Hamilton was the first 'area of concern' made subject to the process. Consequently, the process has involved a drawn-out contest over the institutional rules for water-quality management for the harbour.

Finally, it should be noted that the federal government has established few rules regarding non–point source pollution of the harbour. The federal government possesses no constitutional authority to affect land uses and their regulation. The most important federal statute is the Transportation of Dangerous Goods Act, 1980, which regulates the transport of most products across provincial and international boundaries by road, rail, or airline. Atmospheric transportation of residuals is potentially subject to the Environmental Protection Act, but no federal rules regarding the depositions into or out of the harbour watershed have been formulated. Point-source air-emission rules rather than non–point source air-transportation rules are a feature of Ontario's regulation under its Environmental Protection Act.

Institutional-Rule Configurations

We have reviewed the plethora of institutional rules of both levels of government as they are in use for Hamilton Harbour. That they represent a richer network of rules than was found for our two previous case-studies reflects the multiple attributes or dimensions of water quality and its ecosystemic linkages. The institutional rules are, however, asymmetrically 'tilted' towards provincial dominance. Before we examine the operational rule effects of this configuration, we must first review the current state of knowledge about harbour water quality and its causes and effects.

---

9 The RAP writing team hired a consultant to identify and organize the stakeholders and to involve the general public (2,500 persons were involved through the dissemination of information and the holding of four public meetings). The contract of the consultant was subsequently allowed to lapse. Federal officials were, not surprisingly, active proponents of the open deconcentrated process.

The State of Harbour Water Quality

Harbour water quality may be described in terms of five sets of parameters measurable in the water column and, on occasion, in the sediments (Sproule-Jones 1981): dissolved-oxygen levels; suspended solids; pathogens; nutrients; and heavy metals and toxic chemicals. Each of the five is described, as is its effects in terms of its correspondence with the man-made standards of quality embodied in the Ontario Ministry of Environment 'objectives' and in terms of its linkages with biological species. Evidence as to the contributing sources or causes of their exceeding standards will be described. The causes, effects, and variations in the presence of any set of parameters are subject to much scientific uncertainty, and any discussion of water quality in any site will thus remain incomplete and potentially subject to newer scientific evidence and newer methods of investigation.[10]

Dissolved-Oxygen (DO) Levels

Dissolved-oxygen levels in Hamilton Harbour vary by site, season, and levels in the water column. A large body of open water like Lake Ontario will have DO levels at saturation, with continuous re-aeration from the atmosphere into the upper level (the epilimnion) sufficient to take account of temporary demands on the oxygen from, say, the decay of plankton. Harbour waters, however, are rarely at saturation, especially in the lower level (the hypolimnion), because the 'natural' re-aeration from the atmosphere and the inflow of oxygenated waters from tributaries and Lake Ontario are all insufficient to take account of biochemical oxygen demands (BOD) and chemical oxygen demands (COD) placed on DO levels. These processes are exacerbated by seasonal climate variations, which lead to thermal

---

10 The data in this section are based on a number of sources. Of particular value is the RAP writing team report, *Goals, Problems and Options for Hamilton Harbour* (1987); their 1989 update, *Environmental Conditions and Problem Definition*; and the Ontario Ministry of Environment report (1985), all of which summarize site-specific research conducted on the harbour since 1972. These data are supplemented by studies conducted under contract for or directly by the Ontario Ministry of Environment, by studies published in scientific journals, and by independent evidence gathered from waste dischargers.

stratification of water levels in summer months, preventing the more-saturated epilimnion from mixing with the less-saturated hypolimnion; a temperature barrier called the thermocline at a depth of 6–7 metres limits the natural circulation of waters from June through September. The particular location of outfalls affects BOD and COD loadings by site, and the particular location and composition of sediments also affects COD loadings by site (and water sampling area). Thus residuals disposal, the physical characteristics of the harbour, and the 'natural' assimilative characteristics of the environment interact to affect DO levels. Figure 9 depicts these major characteristics, and the seasonal variations in water circulation.

Dissolved-oxygen levels are measured in milligrams per litre of water, and the provincial 'objectives' cite 6 mg/L of DO as the minimum amount necessary for the support of aquatic biota when the water temperature is between 10° and 15° Celsius. These 'objectives' are exceeded for most of the harbour waters during summer months, when the average values are 0.5 mg/L (10 per cent saturation) in the hypolimnion and 7.0 mg/L (80 per cent saturation) in the epilimnion. As a result, cold water biota are mostly absent from harbour waters, excepting the occasional migrating fish during spring and fall. As late as 1979, certain sites in the harbour displayed complete anoxia in the hypolimnion, regardless of season. However, *all* sites sampled in 1988 recorded saturation levels sufficient to support oligochaete worms, one of the simplest forms of benthic invertebrates at the bottom of the aquatic chain (DO levels of 1 mg/L are satisfactory for most benthic invertebrate populations). Higher up the food-chain, some 59 warm-water fish species survive in harbour waters, especially on the northern and western waters. Indeed, the numbers of carp are destructive of wildfowl habitat and have and are being deliberately reduced. Somewhat paradoxically, the low DO levels limit the 'polluting' effects associated with the decay of particulate phosphorous, one of the major nutrients in the harbour (see below). They also appear to limit the chemical conversion of some toxic substances found in the sediments and attached to suspended solids. In sum, the DO levels inhibit the regulation and production functions of the natural ecosystems.

The BOD and COD on the harbour waters come from a variety of sources. Nitrification of ammonia accounts for 40 per cent of total water-column oxygen demand, and 85 per cent of ammonia loadings are associated with the two municipal waste-treatment plants

Figure 9. Water circulation in Hamilton Harbour: Seasonal and water-column-level variations
Source: Adapted from Ministry of Environment (1979: 25, with additional information)

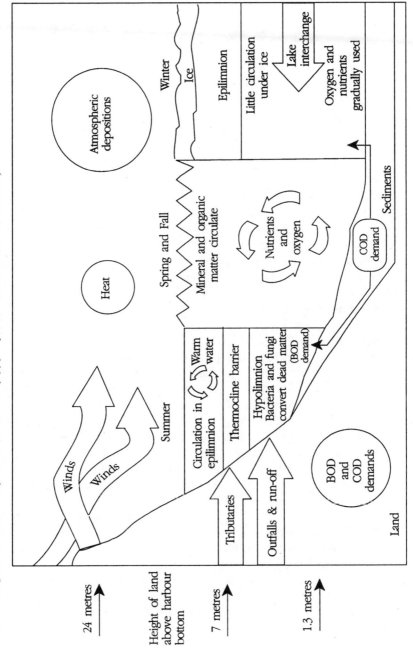

(measured in kilograms per day from point sources). The sediments also produce nitrogen gas associated with ammonia, and these account for 7–14 per cent of hypolimnion oxygen demand.

The second major source of oxygen demand is plankton decay (40 per cent of total water-column demand), which again is partly associated with nutrient discharges (discussed below). Total phosphorous loadings as a major nutrient are primarily associated with the municipal waste-treatment plants. Twenty-five per cent of the oxygen demand is attributable to the decay of particulate phosphorous and organic matter. Most of the remaining oxygen demand is currently attributable to the oxidation of methane gas produced in the harbour sediments. Considerable scientific uncertainties remain about the potential oxygen demands from the sediments in terms of the oxidation of some trace metals, the conversion of some persistent organic compounds, and the bacterial metabolism of non-persistent organics. There is, in other words, no one-to-one relationship between point-source controls on, say, the municipal waste-treatment plants and DO levels in the harbour.

Suspended Solids (SS)

Suspended solids are 'conventional' contaminants of water systems in the sense that their presence is discernible to the human eye in terms of water clarity, scum, and debris. Their association with and physical attachment to other pollutants like pathogens and trace metals are of most scientific concern, because of their linkages with the regulation and production functions of natural ecosystems. However, they are directly linked with the inspirational function of ecosystems and thus of immediate concern to human populations.

Suspended solids are measured in kilograms per day, and there are no provincial 'objectives' regulating suspended-solids loadings in effluent. There are 'objectives' for swimmable waters, such that they should be devoid of substances producing 'an objectionable deposit, color, odor, taste or turbidity' (section 41) and water clarity should have a Secchi-disk transparency of at least 1.2 metres. Water-clarity levels also affect light transparency and, consequently, the distribution, abundance, and diversity of submerged aquatic plants necessary as fish habitat. However, water clarity is also affected by phytoplankton and dissolved organic substances, so there is no one-to-one relationship between ss loadings and Secchi-disk transparency measures.

The harbour is generally free of floating debris. The occasional accidental oil spill (seven reported incidents between 1974 and 1986) is small in size, containable, and 60–90 per cent removable within forty-eight hours by the coordinated responses of the Port of Hamilton Spill Control Group.[11] Water clarity averages 1.4 metres by Secchi-disk transparency, with lower readings closer to shore. At best only 30 per cent of this clarity appears to be associated with algal biomass; the remainder is the result of suspended-solids inputs to the harbour and to resuspended sediments caused by wave actions. Inputs from the treatment plants and the steel mills reduced ss loadings by two-thirds between 1977 and 1987, and now 63 per cent of the inputs comes from soil erosion flushed through the tributaries to the harbour. No information is currently available on the chemical and biological composition of eroded soil.

Pathogens

Pathogens are a set of bacteria and viruses that cause infectious diseases in human beings through direct contact. Many of these are water-borne, and they are considered a 'conventional' pollutant because of their association with human and animal sewage released into lakes, rivers, harbours, estuaries, and marine environments. A rough approximation of the presence of these pathogens is given by measuring the concentrations of the coliform bacterium, which are easily collectible and stable enough for simple analysis. The provincial 'objectives' suggest that a fecal-coliform count in excess of 100/100 mL and a total coliform count in excess of 1000/100 mL requires the disinfection of water for consumption and contact-recreational purposes. It is simpler to ban these uses for most water bodies, including Hamilton harbour. More generally, most aquatic environments rely on a 'natural die-off' of bacteria and viruses as a method of control.

11 This voluntary cooperative team is made up of commissioners and representatives of the Coast Guard and local industry. Additional small spills occur, as evidenced by the slicks on the water. These are generally less than one molecule thick.

Coliform counts vary from site to site in the harbour, with higher counts exhibited in the south and east than in the north and west. In the last decade, the geometric-mean fecal-coliform counts have been below provincial 'objectives' in samples taken in the west and centre of the harbour, but have exceeded the 'objectives' at other sampling sites. New near-shore sampling sites recorded summer counts that exceed the 'objectives' on rainy days. Total coliform counts have not been taken since 1975, largely because the testing procedures are less accurate than for fecal-coliform counts.

The sources of pathogenic pollution are many, and no data exist on the relative contributions from different sources. The higher fecal-coliform counts recorded during rainy summer days suggest that the overflows from the combined sewage and storm-water system that exists in Hamilton are a major contributor, as are the by-passes engineered into all sewage-treatment plants. On days of average rainfall, all sewage is disinfected with chlorine,[12] although storm water itself often carries relatively high coliform counts from materials deposited on urban road surfaces.

The relationships between pathogens and the regulation and production functions of nature ecosystems are, at best, dimly understood. Some bacteria and viruses have a direct and sublethal effect for most humans. Other bacteria are essential for the assimilation of certain waste residuals. In the case of the harbour, the nitrification of ammonia and the reduction of dissolved organic carbon rely, for example, on the mediation of different groups of bacteria. Such scientific uncertainties are exemplified for all harbours and water bodies, not just Hamilton Harbour.

Nutrients

Nutrients are an essential component of ecological processes and life-support systems, and they hence facilitate the performance of the regulation function of natural ecosystems. Wetlands, including those to be found around lakes, harbours, and estuaries, are im-

---

12 Data collected before and after the chlorination of sewage at the two municipal treatment plants indicate that mean coliform concentrations were reduced tenfold between 1961 and 1979. However, samples recently taken in the vicinity of the treatment diffusers still indicate that provincial 'objectives' are being greatly exceeded.

portant sites in which aquatic plants (including algae) use nutrients that make their way through the food-chain to end up as protein in fish and waterfowl. All wetlands ultimately become eutrophic; the aquatic plants use nutrients in the water and in the atmosphere to grow, expand, and decay, with the aid of dissolved oxygen. But the levels of dissolved oxygen are insufficient to sustain these processes through time. Residual wastes that contain nutrients can accelerate these natural processes and, by accelerating the use of dissolved oxygen, create additional difficulties for natural ecosystems, at least in a site-specific sense. Nutrients can thus become pollutants, but the 'fine-tuning' of waste residual nutrients to the natural eutrophication of water bodies is beyond current scientific and engineering capabilities. The traditional 'solution' is to reduce nutrient loadings by point-source waste dischargers as much as is technically and economically feasible.

A traditional indicator of overly rich nutrient conditions in fresh waters is that of chlorophyll *a* concentration, a measure of algae abundance. Values for Hamilton Harbour (which average 13.5 micrograms per litre [μg/L] for all sites, depths, and seasons) are similar for other fresh water bodies when controlling for phosphorous loadings (a key nutrient) and basin retention times. Higher values are recorded in summer months because of improved springtime water circulation and the greater availability of DO in the photic zone.

Measures of phosphorous and ammonia concentrations are two further indicators of possible nutrient 'pollution.' The seasonal average total phosphorous concentration in the harbour is currently 64 μg/L. There are no provincial 'objectives' for phosphorous; instead, site-specific guidelines are suggested, and total phosphorous concentrations exceed the guidelines of 20 μg/L in all seasons. Similarly, ammonia concentrations, which are both directly taken up by algae and also converted by bacteria into nitrate for uptake, exceed the provincial 'objectives' of 20 μg/L (as nitrogen) in most months. Values vary between 300 μg/L and 2,000 μg/L, depending on water temperatures and DO levels.

These data suggest that other water-quality parameters in the harbour limit the nutrient effects of ammonia and phosphorous. DO levels and water-clarity levels inhibit the biological processes of eutrophication, as we have noted. Further, some of the phosphorous loadings are associated with suspended sediments from creeks and point-source outfalls, and these add to the stock of phosphorous in the harbour sediments; there is little or no phosphorous release in anoxic and low-saturated oxygen sediments. Third, elevated concentrations of iron in the hypolimnion and sediments convert some of the phosphorous stock into ferrous phosphate, a non-nutrient. In short, other water-quality parameters (or pollutants) slow down the eutrophication process for Hamilton Harbour.

The point-source loadings of phosphorous and ammonia have been radically reduced since their peaks in the late 1960s. Municipal treatment plants are associated with 85 per cent of the total loadings (measured in kilograms per day) of ammonia and 64 per cent of the total loadings of phosphorous. Controls on the direct dischargers from the steel-milling processes account for a fourfold reduction in ammonia loadings and a fortyfold reduction in phosphorous loadings. In the latter case, some of the loadings are diverted to the Hamilton treatment plant to facilitate the chemical treatment of phosphorous with iron (ferric chloride). More generally, the nutrient-enriched waters of Hamilton Harbour are being modified without direct, but with *potentially* indirect effects, on its natural eutrophication.

Heavy Metals and Toxic Compounds

This category of water-quality parameter encompasses a range of less-traditional waste residuals that are coming gradually to dominate scientific enquiries and regulatory rules. While the progress of environmental sciences is rapid, it often raises as many uncertainties as it forecloses over time. Thus the identification of persistent organic chemicals, such as polyaromatic hydrocarbons (PAHS) in harbour sediments may lead to concerns about their sublethal effects in benthos and their possible biomagnification through the food-chain. Yet the linkages in such processes are poorly understood and also difficult to infer from bioassay experiments. There is some pressing concern to discover these and other linkages to prevent the collapse of all four ecosystem functions, not only in one Great Lakes site but also through its possible interconnectedness with other situational, regional, and global ecosystems. Collapse in this context refers to the lethalities, diminished capacities, reproductive interferences, or mutagenic offsprings of biological organisms.

The International Joint Commission identifies 1,065 hazardous and potentially hazardous substances in the waters in the Great Lakes Basin, but a recent review of the Great Lakes Water Quality Agreement notes that 'the present state of knowledge of the toxicity and exposure of humans and other organisms to chemicals is not adequate to develop hazard and risk assessments for the majority of chemicals found in the Great Lakes Basin' (National Research Council of the United States and the Royal Society of Canada [1985: 70, 72]). Data that identify the presence of heavy metals and toxic compounds in Hamilton Harbour are both partial and of recent origin. Sampling of nine trace metals in the water column around the discharges from the steel mills have been conducted since 1977. Except for iron, these samples now rarely exceed provincial 'objectives' in their liquid concentrations (normally measured in micrograms per litre). Even for iron, only 9 per cent of the samples exceed provincial 'objectives.' Samplings from around the municipal treatment-plant diffusers also meet provincial 'objectives' for these particular contaminants. Sampling of harbour waters for the identification of any persistent organics is also partial and recent (with the exception of phenols, which meet provincial 'objectives'). These compounds, such as PCBS, PAHS, and organochlorine pesticides, are believed to be critical as a catalyst for the presence of mutagens and carcinogens in higher biota.[13] Recent sampling for biphenols and hydrocarbons finds that the one PCB that has an 'objective' (in this case, an 'objective' recommended by the Canadian Council of Environmental Ministers, an interprovincial agency; no Ontario 'objectives' exist) exceeded it in between 14 and 100 per cent of the samples. Total PAH concentrations are also detectable in the water column (especially around point-source outfalls), but no 'safe objectives' are available for evaluation. Commonly found pesticides, such as DDT and Mirex, are not detectable in the water column.

Trace contaminants are more easily tracked through sediment analysis, as persistent organics remain largely in a dissolved state in the water column. Eleven heavy metals are currently analysed in the surficial sediments, and all but one greatly exceed the only 'objectives' available, namely, the provincial 'guidelines for the open-water disposal' of dredge spoils.[14] Measurement is by concentration ratios of micrograms or milligrams per litre. Scientific evidence

---

13 PCBS are polychlorinated biphenols and PAHS are polynuclear aromatic hydrocarbons.
14 The metal below 'guidelines' is cobalt. The ones that exceed 'guidelines' are iron, copper, chromium, nickel, zinc, lead, cadmium, mercury, and arsenic. No guideline exists for manganese deposits.

suggests that oxidation of most of these metals is critical prior to their possible bioavailability; they become benign compounds, as it were.

Many persistent organics are detectable in the harbour sediments. The mean concentration of PCBS is comparable to that in other Lake Ontario harbours, but many samples contain concentrations well above the dredge 'disposal guidelines.' Thirteen PAH compounds are detectable, and in concentrations some twenty times greater in samples distributed near the steel mills. Pesticide levels tend to be low, and DDT concentrations are less than those in other Lake Ontario harbours.

These contaminants are always toxic in elevated concentrations in bioassay laboratory experiments. Their effects in aquatic environments are dimly understood because of the multivariate and synergistic nature of both the aquatic environment and the biochemistry of different biota. Three broad conclusions suggest themselves on the basis of current evidence about the effects of trace contaminants on biota within the harbour.

First, the multiplicity and diversity of benthos in the harbour largely reflect the eutrophic water-quality conditions, although trace contaminants contribute significant oxygen demands to these conditions. Similarly, the relationship between the toxicity of these contaminants and benthic organisms is masked by the adverse effects of low DO levels among other possible variables.

Second, the harbour supports a diverse fishery (fifty-nine species), but community structure is largely confined to smaller, short-lived species (warm-water fish). Analyses of fish tissues indicate the presence of mercury, PCBS and Mirex, in sufficient concentrations in six of twelve sport-fish species that the province's *Guide to Eating Ontario Sport Fish* advises limited annual consumption. However, tissue studies of PCB and pesticide concentrations also suggest that the levels are comparable with those of other Lake Ontario sites. Similarly, the prevalence of fish tumours, while alarmingly high, is comparable with that of most Lake Ontario sites.[15]

Third, the harbour supports a diverse and abundant waterbird population, and most of the shoreline provides nesting and stopover

15 The data vary by year, species, and tumour type. Tumour frequencies range from 3 per cent for liver neoplasms in white suckers to 52 per cent for gonadal tumours in carp and carp hybrids.

sites for large numbers of different species. Some trace contaminants are detectable in herring-gull eggs and in the tissue of flightless domestic ducks, but as nearly all species can feed some miles from their colony sites it is impossible to assess the precise contributions of harbour contaminants.

In sum, the cause-and-effect relationship between trace contaminants and harbour biota are yet to be established. Most evidence suggests that the harbour contributes to the potentially hazardous degradation of ecosystem functions that extend beyond the boundaries of the harbour and its watershed.[16]

Operational Rules-in-Use

The Scope of Operational-Rule Configurations

Our review of the state of the harbour water quality reveals that the liquid inputs into the harbour are partly diluted and partly treated or untreated and that the flows out of the harbour may be characterized in the same way. This 'real world' situation occurs despite, or (better phrased) within, the context of the plethora of rules established by statute by the provincial and federal governments and reviewed above. It points to the fact that the operational rules-in-use include those that facilitate the engaging of individuals, private-sector organizations, and public-sector organizations in myriad socio-economic transactions, and the disposal of their inevitable waste residuals in ways they eparately and/or jointly see fit. In other words, the rules regarding household, commercial, industrial, and agricultural activities in the watershed (in particular) are the dominant operational configurations of rules-in-use.

The regulatory regime that we previously reviewed is, in the light of these comments, a set of marginal rules-in-use that affect but do not determine the decision situations facing at least the half a million watershed residents. And among these marginal rules-in-use, the key operational rule is the point-source-effluent certification

16 The harbour waters are flushed through the ship canal to Lake Ontario and are diluted nine times, on the average, some 1,250 metres from the canal. There is no direct evidence that nearshore pollutant parameters in western Lake Ontario are affected by harbour wastes and sediments compared with ecological sources. The biotic webs are thus probably the major linkage between the harbour and the wide ecosystem.

process, involving primarily the Ontario Ministry of Environment officials and the managers of the industrial and municipal waste-treatment plants and outfalls. The remaining rules-in-use are of lesser and even more marginal operational significance. The rules-in-use that have the potential for increasing their marginal effects are those embodied in the new Canada Environmental Protection Act through which controls of trace contaminants may be made 'at source'; it was under the predecessors of this act that such compounds as DDT were banned.

The current limits of the regulatory rules-in-use are illustrated in figure 10. In general terms, this figure shows that discharges from point sources are partially regulated in terms of the five types of pollutants. In contrast, most pollutants are unregulated if they flow into the harbour from non–point sources or if they simply exist already in the waters or sediments of the harbour (*in situ*). How well does this configuration of operational rules work? Why is the configuration apparently so limited in use? In the next section, we address these kinds of questions.

Some care should be taken in interpretation of figure 10. It retains the fivefold categorization of water-quality parameters described earlier in this chapter, which is, at best, a simplification of the nature of the good because of the multivariate and synergistic nature of the aquatic environment. It also categorizes the pollutant inputs by three broad kinds of sources, namely, point, non-point, and *in-situ* sources. In other words, figure 10 should *not* be examined in terms of an evaluation of the operational rules, but rather in terms of the scope of the regulatory regime of operational rules.

Evaluation in General

The scope of the regulatory rules discussed above demand a different kind of methodology for evaluation and appraisal. Traditional methodologies for evaluating water-quality management appear inappropriate. They fall into three categories:[17]

1 / Measurement of Rule Compliance: In this category are studies that evaluate performance in terms of the number of outfalls

17 The studies referred to in the next three subparagraphs are reviewed and criticized in Sproule-Jones (1981: 81–9).

Figure 10. The scope of regulatory rules

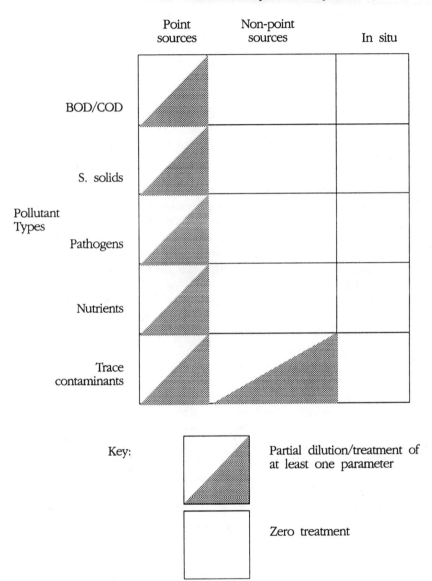

Source of pollution inputs

	Point sources	Non-point sources	In situ
BOD/COD			
S. solids			
Pathogens			
Nutrients			
Trace contaminants			

Pollutant Types

Key:

Partial dilution/treatment of at least one parameter

Zero treatment

under certification or the number of violations of certification rules.

2 / Measurement of Pollution-Control Expenditures: In this category are studies calculating the absolute levels of capital and operating expenditures of treatment plants plus (occasionally) the administrative expenses associated with regulation. Sometimes studies are based on the relative expenditures on pollution control defrayed by different governments. Also, sometimes studies attempt to calculate the remediation costs for particular water-quality parameters (such as DO levels) in order to make a benefit-cost analysis of improving water-quality conditions for particular uses (like a fishery).

3 / Measurement of the Value of Ambient and Effluent Improvements: In this category are studies that calculate the value of improvements in one or more uses from enhanced water-quality conditions. These may be measured by physical indicators, such as fish abundances, or by financial indicators, such as increases in the economic value of increased fishing efforts or in the total travel costs of fishermen to the site in question. 'Contingent valuation' studies fall into this category. These are studies that attempt to measure the attitudes of citizens about their perceived benefits of water-quality uses, including residuals disposal. Often they attempt to translate these perceived benefits into financial indicators, such as the willingness to pay for water-quality improvements.

Each of these three categories of studies assumes that the regulatory rules-in-use can be manipulated by site or sites to produce desired outcomes in terms of the ambient water-quality conditions themselves or in terms of the behaviours of individuals, households, industries, and other persons granted legal status. They make the magnificent unreal assumptions that: 1 / the regulatory rules constitute the full set of operational rules as incentives for changing socio-economic behaviours in myriad decision situations; and 2 / environmental sciences are so well advanced that the predicted effects of regulatory rule changes can be accurately estimated and revealed in aquatic environments. The inherent danger is that collectivities may accept these assumptions and proceed with institutional and operational rule changes that do not produce the desired outcomes, and then proceed to expand the regulatory rules as a form of positive feedback from invalid signals about the relationships between rules and water-quality outcomes. This appears to be one explanation for the rapid increases in the number and range of regulatory rules established by statute since the 1960s.

Given more realistic assumptions about both the marginal significance of regulatory rules in relation to the total set of operational rules-in-use and the dynamic uncertainties of aquatic environments revealed by environmental sciences, the question that must be posed is 'What alternative methodologies may be valid to evaluate water-quality management in a site such as Hamilton Harbour?'

An Evaluative Heuristic

One answer to the question about a valid different evaluative methodology is heuristic, rather than a fully specified theory or model, in which to suggest the pattern of relationships among rules, water-quality parameters, and functioning natural ecosystems. A fully specified theory must be able to spell out the theoretical assumptions and the set of determining conditions in time and place in order to derive testable hypotheses as plausible conclusions or conjectures. The existing knowledge base of the environmental sciences is too small to enable us to spell out valid theoretical assumptions and necessary determining conditions applicable to a site such as Hamilton Harbour. A heuristic, however, suggests a pattern of relationships between the key sets of variables that can act as an organizing framework for later posing, as conjectures, tightly bound analytical constructs such as theories and models. A heuristic is, in other words, a element in the construction of a paradigm about water quality and aquatic ecosystems. Only through such paradigms can plausible conjectures ultimately be derived and tested.

We use, as a basis for the heuristic, the ecosystem approach as outlined at the beginning of this chapter. We take the four ecosystem functions and use them to appraise the current state of harbour water quality. When the water quality (as measured along one of the five parameters) contributes positively or negatively to one of the four ecosystem functions, we indicate such by entering a plus (+) or minus (−) respectively into the cells of figure 11. A positive relationship suggests that, in terms of a particular water-quality parameter, the harbour contributes positively towards an ecosystem function. A negative relationship suggests the opposite. The

Figure 11. Probable relationships between harbour water-quality parameters and ecosystem functions

Harbour water-quality parameters

Ecosystem functions	Dissolved oxygen	Suspended solids	Bacteria + viruses	Nutrients	Trace contaminants
Regulation	−		M^1	+	−
Carrier	+	+	M^2	+	−
Production	−	M^1	M^1	−	−
Information		−			

M^1 = Mixed, depending on use
M^2 = Mixed, depending on organism in question

heuristic and its evaluative capabilities are premissed on the contention that the state of harbour waters is a product of the rules and behaviours of persons in the geographical and historical context of the harbour and its watershed.

In figure 11, the cells in the matrix are either left blank, indicating no probable relationships, or filled, indicating a positive, negative, or mixed relationship between the sets of parameters and the ecosystem functions. The word 'probable' needs emphasis. We cannot be certain that the patterns of relationships are as indicated, and we cannot specify the precise probability of the relationships. Such is the rudimentary state of environmental sciences. Finally, we must re-emphasize that many of the parameters interact in the multivariate context of the harbour waters.

With all these caveats in mind, we note that there appear to be consistently negative relationships between the trace contaminants of metals and toxic chemicals and the ecosystemic functions. Also in only four cells of twenty are the relationships unambiguously positive. The other cells reflect the fact that the harbour waters are deleterious to 'proper' ecosystemic functioning. Improvements in the effectiveness of the subset of operational rules-in-use that we call the regulatory rules may well have to be directed towards remedying most of these parameters of water quality. The negatives shown for toxics suggest that remedies ultimately lie in efforts to improve the dissolved oxygen levels in harbour waters as a form of *in situ* treatment; efforts to reduce the total loadings of toxics discharged through point sources (as is promised by the Ontario Municipal-Industrial Abatement Strategy); and efforts to reduce the non–point source total loadings of toxics (as is possible under the new federal Environmental Protection Act).[18] Needless to say, better scientific information is necessary for these relationships to be clarified, and better social science information is necessary for an evaluation of the appropriate regulatory rules and their implementation.

Impacts

The state of harbour water quality impacts upon other actual and potential uses of the aquatic environment. We have already noted

18 These are not the priority measures formulated in the current remedial action plan for the harbour.

the negative effects on swimming (which is banned), on recreational boating (which is constrained), and on the historical values of a cold-water commercial fishery (which was eliminated).

One approach to assessing the impacts of water quality is to take the cells in figure 11 that display negative signs or mixed signs that have some negative effects and calculate the costs and associated losses to the watershed economy from the negative impacts. Because of the data limitations that result from scientific uncertainties, this approach cannot be pursued in full. Moreover, each cell is permeable over time. However, it may be possible to take a cell or group of cells where data are less limited at any one time and calculate the economic impacts.

To indicate the magnitude of the impacts, this approach is pursued for the cell that is intersected by suspended solids and production ecosystem function. One of the negative impacts in this 'mixed cell' entry is on the sport fishery in the harbour. The ambient suspended solids reduce water-clarity levels, and hence light penetration, for *adult* fish habitat. Given the DO and nutrient levels in the harbour, the potential yields of warm-water sport-fish species are reduced. If we further assume that the two major warm-water sport-fish species that are negatively impacted are Northern Pike and Large Mouth Bass, then we should be able to calculate the economic costs of restoring or enhancing the potential yields to levels made possible with *no other changes* in the water-quality parameters. Note that this approach does not change the edibility of the fish species; we assume no change in the effects of the trace contaminants on the warm-water fishery.[19] Note also that we do *not* assume that the potential yields will result in increased catches or fishing effort; such a result would occur only if additional water-quality parameters were changed or if improved physical access to the harbour were to occur.[20]

Table 16 shows the direct and spin-off costs from the suspended solids in the harbour on the potential yields of the two sport-fish species: annual direct losses amount to $330,000 annual income losses to the watershed are approximately $3 million, and annual employment losses are some 30 person-years.

19 The data were taken from Marshall, Macklin, and Monaghan (1988).
20 It would also imply calculating the non-market benefits of sport fishing for the two species in question. Most of the benefits of sport fishing are intangibles.

TABLE 16
Annualized financial impacts of suspended-solids pollution on the sport fishery[a]

Costs of light penetration[b]	330,000
Income losses[c]	$3.10 million
Employment losses[d]	30 person-years

Notes:
[a] 1987 dollars/year over 20 years
[b] Based on capital and operating costs of six mitigative measures
[c] Multiplier of 0.9
[d] Assumes 10 person-years for $1 m of expenditure

These calculations should be taken as simply one subset of indicators of the set of indicators of the impacts of water quality on the harbour watershed. The indicators are obviously financial in kind; however, the full magnitude of the impacts, financial and non-financial, is currently beyond the state of knowledge in the environmental and social sciences. These figures represent a small part of the opportunities forgone by persons facing residuals-disposal situations under current operational-rule configurations. To repeat, our heuristic suggests a large number of negative impacts of the water quality. One of these is on the sport fishery. We have suggested its magnitude in dollar terms.

Conclusions

Although the title of this chapter is 'Water-Quality Management,' our findings suggest that water quality is not managed, and perhaps might be called mismanaged. Point sources of various polluting parameters are partly treated and partly diluted under operational rules-in-use. But the ambient water-quality characteristics are not managed in the sense of manipulated through rule arrangements, and the results affect the functions of the natural ecosystems in the bay and impact (negatively) upon a number of other uses of the harbour and watershed. We suggested, in our heuristic framework, a way to appraise the state of the harbour waters and a method to calculate the impacts of the water on ecosystemic functions. Within the limits of scientific knowledge, the waters appear to impact negatively on many ecosystem functions.

In the theoretical language of this book, the operational rules-in-use for water-quality management barely touch, let alone fit, the nature of the good. This result is attributable, in part, to the complex characteristics of the good, many of which are dimly understood by current scientific inquiry, and, in part, to the fact that other operational rules-in-use that structure decision situations for watershed residents, industries, and municipalities largely permit persons to dispose of residual wastes in separate ways, irrespective of their consequences and impacts. For the latter reason, the nature of regulatory rules for water-quality management must be rethought. They exemplify an intellectual construct that interprets public policy as the direct and exclusive result of governmental decisions. Instead, they appear to illustrate that public policy is the result of numerous decisions taken jointly and separately by individuals, which governments can influence only indirectly by changing the incentive structures in these numerous decision situations. The configurations of rules-in-use are wider in scope and range throughout the materials-balance processes of a modern urbanized economy.

Those parts of the operational rules-in-use that comprise the regulatory rules for water-quality management flow from the institutional- and constitutional-rules configurations. The rules are 'stacked,' but dominated by provincial rules in an asymmetrical fashion, with federal sources of rules. The rules are 'nested' by multiple sources, especially Canadian and U.S., but, they are dominated by the domestic rule configurations embodied in the interpretations of the Constitution Act.

The nature of the good, with its technical interdependencies with most alternative uses of the harbour, imply that a major allocative consequence of the operational rules-in-use for all goods in Hamilton Harbour is to grant priority to residuals disposal over these other uses. An exception is the case of commercial shipping, which has few technical interdependencies with residuals disposals and which is granted explicit priority by the doctrine of navigable servitude. It is as if commercial shipping is the captain, residuals-disposal the first mate, and all other uses the crew of the 'Good Ship *Hamilton Harbour*' – except that many of the crew have fallen overboard or lie seasick in their bunks.

The next chapter provides a brief summary of the micro-case studies and their implications for governments at work. We proceed with the knowledge that the scope and complexity of rule configurations may correspond in only limited ways with the scope and complexity of a policy such as that of water quality.

10

Rules and Cases

As this book was being written, governments were toppling in Eastern Europe, warfare was raging in the Middle East, civil war was rending in Central America and parts of Africa and the Far East, and Canada was yet again in the midst of a constitutional crisis. The policy cases analysed and explained for one urban watershed in Canada appear very 'small beer' indeed!

Yet commercial shipping, recreational boating, and water-quality management for Hamilton Harbour exemplify the qualities of politics and government in Canada. Goods get transported, leisure pursuits are followed, residual wastes get disposed of – and their institutional foundations are rarely debated by Canadians. Productive decisions get made, disputes get settled, and changes in policy occur with a large measure of orderliness and predictability.

These things do not just happen. Centuries of learning, largely based in Europe, have been distilled by generations of family, kin, and society into norms and rules of conduct to help structure decision situations for productive outcomes. They have been adapted and readapted for the geographical circumstances of different sites and regions in Canada, and for the evolving technologies of different goods. They multiply and intermesh and become configurations of rules. While their meanings may differ for individual Canadians, they pose a basic logic for understanding public policy, whether in Hamilton, Vancouver, Moose Jaw, or Shawinagan. Hamilton has simply 'lucked out' in its selection as a site for understanding the nature of rules in relation to public policies.

Nevertheless, the cases, and this book itself, emphasize the distinction between rules-in-use and rules-in-form. The rules-in-use are the relevant subset of rule configurations for explaining public policies. And the rules-in-use will differ according to site and region. Such is to be expected when many institutional rules are the product of provincial governments. It is also to be expected when the operational rules-in-use are adapted for the conditions of different locations in the country. The rules-in-use for Hamilton, therefore, differ, to some degree, from other places.

Not all of the rules-in-use differ, however. The really important ones are the same for all regions of the country. Most of the constitutional rules-in-use do not vary from region to region. Most institutional and operational rules-in-use can be generalized to apply to different locations and communities. This is the beauty of theory. It bottles and preserves, as it were, the harvest of real-world situations for the nourishment of readers throughout the country and abroad (apologies for that one, dear reader!).

In this chapter, we re-emphasize some of the theoretical conclusions about rules-in-use for the consequences of public policy discovered in our three micro-level cases. We describe what happens when the rules for each policy case converge and conflict. And we tease out of our findings the critical generalizations about rules-in-use for Canadian parliamentary federalism. We leave our evaluation of this system of rules for the final chapter of the book.

Three Cases: Multiple Rules

All three policy cases indicate that rules are both 'stacked' and 'nested.' The rule 'stacking,' in which rules are layered hierarchically, meets many of our common-sense understandings of how policies get provided, produced, or regulated. First, at the lowest level, operational rules are developed. The operational rules are standard operating procedures in the field, with consequences for public policy 'enjoyment' by citizens. Different public policies require different sets of operational rules because the technical attributes of the goods differ. Similarly, we see, at the next-higher level of rules, a variety of institutional rules-in-use that vary by policy and by the processes for policy provision, production, and regulation. Again, institutional rules are developed to meet particular policy needs. The authority contained within the institutional rule configurations for policy making and implementation varies, too, as a function of constitutional-rule configurations. More surprising in light

of our common-sense understanding is the multiplicity of constitutional rules-in-use in Canada. Generations of students and laymen
are accustomed to thinking of the Constitution Act or as previously,
the British North America Act, as the source of political authority
and institutional rules, along with (perhaps) the more obvious parliamentary conventions, such as ministerial and collective responsibility. The fact that there are constitutionally independent sources
of political authority and institutional rules, in the country and
abroad, that can critically determine public policy outcomes may
be both surprising and alarming. Such is the case with commercial
shipping, in particular, which has multiple constitutional sources
domestically and also internationally. It is the multiple sources of
constitutional rules, and the consequent 'nesting' of different stacks
of rules, that is the most surprising.

The rule configurations that are 'stacked' and 'nested' pose com-
plications for the scholar and reader. For instance, if we assume that
there are ten constitutional rules that form a configuration of such
rules, and if each permits two kinds of authority relationships in
terms of institutional rules (such as open or closed), then we have
a range of institutional rules of 2 × 10 factorial. If the process is
duplicated at the operational rule level, then we have (2 × 10!)(2
× 10!) possible solutions at the operational level for each public
policy. Since 10 factorial is 3,628,800, the range of possible policy
outcomes from this hypothesized rule configuration is enormous.
That is why it often appears as if constitutional rules make no difference in policy outcomes. Some policies appear no different in a
federal or in a unitary state, for example. This is a beguiling but
erroneous conclusion.

The complexity and range of possible policy outcomes can be
reduced by describing, from an evaluation of each policy outcome,
the basic logic of the rule configurations for that policy. So we saw
that the basic logic of rule configurations for shipping was that of
competition between ports and, within ports, over the foreshore
uses. In the case of recreational boating, the basic logic was that
pleasure boaters were essentially 'squatters' who enjoyed the use
of harbour waters but had no legal property rights to maintain,
increase, or guarantee their activities. There were economic opportunities forgone as a consequence. There also appear to be substantial opportunities forgone for rival uses of the harbour as a
consequence of residuals disposal. And the basic logic for water-

quality management pointed to potential threats to many ecosystem functions because of the rule configurations for residuals disposal in the bay. These basic logics do, indeed, vary from one policy to the next. But they summarize and synthesize the consequences of rule configurations for each policy case, and they make tractable an understanding of the workings of constitutional and institutional rules in practice rather than in theory.

The significance of the previous paragraph for the development of political science as a discipline merits extra emphasis. Rules-in-use can link the micro to the macro for public policies in many countries. Their analysis and explication may be the new agenda for the discipline.

The complexity of rule configurations is amplified by the existence of both rules-in-form and rules-in-use. If the total set of rule configurations were rules-in-use, then the scholar and reader would be greatly aided in their understandings of how governments work. It would make possible a 'top-down' methodological strategy or make possible an analysis of federal-provincial relationships with some assurance that the policy conclusions reached through those relationships actually lead to predictable policy outcomes.

But, rules-in-use do not constitute the full set of rule configurations, and probably could not in any diverse society with political traditions. Rules-in-form play some role in establishing meanings of political association for different individual citizens, and rules-in-form also record many past meanings that signal the policy solutions of previous generations. For example, the anathema, for many citizens, that the jumble of buildings, smokestacks, and piles of coking coal on the waterfront in Hamilton Harbour represents, may signal times passed industrially and times ignored environmentally. For others, that jumble may signal times passsed in productive work and time devoted to technological adaptation to world steel markets. However, such conceptions complicate our understandings of rule configurations and their relevance for public policy.

Rule configurations and their basic logics for different policy cases may not be systematically constructed. The logics may converge and conflict, and the rule configurations may not form a 'seamless web' of arrangements. This is to be expected when rule configurations are not preordained by an ethical observer who 'maps out' their interrelationships. Rules have grown and changed in the light of historical and geographical circumstances, and it is always unlikely that they can predict future circumstances and the future needs of a diverse population. But we need to review how they diverge in the case of Hamilton Harbour and what lessons they teach us about governments at work.

Basic Logics and Allocational Rules

Our three policy cases indicate that commercial shipping is the priority use of Hamilton Harbour, followed, in turn, by that of residuals disposal and recreational boating. Other uses of the harbour, such as sport fishing and ice boating, are sporadic and of even less priority. The priority of commercial shipping is based on the rule of navigable servitude, which the courts have used to resolve conflicts between rival sources of constitutional authority over the legislative and property relationships in the bay. The rule of navigable servitude represents the historical allocational principle for Hamilton Harbour uses. It, in fact, is a medieval rule transferred from England. At the time of the Magna Carta, the Barons agreed to remove their fishing weirs from the River Thames to allow the unobstructed passage of the King's Navy in those navigable waters (Moore and Moore 1903). This is still the primary constitutional rule on navigable waters in Canada. It challenges and, when in conflict, supersedes the rules for shipping in the rival Constitution Act. Some persons question its modern-day relevance; it is, nevertheless, also the explicit formal priority of the harbour commissions.

The second priority of residuals disposal is an unplanned consequence of the technical interdependencies between this use and its rivals. Many polluting residuals drive away rival uses such as swimming, water-contact recreation, and fishing for cold-water species. The rules-in-use do not explicitly state the priority of residuals disposal. But the basic logic of the rules for rival uses, given the technical attributes of these rival goods, results in this allocational decision where any one use can drive out any other use. It is a cause of concern for many watershed residents who publicly support plans for remediation of the harbour. Unfortunately, the plans for remediation to be undertaken through the Canada-Ontario Agreement and the International Joint Commission do not envisage changes in the major rule configurations; they represent greater expenditure outlays of the provincial and federal governments through some changes in the operational rules of what we called the regulatory rules, a fraction of the configuration of rules in use. Again, there is no simple or single stack of rules from which policy outcomes can be predicted. However, the basic logic of the configurations of rules-in-use can be suggested by focusing initially on policy outcomes and their impacts.

The third priority of recreational boating is a consequence of the rule configurations including the property rights for the foreshores and harbour waters. Recreationists possess no property rights and, given the greater priorities of commercial shipping and residuals disposal, have limited means to negotiate alternative rule arrangements. They must rely on the benevolent discretion of public agencies, including the Harbour Commissioners. The benevolent discretion is most visible in the subsidization of moorage facilities and marinas, but the operational rules for this policy are fragile and dependent on rule configurations for alternative goods.

The allocational principles for Hamilton Harbour thus represent the intermeshing and interlocking of rule configurations for different public policies. In the one instance, these rule configurations mesh by deliberate design, through the application of the doctrine of navigable servitude. In the other cases, no design rules exist. Policy outcomes appear to emerge from the rule configurations rather than to be produced by explicit design.

Economists like to pose a grand objective for explicit design principles for alternative uses of a natural resource. They suggest that the marginal value to resource users from any single use should equal the marginal value of all alternative uses. This objective is based on utilitarian assumptions that all users can rank their preferences on a common scale. It is to be implemented, it is assumed, by a benevolent-despot form of government, one that can ascertain and aggregate the revealed preferences of users and then has the power to implement the objective. At a minimum, the benevolent despot can alter the property-rights arrangements so that users can negotiate and bargain for their preferred solutions. Such utilitarian assumptions imply, in other words, rule configurations that currently do not exist and probably will never exist in a society committed to some elements of democratic, individualistic, and egalitarian beliefs. Perhaps, more fundamentally, they raise the question of whether rule configurations can be synoptically designed. Perhaps the task of design is beyond the capabilities of any single community and its political agents.

This does not mean that the allocational principles for the harbour or for any water resource in Canada should be accepted as given. It means, however, that the rule configurations may have to be analysed and disaggregated for possible change. We do know, for instance, that the rule configurations currently permit a variety of operational-rule changes, but many of these are contingent on the exercise of discretionary authority by public agencies. More fundamental changes would require changes at the institutional and constitutional levels, such as any change contemplated for the rule of navigable servitude. Significant marginal changes in rules-in-use may result from understanding the basic logics behind policy outcomes. There are implications for our understandings of parliamentary federalism in these statements. To these we now turn.

Parliamentary Federalism and the Cases

Does the nature of Canadian parliamentary federalism make a difference for public policies? A superficial answer to this question, based on the evidence of our three cases, is: perhaps. The nature of the good and the particular configurations of rules-in-use for these goods seem to suggest that the configurations of rules-in-use could have as easily been predicated on a unitary system of government or on a presidential system. For example, the kinds of attentuated property rights for recreational boaters could as easily exist within the French and British systems of governance as within the Canadian. Similarly, the marginal effects of the regulatory rules in conjunction with the wider rules-in-use for residuals disposal could as well be as manifest in harbours in Marseilles or Bristol as in Hamilton, as polluted sites world-wide would suggest. Finally, the competitive dynamics of commercial shipping have an international basis that makes Canadian domestic rules appear marginal in impact.

By contrast, we have indicated that the constitutional-rule configurations of Canadian parliamentary federalism permit a wide variety of institutional-rule configurations for the two levels of government, albeit with asymmetries among federal and provincial powers for different public policies. The club or cartel of governments plays a grand metagame, but within which a variety of institutional subgames may be developed. In turn, the particular institutional-rule configurations adopted in Canada at any particular time permit, in turn, a range of operational-rule configurations to be selected for the many different public policies provided, produced, or regulated by government. Thus commercial shipping and pleasure boating are asymmetrically the concern of the federal government, albeit mediated by the independent constitutional status of the harbour commissions. And water-quality management is asymmetrically the concern of the provinces, albeit mediated by the interaction of rules over economic and non-economic decisions other than those that form the regulatory rules for the aquatic environment.

We have what appears, superficially, to be a paradox. Canadian parliamentary federalism appears, in one view, to make no difference, but appears, in another view, to make a difference in public policy outcomes 'in the field' (as it were); it is the end-product of multiple rules and multiple games.

Theory and evidence suggest that the configurations of rules in use in Canadian parliamentary federalism make critical differences in three important respects. First, recall the nature of rule configurations. In any decision situation involving multiple rules there are a variety of potential outcomes, depending on the configuration in place at any one time. Ten constitutional rules with two possible institutional rule solutions at any one time will yield $2 \times 10!$ possibilities. A further ten institutional rules with two possible operational-rule solutions will yield $(2 \times 10!)(2 \times 10!)$ operational outcomes. Canadian parliamentary federalism, like all systems of governance, permits some variety and diversity in the rules for decision situations about policy outcomes. There will likely be some overlap in the incentive structures of these rules for decision situations in Canada with the comparable incentive structures of the rule configurations existing in other governance systems, such as those in Britain, France, or the United States. At times, policy outcomes between countries will appear to converge. At other times, they will diverge.

Second, remember that rules interact with the nature of goods and the nature of individuals in establishing decisions about public policies. The nature of many goods is technically invariate across governance systems. And, to some degree, individuals share commonalities of interest, regardless of governance systems. At a minimum, the biochemical composition of the human species has a definable range of physiological behaviours. Thus there will be some overlap in the character of policy decisions made in Canada and in other countries.

Finally, it is worth noting how public policy is the product of collective behaviour that is normally wider than the collective behaviour of governments. Persons can organize much of their collective activities without governmental provision, production, and regulation of their activities. Governments do not possess a monopoly on collective action. Thus recreational boating or residuals disposal or commercial shipping takes place as the result of the activities of many legal persons, only some of whom are governmental agencies. Governments do help provide institutional rules, and the rules regarding the security of persons and remedies available for breaches of contract and tort are especially significant rules influenced by governmental collective action.

But more direct provision, production, and regulation by governments exclusively need not be a necessary concomitant of collective decision making. Some of the epistemological foundations for our understanding of governments at work in the light of this broader view of collective action will be examined in the concluding chapter. I wish here simply to suggest that rules-in-use include rules developed outside governmental institutions. These rules can result in policy outcomes that converge or diverge from outcomes that are the product of systems of governance that are neither parliamentary nor federal.

We can, as a consequence, conclude that Canadian parliamentary federalism appears to make *some* difference in public policy outcomes. The difference may be captured by the phrase 'a constitutive principle.' This phrase denotes the principles at work behind the basic logic of the configurations of rules-in-use. We examine the 'constitutive principles' of Canadian parliamentary federalism in the final chapter, which undertakes an evaluation of governance and public policy. In the interim, we return to the heuristic framework for policy analysis discussed in chapter 1.

Conclusion: A Policy Framework

Chapter 1 presented a framework for understanding the connections between what we have variously called the basic ingredients or the hard core of policy analysis (namely, rules, goods, and individuals) and the outcomes and impacts of policies among citizens. We saw that the basic ingredients combined in multiple decision situations resulted in policy outcomes and impacts, albeit mediated by the historical and geographical contingencies of any community. In turn, these contingencies and the policy outcomes and impacts could alter the character of the basic ingredients in the sense of establishing a feasible set of rules, a workable range of policies or goods, and a limit to the variety of individual motivations to engage in collective action. The process of policy analysis as depicted in the framework is circular and dynamic. Fortunately, in many Western cultures, the process is circular, dynamic, and productive. In other cultures, the process has produced non-productive or unproductive consequences of collective action. Parts of Ethiopia and Sudan may be apt modern examples of the latter consequences. There is, of course, a danger that the unpredictable consequences of the processes can alter the productive circumstances of life in Canada. Canada could become an Argentina without conscious forethought of the ways in which the basic ingredients could produce unfortunate outcomes.

What is apparent from our empirical studies and from our identification of the rules-in-use is that rules in general provide a way in which experience with productive policy outcomes can be stored as capital assets for current and future generations. Rules are a form of cultural endowment. The cultural endowment of parliamentary federalism appears, when considered in tandem with other rules-in-use, to produce generally positive outcomes and impacts. Experience with water-quality management would, however, suggest that outcomes and impacts are not always positive. The rules-in-use attached to the rules of parliamentary federalism in Canada can result in rule configurations that belie the benefits of collective action. A fuller evaluation of the basic logic of rule configurations in Canada will be addressed in the next chapter. Here we wish to emphasize the surprises and apparent unpredictabilities of the consequences of Canadian rules. What appears on the surface to be the same set of rules results in some beneficial and some deleterious policy outcomes. Why?

The answer is twofold. First, we have examined rules-in-use and not rules-in-form. Some of the rules-in-use have been unusual, to say the least, like the rule of navigable servitude and the rule of squatters. In the second place, the configuration of rules rather than the rules per se makes a difference. The 'stacking' and 'nesting' of rules in particular configurations was unusual, such as the 'nesting' of domestic and international rules for commercial shipping and the 'stacking' of rules such that some Canadian harbours have rules 'stacked' to the constitutional level but the domestic constitutional level is that of pre-1867 Canada. These two factors, the actual rules-in-use and their particular configurations, appear to account for the fundamental differences in the ways that governments work in Canada.

It is important to emphasize the differences between rules for another quite distinct reason. If all group behaviour – in political, economic, or social decision situations – is a product of rules, then the concept of rules has no explanatory power. Rule-ordered behaviour becomes a logical tautology. However, if different types and configurations of rules produce different behaviour and policy consequences, then the differences can be explained in a non-tautological fashion.

Finally, it is worth noting that the heuristic framework and the propositions advanced in this book cast a different light on the intellectual stream of ideas known as public choice analysis. The term 'public choice' has been eschewed until now; it is often misleadingly perceived as an economic interpretation of individual behaviour in decision situations in which governmental officials are involved. Our analysis and the elements in the framework demonstrate that individuals act in diverse ways with diverse consequences, depending on the rule configurations and nature of the good. Public choice is thus better viewed as a liberal individualistic approach to collective action and public policy. More important for the informed layman than disputes about nomenclature and approaches is the insight that this kind of analysis can provide. It is to be hoped that the reader now possesses a better understanding of governments at work in Canada. It now remains for us to assess the value of governments at work.

PART III : Conclusion

11

Evaluation

Paradigm Lost

In chapter 3, the limits of the orthodox ways to assess public policies were exposed. We saw there that the orthodoxy or established paradigm viewed policy outcomes as the consequence, in part, of rules, and that policy outcomes could be improved by appropriate rule changes. Criteria for assessing improvements were the most developed in the economics literature that used either utilitarian or 'Paretian' criteria for evaluation.

The limits of the paradigm were revealed through a discussion of their ontological assumptions or *raison d'être*. Rules, we argued, were not simply instrumental devices to be manipulated at will to get preferred policy outcomes. Rules at all levels (constitutional, institutional, and operational) had multiple meanings for individuals, and some of these meanings went beyond the more instrumental and tapped into some basic presuppositions about the social world.

We also argued that individuals enjoy some measure of personal autonomy from rules, and were neither the exclusive authors of rules nor the exclusive product of rules. Consequently, rules could never be accurately manipulated by individuals with the certainty that desired policy outcomes would ensue. Rules limited the range of possible policy outcomes envisaged within any community, and, in turn, they were only incentives rather than commands for individuals to obey.

Third, we noted that, in an historical sense, rules represent the preferred state of community affairs for successive generations. Rules will always lag behind individual and collective requirements, as persons develop and evolve new meanings about the world around them.

Beyond these ontological difficulties with policy evaluations, our examination of the basic logic of rules-in-use in Canada revealed another major difficulty. We saw that rules rarely, if ever, stood alone and had predictive policy consequences. Rather, rules were multiple in number and configurative in shape. Indeed, the configurative nature of rules is built into the federal system where both levels of government have *de facto* access to the same policy fields. Because of the configurative nature of rules-in-use, any single rule and its policy outcomes can be replaced by other rules with comparable outcomes, or consequences of any single rule can be offset by the combined operation of other rules in a configuration.

Take, for example, some of the operational rules for public policies we examined in chapters 7, 8 and 9. A rule that regulates the concentrations of oxygen-demanding wastes in any municipal sewage outfall can be offset by rules regulating the assimilative capabilities of the receiving waters. Or a rule designed to speed up vessel turn-around time, for example, through a system of flexible shifts for those involved in the activity, can be replaced, with the same consequences, by a rule facilitating the reservation of berthage by radio contact between captain and harbour-master. Indeed, conversely, rules may negate each other or work at cross purposes.

The 'nesting' of rules suggests that there are multiple sources of operational rules, such as the institutional rules of province and nation, and multiple sources of institutional rules, such as constitutional rules embodied within the Constitution Act, within rival domestic sources (such as the Magna Carta), and within rival international regimes. In other words, on strictly empirical grounds, rule configurations and their policy consequences are highly complex, and it may be beyond the limits of our current understanding to disentangle the effects of any one rule within a rule configuration in the interests of assessment and evaluation. So, for example, we were able to assess the policy outcomes and impacts of our three case-studies, but we were not able to delimit the precise contribution of each and every rule within the rule configurations to the policy outcomes and impacts in question.

Does this all mean that policy evaluations should be abandoned? Can we ever prescribe appropriate rules and rule changes? Are Meech

Lake and all the various constitutional proposals essentially fruitless endeavours in terms of their effects on public policies for individual Canadians? The answers to these questions require a newer perspective on the nature of evaluation.

Paradigm Sought

A solution to the problems of evaluation may lie in two concepts, both of which have been discussed in some form in this book. Let us review these two concepts before they are applied to the particular governance regime in Canada.

Basic Logic

We have referred a number of times to the basic logic of the rule configurations in Canada. The 'basic logic' of rules refers to their predictable set of consequences if they are working as they are supposed to work. Let us disentangle this definition, using some examples to clarify.

Rules are major causal factors that lead to effects, some of which show up in the form of policy outcomes and impacts. This statement needs little justification. It is the working premiss of evaluation studies. It is verified by the policy analysis provided in this book, and in many others. Over time, regular patterns of consequences emerge from the operation of rules as causal factors. We come to accept these consequences as predictable effects. On occasion, however, our expectations are not met. The regular patterns do not emerge. Something has happened to the ways that the rules operate. We must revise our expectations, perhaps by including these new exceptions in our predicted range of consequences or by revising our understandings of the rule configurations themselves (perhaps a new rule has emerged or perhaps an interaction of existing rules has not occurred previously). However, when we revise our expectations, we now reach a new resolution of the ways in which the rules are supposed to work. In short, rules do not have an unvaried one-to-one relationship with effects over all time-and-place circumstances. They have predictable effects, but there are boundaries of time and place – of context, if you will – on these predictions.

The reasons for these limitations on perfect predictions may be obvious in the light of our discussions, in chapters 1 and 2, of the nature of the individual. People are creative, adaptable, learning and exploring creatures. They constantly seek for ways to apply old rules to new problems (including new technological problems of goods) and for ways to devise new rules for better resolution of old problems. We would not expect, therefore, the range of predictable consequences of rules to stay static. However, for long-enough periods of time, we hope to be able to describe these predictive consequences, and hence the basic logic of rules.

Let us explore this reasoning with some examples. The first example is far-fetched, but it deals essentially with the problem of predictability. It is the example of my grandmother's big toe. Whenever the atmosphere is humid and rain is predicted, my grandmother's big toe begins to ache. Grandmother and I come to accept a basic logic about the rule 'if G's toe aches, then it will rain.' The basic logic always seems to occur. However, we notice that sometimes rain does not result when the toe aches, and that, on occasion, the toe does not ache even when the rain is falling. We have to revise our rule. Tentatively we hypothesize that 'if elderly people are susceptible to arthritic pain, then humid and rainy conditions will increase this susceptibility.' The range of predictable consequences has been increased by this new rule. A revised 'basic logic' of the rules of physiology, at least for my grandmother, has emerged.

A better example are the four-way-stop-sign rules at the intersections of minor roads. The example points out the limits to the basic logic of those rules that coordinate individual drivers into a kind of collective action. The rules are rules-in-use. They are mostly enforced by each driver. Each driver takes his or her turn to enter the intersection after slowing down or stopping at the sign. Occasionally a driver violates these rules and pushes ahead out of turn. The rules can tolerate these occasional violations. More than one violation at a time leads, however, to accidents. The rules have become unenforced: they have become rules-in-form. The solution is for continued enforcement by a police officer or for devising new rules, embodied in either traffic lights or in giving priority to some routes over others (rather than the rule of 'each in turn'). Individuals – in this case, the violators – demand new rules of collective action.

The third example is more obviously political. In 1832, the British government began a process of franchise reforms that continued for almost one hundred years and whose effects are still being felt. The rules for selecting MPS were changed as, *inter alia*, the franchise was extended to millions of adult, male property owners. The basic logic of the pre-1832 rule configurations at both an institutional and a constitutional level (remember, the two levels are largely fused under British parliamentary practice) were leading to continuous and negatively viewed consequences for many individual citizens. On pain of more radical changes in the constitutional-rule configurations, the franchise changes were enacted, and a new basic logic began to be established. The new basic logic gave incentives to the existing political parties and to new political parties to seek out minimum winning coalitions at election time. Plurality rule and, less frequently, majority rule became enduring elements of the basic logic of British parliamentary government. This example suggests how the character of the rule configurations may be changed by changing a subset of their component rules. More important, it suggests that the basic logic and its predictable set of consequences may only emerge over time as large groups of individuals adjust their behaviour to the incentives of the new rules-in-use.

All three examples imply that the complexity of rule configurations may be made tractable by using the concept of 'basic logic.' The concept focuses our attention on the enduring patterns of consequences that flow from multiple rules that are 'nested' and 'stacked' in configurative patterns. It describes, at a macro-level of analysis, the simultaneous effects of lots of rules-in-use, many of which are micro in scale. The concept does not lead to perfect predictability. Indeed, perfect predictability is unlikely unless and until individuals can be perfectly programmed! The concept of 'basic logic' does, however, capture the essential core workings of rules and rule configurations.

Community of Understanding

In our discussion of parliamentary sovereignty in chapter 3 and of federalism in chapter 4, we reviewed the major interpretations of these two fundamental sets of institutional rules within the Canadian governance system. The latter discussion in particular showed that there is no standard view on interpreting of how federalism can and should be understood to work in Canada. Another way of putting this point is that there exists no single 'community of understanding' about this essential part of the rule configurations.

A 'community of understanding' therefore refers to the acknowledged beliefs existing within any governance system about the basic
logic of its rule configurations. Communities possess, as it were, an
epistemology of how their rule configurations can and should operate. The 'community of understanding' may include suppositions
about the concepts of comprising the basic logic, about the causal
connections between the concepts and their policy outcomes and
impacts, and about the standing of individuals in relation to the
basic logic of rules. In other words, an ideology or creed may in
fuse the design principles of rules and their reform.

By way of example, de Tocqueville described some of the elements of a 'community of understanding' that existed in early nine-
teenth-century New England:

> The native of New England is attached to his township because it is
> independent and free: his cooperation in its affairs ensures his attach-
> ments to its interests; the well being it affords him secures his affection;
> and its welfare is the aim of his ambition and of his future exertions. He
> takes part in every occurrence in the place; he practises the art of gov-
> ernment in the small sphere within his reach; he accustoms himself to
> those forms without which liberty can only allow by resolutions; he
> imbibes their spirit; he acquires a taste for order, comprehends the bal-
> ance of powers, and collects clear practical notions on the nature of his
> duties and the extent of his rights. (1960, 1: 68)

For de Tocqueville, a 'community of understanding' had emerged
in these townships. It was grounded in the sovereign equality of
individuals and their equal standing in relation to the construction
and adaptation of the rules of collective action.

It is an empirical matter as to whether a 'community of understanding' has emerged in any governance system. An immediate test
is for the reader to reflect on the shared understandings he or she
enjoys with fellow citizens. In Western countries at least, it appears
that major parts of a community of understanding exist.

In most communities, too, there is a general agreement about the
meaning and importance of the rules-in-use and the rules-in-form.
Communities tend to develop, over time, shared understandings
about the rules and about the relationships between individuals and
the rules.

For example, in some communities, such as Canada in 1962, it became very important to establish a bill of rights as a statutory set of rules, even though the bill had no more instrumental value than the pieces of legislation and common law it packaged together in one act of Parliament. It tapped a deeply held meaning about the limits of collective action and about the personal autonomy of citizens in relation to those rules of collective action. In Canada, the bill's successor, the 1982 charter, while it extended the range of the rules, was also given an instrumental status as a set of rules-in-use by virtue of its entrenchment as amendments to the Constitution Act. Canada now has constitutional rules-in-use of both an instrumental and a non-instrumental kind. This is one of many reasons why it became difficult to formulate a so-called Canada clause as one of the constitutional amendments of 1991 and 1992. The clause was supposed to incorporate a variety of deeply held ontological beliefs about the state and its citizens.

In sum, it is at the level of community of understanding that people reflect upon and share their concerns about the basic logic of their political regime.

Constitutive Principles

I have suggested that the two elements of evaluation consist of the basic logic of rules and a community of understanding about this basic logic. The two elements form the 'constitutive principles' of a governance system. The 'constitutive principles' enable citizens to share a commonality of ideas about how a governance system is designed and how it may be redesigned. The paradigm or method of uncovering the constitutive principles for any governance system provide a way to assess the rule configurations that have consequences in terms of policy outcomes and impacts.

Paradigm Found: The Canadian Case

What are the constitutive principles of the Canadian governance system? Let us review the two components in turn.

Basic Logic

The basic logic of rules in Canada may be summarized in the light of the more extended discussions in this book. At this time, we should also highlight those elements in the basic logic that are newly developed or reconceptualized by the theory presented in this book. In so doing, the originality of the concepts in the basic logic may be made more apparent.

First, the rules consist of rules-in-use and rules-in-form. Only the former have a direct role in providing Canadian governments with opportunities and constraints, as these are the enforced rules. Rules-in-form have an indirect significance in so far as they influence the motivations of citizens and political actors.

Second, the rules-in-use are 'stacked' by scope of authority. Thus constitutional rules are rules about institutional rules, which are rules about the operational rules for deliverying public policies. These two key concepts of rules-in-use and rule 'stacking' enable us to identify, at a constitutional, institutional, and operational level, the linkages between the macro and the micro levels in the Canadian sociopolitical economy. We can then state, for example, that the squatters' rights enjoyed by recreationists on the harbour waters of a bay like Hamilton's are a product of the basic logic of the Canadian rules. These rules grant a harbour commission independent constitutional and institutional authority to make rules about the operation of boats on its waters.

The rules-in-use link the constitutional, institutional and operational rules with public policies in different parts of Canada. In many cases, the rules 'nest' as well as 'stack.' That is, they have multiple sources and are configurative in form. In policy terms, Canadian public policies and their rules are interdependent with the rules of other countries, as indeed we found with water-pollution issues. The degree of interdependence will vary with the policy in question. Canadian public policies and their rules must also include the enforced socio-economic norms – as rules-in-use – of communities within the country. Put another way, these norms are often rivals to the governmental rule arrangements. Thus fishers will develop their own norms about allowable catches, and enforce these norms rather than comply with governmental operational rules about allowable catches. In this case, the governmental operational rules can become mere rules-in-form, like all of those municipal by-laws prohibiting polluting materials from storm and sanitary sewers.

At the top of the stack of governmental rules in Canada are the constitutional rules, which, in practice, permit both the federal and the provincial governments to enter policy fields of their choice. The reason for the *de facto* concurrent jurisdictions lies with the nature of public policies – they overlap the heads of jurisdictional powers established in the division-of-powers sections of the Constitution Act.

Further, major constitutional change requires the unanimity of the eleven governments, despite increasing pressures for and newly developed strategies of governments to resort to public-consultation processes, including referenda. The process models the process of decision making in cartels or in clubs. The major decision rules require unanimity and preclude the exclusion of any one member. Cartels are notoriously unstable. However, the Canadian constitutional regime has remained a stable metagame, despite the recurring brinksmanship and 'dog-in-the-manger' strategies played by one or more of the participants. The participants remain as both rivals and collaborators.

Within the grand metagame of the cartel, the federal and provincial governments act as joint or single suppliers of a range of public policies, with the precise situations for any *single* policy at any *single* period of time subject to both the asymmetrical bargaining powers inherent in the Canadian federation and the displacement of governments through general elections. The result is instability at the level of operational rules as federal and provincial institutions negotiate and renegotiate, and as institutional solutions swing between the joint supply by both levels and the single supply by either level of government.

It is moot whether the instability in operational rules is in those rules-in-use or those rules-in-form. Frequently operational rules of government do not synchronize well with the nature of the good, and the rules get displaced by rival social norms, many of which are later codified into common law. Governmental operational rules become essentially rules-in-form. Public policies become neither the pronouncements of a government nor the rules promulgated by a government, but rather the end-product of social decision making. There are non-governmental 'market-like' processes that result in public policies in the field. The scope of these processes or of more traditionally conceived governmental processes is simply a matter of empirical investigation. We discovered, through our case-studies, that environmental policies fell largely outside the domain of the governmental laws and regulations. We found that shipping policies and pleasure-boating policies were much more within the domain, but subject to competition from other sites in the region and, in the former case, in the northeastern portions of North America. The basic logic is essentially an attempt to accommodate Crown sovereignty with representative democratic government, without resorting to the revolutionary principles inherent in popular sovereign models of the polity.

The reader who has been skimming this book and reads this summary of the basic logic of Canadian parliamentary federalism is surely asking why 'x factor' is not included, why 'y factor' is only partially correct, and why 'z factor' needs further qualification and elaboration. He or she is referred back to the general theoretical statements about the basic logic made earlier in this chapter. Basic logics appear to be 'bold statements'; they are, in fact, 'bold statements' deliberately posed as an analytic tool.

Community of Understanding

Canadians have been spectators at a series of constitutional conferences, agreements, and (in the 1981 case) amendments for over twenty years. Constitutional change has also been a continual if infrequent topic on the agenda of governments since 1926. This series of debates has led – increasingly, in the views of some commentators (e.g., Cairns 1988) – to the mobilization of large segments of the Canadian population around the wisdom, or lack of it, about the process of constitutional design and redesign. The debates in Quebec after the election of the Parti Québécois in 1976 were followed by debates throughout the rest of Canada after the Meech Lake Accord of 1987. There appears to be general agreement about the nature of the club process as the basic logic of the constitutional metagame. There is yet to evolve any non-governmental agreement or community of understanding about an alternative process, other than a concern that governments must consult through advisory referenda, legislative committees, or ad hoc special commissions.

At the root of the lack of any single community of understanding in Canada about how the constitutional-rule configurations should be framed is the mixed and muddled nature of the constitutional provisions of sovereignty, representation, federalism, and individual and group 'rights' that find credence in some parts of the constitutional rules. The particular accommodation that has resulted is unsatisfactory in terms of any priority accorded to these premisses in the minds of the observer. The club supergame was not the conscious result of ratiocination by 'framers'; rather, it was the product of power politics by majoritarian governments and their allies at different times in Canadian history.

One result of the lack of any single community of understanding is that individuals and groups are free to infuse the rules-in-use and rules-in-form with their own distinctive ontological meanings. It becomes impossible to conduct evaluations of one or more parts of the regime, particularly at the constitutional level, that do not impinge on some more deeply held meanings abôut the rules at issue. Consequently, reforms, particularly at the institutional and constitutional levels, become extremely difficult to advance. They are judged, by some, in non-instrumental terms.

There is some value, nevertheless, in the constant quest for a community of understanding. The rivalry of ideas represents part of the best traditions of Western civilization (Berman 1984). However, the rivalry of ideas or competing visions can lead to frustration, and even revolution, if the assumptions behind the ideas do not converge. A rivalry of ideas may simply degenerate into a contest of competing visions, with the view that the contest must produce a winner. Constitutional reform may be looked on as a 'common pool' in which the gains advanced by one vision of Canada may be perceived as losses by another vision. It is the contention of this book that it is the individual Canadian, and the individual reader of the work, who must provide the understanding to judge the governance system and its 'constitutive principles.' A community of understanding can be successful only if it is grounded upon individual understandings about the 'basic logic.' One hopes that a community of understanding will develop from such individual understandings. If not, the constitutive principles will be subject again to the power politics of organized groupings – the traditional power politics of the organized club or, more likely, the modern power politics of groups organized under such self serving-banners as those of French Canadians, English Canadians, multicultural communities, First Peoples, women, and other collective groupings.

Conclusion

The 'constitutive principles' of any governance regime consist of its basic logic and its community of understanding. The principles provide a paradigm or method for evaluating rules and their consequences in terms of public policy outcomes.

The basic logic of the Canadian governance system can be described as a muddled extension of Crown sovereignty, within which governments and citizens work at providing, producing, and regulating public policies. Further, no single community of understanding appears to have emerged in Canada as a constitutive principle. Indeed, there may be threats to its emergence in the face of the organized groupings of governments and of society. Meanwhile, one hopes that the reader will reflect upon and form his or her own understandings about the rule configurations and their policy consequences. The survival of liberty and community may be at stake.

References

Ackerman, B.A.; S.R. Ackerman; J.W. Sawyer, Jr.; D.W. Henderson. 1974. *The Uncertain Search for Environmental Quality*, New York: Free Press

Alchian, A.A., and H. Demsetz. 1972. 'Production, Information Costs and Economic Organizations,' *American Economic Review* 62, 777–95

Axelrod, R. 1984. *The Evolution of Cooperation*. New York: Basic Books

Bagehot, W. 1964. *The English Constitution*. London: Watts and Co.

Bellan, R.C. 1972. *The Evolving City*. Toronto: Copp Clark

Bennathan, E., and A.A. Walters. 1979. *Port Pricing and Investment Policy for Developing Centres*. Oxford: Oxford University Press

Berman, H.J. 1984. *Law and Revolution*. Cambridge, MA: Harvard University Press

Bish, R.L. 1985 'Improving Productivity in the Government Sectors: The Role of Contracting Out. In D. Laidler, ed., *Responses to Economic Change*, ch. 7. Toronto: University of Toronto Press

Black, E.R. 1975. *Divided Loyalties*. Montreal and Kingston: McGill-Queen's University Press

Borins, S. 1988. 'Public Choice,' *Canadian Public Administration*, 31, 12–26

Breton, A. 1985. 'Supplementary Statement.' In *Report of the Royal Commission on the Economic Union and Development Prospects for Canada*, 485–526. Ottawa: Ministry of Supply and Services

– 1987. 'Competitive Federalism Once Again,' *Liberty Fund Conference paper*, Niagara-on-the-Lake, ON

Breton, A., and A.D. Scott. 1978. *The Economic Constitution of Federal States*. Toronto: University of Toronto Press

Breton A., and R. Wintrobe. 1979. 'Bureaucracy and State Intervention,' *Canadian Public Administration* 22, 208–26

– 1982. *The Logic of Bureaucratic Conduct.* Cambridge: Cambridge University Press

Buchanan, J.M. 1979. 'Natural and Artifactual Man,' In H.G. Brennan and R.D. Tollison, eds., *What Should Economists Do?* 93–112. Indianapolis: Liberty Press

Buchanan, J.M., and G. Tullock. 1962. *The Calculus of Consent.* Detroit: University of Michigan Press

Buchanan, J.M., and V. Vanberg. 1989. 'Interests and Theories in Constitutional Choice,' *Journal of Theoretical Politics* 1, 49–62

Cairns, A.C. 1970. 'The Living Canadian Constitution,' *Queen's Quarterly* 77, 1–16

– 1988. 'The Limited Constitutional Vision of Meech Lake.' In K.E. Swinton and C.J. Rogerson, eds., *Competing Constitutional Visions,* 247–62. Toronto: Carswell

Campbell, C., and G.J. Szablowski. 1979. *The Super Bureaucrats.* Toronto: Macmillan

Campbell, M.F. 1966. *A Mountain and a City.* Toronto: McClelland and Stewart

Campbell, R.S.; A.D. Scott; and P. Pearse. 1974. 'Water Management in Ontario,' *Osgoode Hall Law Journal* 12, 475–526

Canadian Tax Foundation. 1987. *The National Finances.* Toronto

Careless, J.M.S. 1967. *The Union of the Canadas 1841–57.* Toronto: McClelland and Stewart

Carter, G.E. 1971. *Canadian Constitutional Grants Since World War II.* Toronto: Canadian Tax Foundation

Chalmers, A.F. 1981. *What Is This Thing Called Science?.* Saint Lucia: University of Queensland Press

Commons, J.R. 1924. *The Legal Foundations of Capitalism.* Madison: University of Wisconsin Press

Copithorne, L. 1979. *Natural Resources and Regional Disparities.* Ottawa: Economic Council of Canada

Cowan, P.J. 1935. *The Welland Ship Canal.* Ottawa: Minister of Railways and Canals

Craig, J.M. 1963. *Upper Canada.* Toronto: McClelland and Stewart

Crawford, K.G. 1961. *Canadian Municipal Government.* Toronto: University of Toronto Press

Davis, O.A. 1969. 'Notes on Strategy and Methodology for a Scientific Political Science.' In J.M. Bernd, ed., *Mathematical Applications in Political Science* 14, 22–38. Charlottesville: University Press of Virginia

de Groot, R. 1986. *A Functional Ecosystem Evaluation Method as a Tool in Environmental Planning and Decision Making.* Wageninen: Agricultural University of Wageninen, Netherlands

Dewey, J. 1927. *The Public and its Problems.* London: Allen and Unwin

Doern, G.B., ed. 1978. 'Introduction,' *The Regulatory Process in Canada*, 1–34. Toronto: Macmillan

Dominion Bureau of Statistics. *Census of Canada.* Ottawa, various years

Dorcey, A.H.J. 1985. 'Coastal Management as a Bargaining Process,' *Coastal Zone Management Journal* 11, 13–40

Dupré J.S. 1965. 'Tax Powers versus Spending Responsibilities.' In A. Rotstein, ed, *The Prospect of Change*, 75–95. Toronto: McGraw-Hill

Dworsky, L.B. 1986. 'The Great Lakes: 1955–1985,' *Natural Resources Journal* 26, 291–337

Dye, T.R,. (ed.) 1979. 'Symposium on Determinants of Public Policy,' *Policy Studies Journal* 7, 652–803

Eby, P., and Partners. 1979. *Recreational Boating Facility Requirements to 1985 in British Columbia.* Ottawa: Small Craft Harbour Branch, Fisheries and Oceans Canada

Environment Canada. 1987. *Goals, Problems and Options for the Hamilton Harbour Remedial Action Plan.* Burlington

– 1989. *Environmental Conditions and Problem Definition for Hamilton Harbour.* Burlington

Feldman, E.J., and M.A. Goldberg, eds. 1987. *Land Rites and Wrongs.* Lincoln, NA: Lincoln Institute of Land Policy

Fenge, T., and L.G. Smith. 1986. 'Reforming the Federal Environmental Assessment and Review Process,' *Canadian Public Policy* 12, 596–605

Forde, A.H. n.d. *A Historical Study of the Pollution of Burlington Bay.* Hamilton: Department of Municipal Laboratories

Friedman, M. 1953. 'The Methodology of Positive Economics.' In M. Brodbeck, ed, *Readings in the Philosophy of the Social Sciences*, 508–28. New York: Free Press

Gettys, L. 1938. *The Administration of Canadian Conditional Grants.* Chicago: Public Administration Service

Gibson, R.B., and B. Savan. 1986. *Environmental Assessment in Ontario.* Toronto: Canadian Environmental Law Research Foundation

Golembiewski, R.T. 1977. 'A Critique of "Democratic Administration" and Its Supporting Ideation,' *American Political Science Review* 71, 1488–1507

Goodwin, R.F. 1982. *Recreational Boating in Washington's Coastal Zone*. Riverton, VA: Institute of Marine Studies, University Press of Washington, DC

Goss, R. 1983. 'Policies for Canadian Seaports,' *Research Seminar Series* 10. Ottawa: Canadian Transport Commission

Great Lakes Water Quality Board. 1984. *Report on Great Lakes Water Quality 1983: Appendix*. Ottawa: International Joint Commission

Gregg, P.M. 1974. 'Units and Levels of Analysis,' *Publius* 4, 59–86

Gunton, T., and J. Richards, eds. 1987. *Resource Rents and Public Policy in Western Canada*. Ottawa: Institute for Research on Public Policy

Hamilton, City of. 1984. *General* n.d. *Background Information*. Hamilton

Hamilton Harbour Commissioners. *Milestones in the History of Hamilton Harbour*. Hamilton

– 1978. *Hamilton Harbour Master Plan*. Hamilton: Planistics Inc, for Hamilton Harbour Commissioners

Hayek, F.A. 1948. *Individualism and Economic Order*. New York: Gateway

Hempel, C.G. 1965. *Aspects of Scientific Explanation*. New York: Free Press

Hodson, P.H., and R.W. Threader, n.d. *Historical Review of the Water Quality of Hamilton Harbour, Cootes Paradise and Western Lake Ontario*. Ottawa: Fisheries and Oceans Canada

Holden, M. 1966. *Pollution Control as a Bargaining Process*, Cornell University Water Resources Centre, Research Paper No. 9. Ithaca, NY

Holmes, J.A., and T.H. Wil. 1984. *Historical Review of Hamilton Harbour Fisheries*, Technical Report No. 1257. Ottawa: Fisheries and Oceans Canada

Hough M., and Partners. 1979 and 1985. *Recreational Boating in Ontario*. Ottawa: Small Craft Harbour Branch, Fisheries and Oceans Canada

Johnson, J., and Partners. 1985. *The Metropolitan Toronto Waterfront Boating Demand Study Update*. Toronto: Metropolitan Toronto and Region Conservation Authority

Johnston, C.M. 1958. *The Head of the Lake*. Hamilton: Wentworth County Council

Kaminski, A.Z. 1989. 'Coercion, Corruption and Reforms,' *Journal of Theoretical Politics* 1, 77–102

– 1992. *An Institutional Theory of Communist Regimes*. San Francisco: Institute for Contemporary Studies Press

Kingsford, W. 1865. *The Canadian Canals*. Toronto: Rollo and Adam

Kiser, L.L., and E. Ostrom. 1982. 'The Three Worlds in Action' In E. Ostrom, ed., *Strategies of Political Inquiry*, 179–222 New York: Sage

– 1987. 'Reflections on Elements of Institutional Analysis,' Workshop in Political Theory and Policy Analysis Working Paper, Indiana University

Klevonick, A.K., and G.H. Kramer. 1973. 'Social Choice on Pollution Management,' *Journal of Public Economics* 2, 101–46

Kneese, A.V., and B.T. Bower. 1968. *Managing Water Quality* Baltimore: Johns Hopkins University Press

Kneese, A.V., R.U. Ayres and R.C. D'Arge, 1970. *Economics and the Environment*. Baltimore: Johns Hopkins University Press

LaForest, G.V. 1969. *National Resources and Public Property under the Canadian Constitution*. Toronto: University of Toronto Press

Laing, R.D. 1965. *The Divided Self*. Baltimore: Penguin

Lakatos, I. 1974. 'Falsification and the Methodology of Scientific Research Programs.' In I. Lakatos and A. Musgrave eds. *Criticism and the Growth of Knowledge*, 91–196. Cambridge: Cambridge University Press

Langford, J.W. 1976. *Transport in Transition*. Kingston: McGill-Queen's University Press

Law Reform Commission of Canada. 1988. *Pollution Control in Canada*, Administrative Law Series, Ottawa

Lipset, S.G. 1965. 'Revolution and Counterrevolution.' In T. Ford ed., *The Revolutionary Theme in Contemporary America*, 21–64. Lexington: University Press of Kentucky

Lucas, A.R. 1976. 'Legal Foundations for Public Participation in Environmental Decision Making,' *Natural Resources Journal* 16, 73–102

– 1981. 'The Canadian Experience.' In S.D. Clark, ed., *Environmental Assessment in Australia and Canada*, 39–48. Vancouver: Westwater Research Centre, University of British Columbia

McCann, L.D., ed. 1981. *A Geography of Canada*. Scarborough, ON: Prentice Hall

McDavid J.C. 1985. 'The Canadian Experience with Privatizing Solid Waste Services,' *Public Administration Review* 45, 602–8

McDavid J.C., and G.K. Schick 1987. 'Privatization versus Union Management Cooperation,' *Canadian Public Administration* 30, 472–87

Macdonald Commission. 1985. *Report of the Royal Commission on the Economic Union and Development Prospects of Canada*. Ottawa: Ministry of Supply and Services

MacKinnon, S. 1988. 'First Ministers' Conferences,' *Fifth Conference on Public Policy and Administrative Studies*, University of Guelph

McRoberts, K. 1985. 'Unilateralism, Bilateralism and Multilateralism.' In
R. Simeon, ed., *Intergovernmental Relations*, 78–93. Toronto: University of Toronto Press

Mallory, J.R. 1971. *The Structure of Canadian Government*. Toronto:
Macmillan

March, J.G., and H.A. Simon. 1958. *Organizations*. Toronto: Wiley

Marshall, Macklin and Monaghan Ltd 1988. *Assessment of Proposed Remedial Action Plans for Hamilton Harbour*. Toronto: Ontario Ministry of Environment

Miles and Co., 1879. *The New Topographical Atlas of the Province of
Ontario*. Toronto

Ministry of Railways and Canals. 1935. *The Welland Ship Canals*.
Ottawa

Ministry of State for Urban Affairs. 1978. *The Urban Waterfront*. Ottawa

Montreal, Port of. 1973. *Highlights of the Economic Impact of the Port
of Montreal*. Montreal: Port of Montreal Authority

Moore, S.A., and H.S. Moore. 1903. *The History and Law of Fisheries*.
London: Stevens and Haynes

Nagel, E. 1961. *The Structure of Science*. New York: Harcourt, Brace and
World

National Research Council of the United States and the Royal Society of
Canada. 1985. *The Great Lakes Water Quality Agreement*. Washington,
DC: National Academy Press

Niskanen, W.A. 1971. *Bureaucracy and Representative Government*.
New York: Aldine-Atherton

Norcliffe, G. 1982. *'Hamilton's Industrial Central Waterfront': Industrial Developments in Canadian Ports*. University of Toronto/York
University Joint Program in Transportation, Report 86

Oakerson, R. 1988. 'Reciprocity.' In V. Ostrom, D. Feeny, and H. Picht,
eds., *Rethinking Institutional Analysis and Development*, 141–58.
Institute for Contemporary Studies Press

Olson, M. 1965. *The Logic of Collective Action*. Cambridge, MA: Harvard
University Press

– 1969. 'The Principle of "Fiscal Equivalence." ' *American Economic
Review*, Papers and Proceedings, 479–87

Ontario Ministry of Environment. 1979. *A Guide to the Great Lakes
Water Use Map*. Toronto

– 1984. *Water Management*. Toronto

– 1985. *Hamilton Harbour: Technical Summary and General Management Options*. Toronto

Ontario Ministry of Tourism. *Ontario Recreational Survey 1975–1979*.
Toronto: Tourism and Outdoor Recreation Planning Study Committee
Ostrom, E. 1986. 'An Agenda for the Study of Institutions,' *Public Choice*
48, 3–25
– 1989. 'Micro Constitutional Change in Multi-Constitutional Political
Systems,' *Rationality and Society* 1, 11–49
Ostrom, V. 1980. 'Artisanship and Artifact,' *Public Administration Review* 40, 309–17
– 1989. *The Institutional Crisis of American Public Administration*,
rev. ed., University, AL: University of Alabama Press
– 1991. *The Meaning of American Federalism*. San Francisco: Institute
for Contemporary Studies Press
Ostrom, V.; C.M. Tiebout; and R. Warren. 1961. 'The Organization of
Government in Metropolitan Areas,' *American Political Science Review* 55, 831–42
Peat Marwick and Partners et al. 1984. *Ontario Ports Study*. Ottawa:
Transport Canada and Ontario Ministry of Transportation and Communications
Pross, A.P. 1986. 'Parliamentary Influence and the Diffusion of Power,'
Canadian Journal of Political Science 18, 235–66
Public Works Canada 1976. *Preliminary Engineering Study of Marina
Facilities in Hamilton Harbour*. Ottawa: Government of Canada
Putman, D.F., and R.G. Putman 1979. *Canada: A Regional Analysis*.
Toronto: Dent
Rawls, J. 1971. *The Theory of Justice*. Belknap Press
Regional Municipality of Hamilton-Wentworth. 1981. *Information Hamilton '81*. Hamilton
Resnick, P. 1987. 'Montesquieu Revisited, or the Mixed Constitution and
Separation of Powers in Canada,' *Canadian Journal of Political Science* 20, 97–116
Roberts, R.D. 1964. The Changing Patterns of Manufacturing Activity in
Hamilton between 1861 and 1921, MA Thesis, McMaster University
Roman, A.F. 1983. 'How Fair Are Existing Environmental Assessment Processes in Ontario.' In E.S. Case; P.Z.R. Finkle; and A.R. Lucas. *Fairness
in Environmental and Social Impact Assessment Processes*, 39–48.
Calgary: Canadian Institute of Resource Land
Ruppenthal, K.M. 1983. *Canada's Ports and Waterborne Trade*. Vancouver: Centre for Transportation Studies, University of British Columbia
Russell, P.H.; R. Knopff; and T. Morton. 1989. *Federalism and the
Charter*. Ottawa: Carleton University Press

Sabetti, F. 1980. 'Covenant Language in Canada,' Workshop on Covenant and Politics, Center for Study of Federalism, Temple University
– 1982. 'The Historical Context of Constitutional Change in Canada,' *Law and Contemporary Problems* 45, 11–32
Samuels, W.J., and J.D. Shaffir. 1981–2. 'Deregulation,' *Policy Studies Review* 1, 436–69
Sawyer, A. 1992. *The Emergence of Autocracy in Liberia.* Institute for Contemporary Studies Press
Schlager, E., and E. Ostrom. 1987. 'Common Property, Communal Property and Natural Resources,' Workshop in Political Theory and Policy Analysis, Indiana University
Schumacher, J.A. 1984. 'The Model of a Human Being in Public Choice Theory,' *American Behavioral Scientist* 28, 211–31
Simeon, R.S.B., and D. J. Elkins 1974. 'Regional Political Cultures in Canada,' *Canadian Journal of Political Science* 7, 397–437
Simon, H.A. 1948. *Administrative Behavior.* New York: Macmillan
Smiley, D.V. 1969. 'The Case Against the Charter of Human Rights,' *Canadian Journal of Political Science* 2, 270–91
– 1977. 'Cooperative Federalism.' In J.P. Meekison, ed., *Canadian Federalism*, 259–77. Toronto: Methuen
– 1980. *Canada in Question.* Toronto: McGraw-Hill Ryerson
– 1987. *The Federal Condition in Canada.* Toronto: McGraw-Hill Ryerson
Smith, A. 1937. *The Wealth of Nations.* New York: Random House
Smith, D. 1969. 'President and Parliament,' Priorities of Canada Conference, Niagara Falls, October
Smith, J.C. 1983. 'The Processes of San Francisco: Adjudication and Regulation.' In T.R. Machan and M.B. Johnson, eds., *Rights and Regulation*, ch. 3. Pacific Institute for Public Policy Research
Smith, L.G. 1983. 'Electric Power Planning in Ontario,': *Canadian Public Administration* 26, 378–401
– 1987. 'Mechanisms for Public Participation at a Normative Planning Level in Canada,' *Canadian Public Policy* 8, 561–72
Smith, P.J. 1984. 'The Ideological Origins of Canadian Confederation,' *Canadian Journal of Political Science* 20, 3–30
Sproule-Jones, M.H. 1972. 'Strategic Tensions in the Scale of Political Analysis,' *British Journal of Political Science* 2, 178–92
– 1973. 'Toward a Dynamic Analysis of Collective Action,' *Western Political Quarterly* 26, 414–26

- 1974a. 'An Analysis of Canadian Federalism,' *Publius* 4, 109–36
- 1974b. 'Citizen Participation in a Canadian Municipality,' *Public Choice* 17, 73–83
- 1975. *Public Choice and Federalism in Australia and Canada.* Canberra: Australian National University Press
- 1978a. 'Coordination and the Management of Estuarine Water Quality,' *Public Choice* 33, 61–53
- 1978b. 'The Social Appropriateness of Water Quality Management,' *Canadian Public Administration* 21, 176–94
- 1979. 'A Fresh Look at an Old Problem: Coordinating Canada's Shore Management Agencies,' *Western Political Quarterly* 32, 278–85
- 1981. *The Real World of Pollution Control.* Vancouver: Westwater Research Centre, University of British Columbia
- 1982. 'Public Choice and Natural Resources,' *American Political Science Review* 76, 790–804
- 1983. 'Institutions, Constitutions and Public Policies.' In M.M. Atkinson and M.A. Chandler, eds., *Canadian Public Policy*, 127–50. Toronto: University of Toronto Press
- 1984a. 'The Enduring Colony: Political Institutions and Political Science in Canada,' *Publius* 14, 93–108
- 1984b. 'Methodological Individualism,' *American Behavioral Scientist* 28, 167–83
- 1985. *The Legal Foundations of the Multiple Uses of Hamilton Harbour*, Copps Chair Occasional Report. Hamilton: McMaster University
- 1986a. *An Historical Profile of Hamilton and its Harbour*, Copps Chair Occasional Report. Hamilton: McMaster University
- 1986b. *Pleasure Boating and Hamilton Harbour*, Copps Chair Occasional Report. Hamilton: McMaster University
- 1988a. *Commercial Shipping and Navigation and Hamilton Harbour*, Copps Chair Occasional Report. Hamilton: McMaster University
- 1988b. 'Science as Art and Art as Science,' *Canadian Public Administration* 31, 34–41
- 1989a. 'Multiple Rules and the "Nesting" of Public Policies,' *Journal of Theoretical Politics* 1, 459–77
- 1989a. 'Urban Policy Making in Canada.' In W.M. Chandler and C. Zollner, eds., *Challenges to Federalism*, 203–15. Kingston: Centre for Intergovernmental Relations, Queen's University
- 1990. 'Institutional Design for the Environment and the Economy.' In B. Sadler, ed. *Integrating Environmental and Economic Assessment*,

ch. 8. Ottawa: Canadian Environmental Assessment Research Council

Sproule-Jones, M.H., and K.D. Hart. 1973. 'A Public Choice Model of Political Participation,' *Canadian Journal of Political Science* 6, 175–94

Sproule-Jones, M.H., and P.L. Richards. 1984. 'Toward a Theory of the Regulated Environment,' *Canadian Public Policy* 10, 305–15

Stanbury W.T., and G. Lermer. 1983. 'Regulation and the Redistribution of Income and Wealth,' *Canadian Public Administration* 26, 378–401

Thorburn, H. 1984. *Planning and the Economy*. Ottawa: Canadian Institute for Economic Policy

Tickner, G., and J.C. McDavid. 1986. 'Effects of Scale and Market Structure on the Costs of Residential Solid Waste Collection in Canadian Cities,' *Public Finance Quarterly* 14, 371–93

Tocqueville, A. de. 1960. *Democracy in America*, 2 vols, ed. by P. Bradley. New York: Knopf

Tullock, G. 1965. *The Politics of Bureaucracy*. Washington, DC: Public Affairs Press

Vile, M.J.C. 1967. *Constitutionalism and the Separation of Powers*. Oxford: Oxford University Press

Walter, G.R. 1978. 'Market Methods of Multiple Use Reconciliation,' *Journal of Environmental Management* 7, 291–6

Watson, J.W. 1964. 'Industrial and Commercial Development.' In A.H. Wingfield, ed., *The Hamilton Centennial*, 32–46. Hamilton: Hamilton Centennial Committee

Weaver, J.C. 1982. *Hamilton*. Toronto: James Lorimer

– 1983. The Location of Manufacturing Enterprises.' In R.A. Jarrell and A.E. Ross, eds., *Critical Issues in the History of Canadian Science, Technology and Medicine*, 197–217. Ottawa: HSTC Publications

Webb, K. 1987. 'Between the Rocks and Hard Places,' *Alternatives* 14, 4–13

Weinrib, L.E. 1987. 'Two Models of Constitutionalism,' Liberty Fund Conference paper, Niagara-on-the-Lake, ON

Wilson, V.S. 1981. *Canadian Public Policy and Administration*. Toronto: McGraw-Hill Ryerson

Winch, P. 1958. *The Idea of a Social Science*. London: Routledge and Kegan Paul

Woodhouse, R.T. 1967. *History of the Town of Dundas*. Dundas Historical Society

Yang, T.S. 1987. 'Property Rights and Constitutional Order in Imperial China,' PhD dissertation, Indiana University

Index

administrative law, 118–19
Arctic Waters Pollution Prevention
  Act, 217
artefacts: 56, 63–5, 67–8, 70, 77;
  defined, 59; and Hamilton, 141;
  and Hamilton Harbour, 139,
  150, 152, 206

Bagehot, Walter, 5
basic logic of government: efficient
  versus dignified parts, 12–14;
  and de Tocqueville, 12
Bay Area Restoration Council, 227
Black, Ed, 95
boating industry. See pleasure
  boating
Boundary Waters Treaty, 1909, 226
British Columbia, 8, 90, 101
British North America Act. See
  Constitution Act, 1867
Buchanan, James, 13, 69
Burlington, municipality of, 140,
  190, 192, 221–3, 225
Burlington Bay, 142, 143
Burlington Ship Canal, 135, 161,
  162

Canada Act, 1981, 60

Canada Assistance Plan, 92
Canada Ports Act, 1982, 160
Canada Ports Corporation (previously National Harbour Board),
  160
Canada Shipping Act, 1970, 160,
  162, 163, 191, 225
Canada Water Act, 1970, 224
Canadian Council of Environmental Ministers, 237
Canadian government: basic logic
  of, 5, 269–72; Charter of Rights
  and Freedoms, 81, 93, 103;
  courts, role of, 82–3; Crown prerogative powers, 80, 104, 118;
  executive-centred federalism,
  7–8, 88, 111, 114; First Ministers'
  Conferences, 89; House of Commons, 87; institutional politics,
  15; parliamentary system/sover-
  eignty, 6, 8, 12, 80–2, 86,
  98–102, 128, 150, 152–3, 208,
  212–13, 255–8, 267, 272; political system, 77; prime minister,
  60, 72, 106; Supreme Court, 80,
  87, 90–3, 98; see also federalism
Canadian Intergovernmental Conference Secretariat, 89

Canadian National Railways, 148, 222, 225
Canadian Steamship Lines, 148, 149, 162
cartel behaviour, 97–8; consequences of, 87–90; defined, 84–5; logic of, 107; threats to, 90–4; *see also* constitutional rules
commercial shipping: assessing performance, 181–4; constitutional rules, 156–7; institutional rules, 159–63; navigable servitude (doctrine of), 155–6, 159, 163, 191–2, 248, 253; *see also* Hamilton Harbour
common pools, 27
community of interest, 35
community of understanding, 267–9, 272–4; *see also* rule configurations
Conservation Authorities Act, 1970, 222
Constitution Act, 1867, 8, 60, 79, 191; Peace, Order, and Good Government (POGG) clause, 79, 91; sections 90–2, 80, 82; Third Schedule, 156
constitutional concurrency, 82–4; *see also* Constitution Act, 1867
constitutional rules, 60–1; Canada Round, 94; cartel, 84–90; and common-law rules, 80; concurrency, 82–4; conventional authority versus operational authority, 80; conventions, 80; and pleasure boating, 191–4; and port management, 155–9; *see also* rules
Crown Zellerbach case, 1988, 91, 216, 224

decision situations, 26
delegated powers, 110–14; bureaucratic accountability, 112; and executive federalism, 111; impact of, 113–14; quangos, 110; and transaction costs, 111
Department of Transport, 160
de Tocqueville, Alexis, 12, 268
Dofasco, Inc., 149, 169, 176, 184

economic policy evaluations, 65–7
economics, mainstream, 55
ecosystems, functions of, 211–12
Environmental Assessment Act (EAA), 220–1
Environmental Assessment Review Process (EARP), 225–6
Environmental Protection Act (EPA), 1971, 217–19, 221, 222, 228; 1988 (federal), 216, 224, 240, 245
equalization payments, 49, 90, 109
evaluative rules, 63–5; *see also* rules
externalities, 27, 42, 54

federal government: and commercial shipping, 153, 154, 157–61; and equalization payments, 49; legislative powers, 80, 83–4, 90–3, 186; and pleasure boating, 191–2; and port management, 159–63; and water-quality management, 212, 215–16, 223–6, 228
federalism: 61, 85–7, 103, 128; asymmetrical, 114–16; and Charter of Rights and Freedoms, 81; and commercial shipping, 153, 156; cooperative, 109; exec-

utive, *see* Canadian government; impact on public policy, 255–8, 272; and pleasure boating, 207–8; six concepts of, 95–7; and water-quality management, 212, 248

Fisheries Act, 1868, 223–4

Fishing and Recreational Harbours Act, 1977–8, 195; 1964, 160

Fraser River, 9, 37, 52, 54

free navigation, right of. *See* navigable servitude

free-rider strategy, 122

goods: divisibility of, 41–3; durability of, 43; excludability of, 41–2; externalities of, 42; first-order dimensions of, 41–2; measurability of, 43; nature of, 40–4, 51, 256; physical and non-human elements of, 24–5; and rules-in-use, 129, 153–5, 183; second-order dimensions of, 42–4; *see also* public policies; public goods

Government of Ontario, 172, 191, 224; *see also* Ontario, province of

Government Wharves and Piers Act, 1964, 160

Great Lakes, vessel-traffic flows, 171; *see also* Lake Erie; Lake Ontario

Great Lakes ports: as competition to Hamilton Harbour Commissioners, 164–6, 183, 185; and transshipment of goods, 164

Great Lakes Science Advisory Board, 226

Great Lakes Water Quality Agreements. *See* International Joint Commission

Great Lakes Water Quality Board, 226–7

Guide to Eating Ontario Sport Fish, 238

Halton, Regional Municipality of, 140, 193, 217, 221

Hamilton, City of: demographics, 140–1, 146; historical economic development, 141–50; incorporation, 157; rival to Hamilton Harbour Commissioners, 167–9; *see also* Hamilton Harbour

Hamilton By-Products Ltd, 149

Hamilton Conservation Authority, 193

Hamilton Harbour, 10; advantages of, 166; as artefact of human design, 150–1; cargo flows in, 175–81, 183; changes to structure and ecologies of, 135–9; and federal Crown, 158; financial policies related to, 170–1, 172–5; operating rules of, 169–72; physical description of, 130; and province of Ontario, 158–9; rule configurations of, 153–5; uses of, 130–4; water quality in, 229–39; *see also* commercial shipping; Hamilton, City of; pleasure boating; water-quality management

Hamilton Harbour Commissioners (HHC): East Port Development project, 174; establishment of, 146; and Hamilton Conservation Authority, 149; influence on development of harbour, 147–9; jurisdiction and authority of, 155, 158, 160–3, 169–72, 190–1; and pleasure boating, 193–4; revenue and pricing policies of, 172–5; ri-

valry of with other ports, 163–4;
and water-quality management,
212–13, 225
Hamilton Harbour Commissioners
Act, 1912, 160–1, 169–70
Hamilton Regional Conservation
Authority, 140
Hamilton Spill Control Group, 233
Hamilton-Wentworth, Regional
Municipality of, 140
Harbour Commissions Act, 1964,
160, 170

incentive systems, 39–40, 47, 82,
88, 128; between levels of government, 97, 107, 111, 115, 256;
and Hamilton harbour, 154; and
Hamilton Harbour Commissioners, 168, 170–1, 186
individual: as unit of analysis,
25–6; nature of, 44–6; preferences, 51; role of, 39; and rules,
67–8
institutional rules, 62–3; configuration, 61–3; and delegated powers, 110–14; and executive
government, 105–10; and pleasure boating, 191–4; and policy
regulation, 117–21; politicization
of, 118; and port authority,
159–63; and voluntary collective
action, 122–3; see also rules
International Harvester (latterly J.I.
Case Inc.), 169
International Joint Commission
(with the United States), 213,
226–7, 236–7, 253

Judicial Committee of the Privy
Council, 61; see also Supreme
Court

Kaminski, Antoni, 13
Kiser, Larry, 50

La Forest, Mr Justice, 91
Lake Erie, 142, 144, 148, 226
Lake Ontario, 130, 132, 135, 139,
178; and commercial shipping,
148, 149, 164; and development
of Hamilton Harbour, 142–4,
149, 185; and pleasure boating,
190, 199; water quality in, 229,
238, 239

Manitoba, 90, 92
marinas. See pleasure boating
McDavid, J.C., 35
Meech Lake Accord, 21, 93, 272
ministerial (and collective) respon-
sibility, 100–1, 106
Municipal Act, 1983, 192, 223
Municipal-Industrial Strategy for
Abatement (MISA), 219–20, 222,
245

Native peoples, 94
navigable servitude, doctrine of,
253–5; see also commercial shipping; pleasure boating; water-
quality management
Navigable Waters Protection Act,
1882, 162, 163, 192, 222
New Brunswick, 60, 101
Newfoundland, 61, 89, 90
Niskanen hypothesis, 54, 113
North Fraser Harbour Commission,
170
Nova Scotia, 60, 101

Ontario, province of: and asymmetrical federalism, 114–15, 154;
and Hamilton Harbour, 159,

161; and 1982 constitutional changes, 90; and pleasure boating, 191–4; system of local government, 140, 157–8; and water-quality management, 213–15, 217–23
Ontario Ministry of Environment, 218, 221, 239–40
Ontario Municipal Board, 167
Ontario Recreational Boating Studies (RBS), 200
Ontario Recreational Survey, 204
Ontario Waters Resources Act, 1961 (OWRA), 217, 221
operational rules. See public policies
operational rules-in-use. See public policies
Ostrom, Elinor, 50
Ostrom, Vincent, 13
Otis Elevators, 148

Paretian criterion, 67
Parliament. See Canadian government
parliamentary federalism. See federalism
Parti Québécois, 91, 272
Planning Act (provincial), 1983, 192–3, 223
pleasure boaters, rights of, 190, 196
pleasure boating, 188; assessing performance, 203–6; constitutional rules-in-use, 191–4; economic impact, 202–3; extent of, 200–1; facilities in Hamilton Harbour, 195–9; navigable servitude, 191, 207; operational rules-in-use, 189–91; policy, as compared to commercial shipping

policy, 207; season, 200; types of, 205
policy analysis, 31–3; and empiricist epistemology, 75–7; hard-core concepts, 40–51, 56–7
policy delivery, 47, 98
policy production, 116–17; and public bureaucracies, 116
policy regulation, 47, 117–21
political science, mainstream, 52–3; Canadian, 72–5
Port of Hamilton. See Hamilton Harbour
Port Pricing and Investment (World Bank study), 171
ports authority, types of, 159–60
prime minister. See Canadian government
property rights, 47
Provincial Health Act, 1956, 220
Provincial Municipal Act, 167
Provincial Planning Act, 167
provisions systems (public economies), 9, 54, 105, 154
public administration, mainstream, 53–5
public choice, 13, 259
public goods, 27; concept of, 36; and mainstream public administration, 53–5; see also artefacts
public-nuisance action, 214
public policies: defined, 15, 127; impacts and outcomes of, 26–7, 51; influenced by nature of good, 117; intergovernmental provision of, 107–10; operational value, 4; understanding public policies, 56–7

Quebec, province of, 101; and asymmetrical federalism, 114–16;

civil law, 118, 122; and constitutional change, 88–90, 272; as 'distinct society,' 69, 96; ports, 165–6

rational choice, 67
Receiver General of Canada, 170
recreation policy, 188–9; see also pleasure boating
residual clause, 91
residual powers, 93, 96, 106
riparians, 40, 47, 56, 163, 190, 192; defined, 155; rights of, 118, 155, 194, 208, 214, 217
rule configurations, 15, 17, 23, 27–9; as cultural endowments, 30–1; basic logic of, 265–7; Canadian constitutional, 81–2; 'constitutive principles' of, 31; and Hamilton Harbour, 184–7, 194; see also rules
rule design, 59–63, 67–9; and Canadian political system, 77–8
rule nesting, 9–10, 65, 153, 212, 248, 250–1, 259, 267, 270
rule stacking, 48, 65, 124, 154, 187, 190, 207-8, 212, 248, 250–1, 259, 267, 270
rules: basis for, 68; changes in, 64–5; consequences of, 47, 48; constitutional, 4, 49; contextual explanation of, 71–2; defined, 22–4, 46; and goods, 129, 153–5; incentive systems, 47; institutional, 4, 47; instrumental and symbolic character of, 29, 69; linkages among three parts, 7–8; nature of, 46–51; operational (public policies), 4; transaction costs, 47; variety of, 50–1; see also rule nesting; rule stacking

rules-in-form, 24; example of, 95; of recreational policy, 188–90; role of, 252
rules-in-use, 7, 24, 69–71; defined, 58; as opposed to rules-in-form, 29; see also rules-in-form

St Lawrence Seaway, 148, 149, 164, 183, 185
Sawyer, Amos, 13
Small Craft Harbours Branch, 199
sovereignty, theory of, 61
spillovers, 109
Statute of Westminster, 60
Stelco Inc., 148, 149, 169, 176, 184

Toronto Harbour, 203–4
Toronto Harbour Commission, 170–1
transaction costs, 111; of governance, 97; theory of, 113; and provincial Crowns, 119
Transport Canada, 162
Transportation and Dangerous Goods Act, 1980, 228
Treaty of Paris, 60
Tullock, G., 13

water-quality management: and common law, 214–15; constitutional rules-in-use, 215–16; defined, 209–10; dilution criteria (standards), 218–20, 222; ecosystem principle, 210–12, 243–5; evaluation of, 240–5; federal rules, 223–8; impact of, 245–7; in British Columbia, 9; institutional rules-in-use, 216–17; materials balance principle, 210–11; nature of the good, 216; navigable servitude, 248; parameters of, 229–39; provincial rules, 217–23; regulatory process, 219; rule configurations, 213, 228, 247–8; subrules, 219

Weinrib, L.E., 98

Welland Canal, 148, 164